WESTMORELAND GLASS

1950-1984

by Lorraine Kovar

PB ISBN# 0-915410-78-8
HB ISBN# 0-915410-79-6

DEDICATION

This book is dedicated to the hardworking and creative employees who toiled at the Westmoreland factory for so many years. Without these employees, collectors would not have all of the beautiful and creative examples of glass to enjoy for many generations to come.

TABLE OF CONTENTS

5

ACKNOWLEDGEMENTS

This book would not have been possible without all of the kind people who donated their knowledge, time, glass to be photographed, and information. My thanks to all of these kind people who are listed here in no particular order.

Mr. Robert Rupp, Westmoreland's General Manager; Ernest Brown, Head Decorator; Charles West-Wilson; Lillian Szafranski; Margaret & Kenn Whitmyer; Lester Naylor; Shirley & Leonard Graff; Mrs. Shirley Charney; Martha & George Pavlick; Joan & Chuck Wolfe; Delores Drown; Mr. Frank Fenton; Dan Tucker and Lorrie Kitchen; Gerry Gentry; Ray Reichard; Cheryl and Bob Pietrasz; Ron and Connie Doll; Patt Papesh; Robert McNabb; Ted Gasowski; Audrey and Joseph Humphrey; and Edna Barnes.

I would also like to thank Deana Wynn who patiently and expertly photographed the items in this book.

Last, but certainly not least, I would like to thank my husband, David, and my daughter, Denise, who put up with me and did the housework while I wrote this book.

FOREWORD

I have been asked several times how I became interested in Westmoreland Glass. My usual answer is that it was mostly by accident or fate.

My first two pieces of Westmoreland Glass were purchased in May 1985. These pieces were the #1943 Urn in milk glass and #1874 large Wedding Bowl. Both pieces had the Roses and Bows decoration with gold accents. I bought these pieces because I thought the decoration was so beautiful. I knew of Westmoreland at the time, but I really didn't know much about the company or what it produced.

Later, in September 1985, my husband and I took a trip to Gettysburg, Pennsylvania. On the way I wanted to stop in Jeannette, Pennsylvania, to find out anything I could about Jeannette Glass. All of the glassware my grandparents had left to me was made by Jeannette Glass. After navigating through the curves and hills of Jeannette and finding no information, we decided to try to find our way back to Route 30. If one does not know this area it is very easy to get lost. This is actually what had occurred until we spotted an auction sign which pointed up a sharp incline. This sign was pointing to an auction at the Westmoreland factory. There were several pallets of glass in every nook and cranny, as well as several tables of glass. The gentleman who seemed to be running things told us the next auction would be held in October 1985. When we explained that we were just passing through, he told us that we could buy anything we wanted and handed us a wholesale price list.

At this point, I should have mortgaged everything and bought the entire stock,but this didn't occur. I did buy every catalog I could find and quite a few pieces of glass. The gentleman even gave my daughter, Denise, a Lotus bud vase and a crystal bell.

After returning home I kept studying the catalogs. I started finding quite a few pieces for sale and very quickly filled up every nook and cranny in my home with Westmoreland.

In 1987, I contacted David Richardson about publishing a book on Westmoreland Glass. He had told me that he would get back to me. I just assumed that this was a polite way to say "no thanks." Two years later Dave did call back to tell me he was ready to publish such a book.

In some ways I must have known this would happen, because I had always kept a notebook on any pieces I couldn't afford to buy and any reproductions, reissues, etc.

Even sources for this book happened by fate. Richardson Printing Corp. had done the photography on quite a few of the catalogs for Westmoreland. This helped round out my collection of catalogs to tell more of the story.

By working with Westmoreland on the catalogs, Dave Richardson had worked with many of the people at Westmoreland. As a result, I was able to get interviews with several people who had worked at Westmoreland.

I hope fate has been kind, and that this book will help tell the story of the dedicated employees who worked for many years producing a high-quality handmade product which will be cherished for many more generations.

THE HISTORY OF WESTMORELAND

The West Era

In 1883 a group of men in East Liverpool, Ohio, incorporated a company called the East Liverpool Specialty Company. This company is believed to have packed jelly in glass containers. According to the Ohio Department of Commerce, this company was a selling organization, not a manufacturer of glass. This particular company was short-lived due to the company treasurer's embezzlement of company funds and escape to Bermuda.

Five years later the company reorganized and tried again. The Historical Society of East Liverpool has a record of the company's building burning in 1898.

Major George Irwin was a part of this East Liverpool Specialty Glass Company. Major Irwin was responsible for moving the major principals of the East Liverpool concern to the Jeannette, Pennsylvania, area. The major reason for relocating was the expected large natural gas reserves in the Jeannette area. This move occurred in early 1888.

Major Irwin offered the Ohio glassmen a chance to buy land parcels before an auction, at predetermined prices, with the idea that the land would appreciate in price when bids were taken at auction. An auction was later held on remaining lots to help lure glassworkers to the area. Free gas was also an enticement for these workers. Although J.H. Brainard states in his history of the company that the gas only lasted a short time, the gas actually lasted for a period of about 20 years. This saved workers quite a large sum of money each month.

The new Pennsylvania company was named Specialty Glass on the 1888 incorporation papers. For a time this newly formed company did nothing.

In June or July of 1889 state reports show that Specialty Glass started erecting buildings. In October of 1889 the company appears to have run out of money.

At this point, Charles H. and George R. West entered the picture and put up $40,000. At the time, the Specialty Glass interest was valued at about $35,000. The West brothers then owned 53% of the company stock and Major Irwin, along with the other East Liverpool men, owned 47% of the stock. Major Irwin may have been president for a very short time, with George West serving as vice-president. Charles West was shown as secretary and treasurer on the incorporation papers. Shortly after this, George West became president, with Charles holding the same position of secretary/treasurer.

The West brothers had enough money to finance this venture entirely by themselves. Previously the brothers owned a dry-goods store located in East Liberty, Pennsylvania, called West McFarland. They sold the dry-goods store and used the funds to get into the Specialty Glass venture. After the West purchase in 1889 the name of the company was changed to Westmoreland Specialty Company. Throughout this period Ira Brainard's name is nowhere to be found on any legal documents.

In later years, J.H. Brainard wrote a history of the company which stated that Ira A. Brainard had backed the West brothers with money to finance the Specialty Glass venture. If this was in fact true, why wouldn't Ira's name have appeared on the incorporation papers? In 1909 Ira's name does appear on official company documents, which leads me to believe that Ira came into the venture some time after the West brothers bought out the Specialty Company entirely.

Shortly after the West brothers took over Westmoreland Specialty the production of glass began.

Both West brothers were very involved in the company. When Charles married Helen Baker in February of 1893, they honeymooned in New England. Even during his honeymoon, Charles was selling carloads of mustard jars and paperweights.

Although both Charles and George wanted the company to succeed, socially they lived in two different worlds. Charles was very social and associated himself with all of the movers and shakers of the time. Charles would attend golf outings with the Mellons of the Mellon Bank. He also lived very close to Ira and Fanny Brainard. Charles West and his wife played bridge weekly with the Brainards. This relationship was so close that Charles named one son after Ira, Samuel Brainard West. The feeling appeared mutual because Ira's last will and testament was witnessed by Charles and Helen West. Charles appears responsible for bringing Ira into Westmoreland as a stockholder.

George R. West was quite different from Charles. George was more down to earth and probably didn't feel the need to rub elbows with Pittsburgh's high society. George loved the candy containers that Westmoreland manufactured. He felt that since these containers were so profitable (a fact that J.H. Brainard disputes in his version of the history) the company would make these items forever.

Charles felt quite differently. This may have been due to the fact that most of the other hand-made glass houses of the time didn't appear to take Westmoreland seriously. Charles felt the only way to get the respect of people like the Fentons and the people at Fostoria, was to start manufacturing fine handmade tableware.

In 1910, the Keystone lines debuted at Westmoreland. This glass was kept in a separate room from that of the candy containers. The Keystone Line was the start of the "new" direction that Charles felt the company needed.

George West didn't care for the direction the company was now taking. The difference of opinion may have caused the brothers to split. In 1920, George West went over to another venture called West Brothers. By all accounts this company may have been a subsidiary of Westmoreland Specialty, located close to, but not in the same location. The West Brothers Company manufactured the containers in which candy and mustard were placed. George West continued at West Brothers until his death in 1929. The company ceased to exist after George's death.

When George West left Westmoreland Specialty, James J. Brainard was brought in to take over as treasurer. At the same time, Charles West sent for his son, Samuel Brainard West, who was working in the oil fields of Texas. Samuel was then given the title of secretary. Charles then became president, a position which he held until 1937.

At the time of this reorganization in 1920, it is believed that Charles not only bought out all of George West's shares but a portion of Ira Brainard's shares as well. When Ira Brainard died in 1927 his will stated that Ira only owned 12% of the Westmoreland shares. At the time of his death Ira also held two notes. One note was for $10,000 and the other was for $5,000. It is believed the money from these notes was used in the expansion in the 1920's. The expansion added another stack, as well as a boiler room and other improvements.

On March 14, 1924, the board of directors of Westmoreland Specialty Company applied to change its name to Westmoreland Glass Company. The 'Specialty' part of the name had started to create problems by leading customers to believe that the company manufactured anything and everything. The company hoped to alleviate this problem with the name change. The application was approved by the State of Pennsylvania on February 10, 1925.

The next organizational change occurred in 1933, when James H. Brainard graduated from Yale and was appointed assistant treasurer of Westmoreland. This appointment disturbed Charles West because the company could not afford the extra overhead during such a depressed economic time. James H. Brainard stayed anyway and proved to be the lifeblood that Westmoreland needed for many years to come. J.H., as he was called, had what it took to keep a company going through very tough times.

J.H. Brainard met his wife, Stella, at

Westmoreland. Stella was a secretary at the plant. They married in 1948. After they married, Stella quit her job at Westmoreland but returned in the 1970's to run the gift shop. J.H. and Stella never had children, which may be one reason that J.H. was so sad when he later sold Westmoreland.

In 1935, Walter Brainard graduated from Yale, but he didn't immediately go to work for Westmoreland. Walter went with Pittsburgh Plate Glass, where his mentor, oddly enough, was George L. West, son of George R. West, who had left Westmoreland in 1920. After serving in World War II as a second lieutenant, Walter joined Westmoreland in 1945.

The Brainard Era

In 1937, another reorganization took place. Charles West retired from Westmoreland. In J.H. Brainard's history of the company he states that the West financial interest had become worthless. I have not found any documents to prove this fact or, for that matter, to disprove it. At this time James J. Brainard, who was named treasurer in 1920, took over as president, and J.H. Brainard took over as treasurer. It has been said that James J. Brainard was a difficult man to work for.

Phillip Brainard graduated from Princeton in 1940. Phillip joined Westmoreland in 1945 along with his brother Walter. Phillip left Westmoreland early in 1964.

Charles West died in December of 1943.

The company continued on for quite a few years with no changes in management. Other changes which did occur consisted of eliminating all cutting and engraving, reducing all handwork, heavily promoting the glass that was being produced, and not making new molds until the milk glass surge in the 1950's.

James J. Brainard died in 1953 and James H. Brainard took over shortly after his father's death.

In the 1950's, milk glass was at the height of fashion. Westmoreland enjoyed large profits during this time. According to Bob Rupp, who was the general manager, this was the most exciting time to be in the glass industry. Many of the other hand-glass houses started making milk glass also. At first glance this might suggest more competition for Westmoreland's milk glass, but the fact is that the production of milk glass by so many companies only helped Westmoreland sell more.

About 1957, milk glass was such a profitable commodity that J.H.Brainard hired Fran Suli. Mr. Suli was hired to help Westmoreland get more of its product out to more customers. The idea arose that a West Coast factory might help get more product to more people, as well as drastically cut shipping costs. One must remember that although at this time Westmoreland was working two shifts, it would stop representatives from taking any orders after June or July because the factory needed to catch up with the volume of orders. This was another reason the West Coast factory seemed so viable. Walter Brainard, along with plant engineers and accountants, took a trip out to Corona, California. The company was offered a fantastic package to set up shop. This included free gas, a long-term lease and buildings which would be built to the company's specifications. Upon their return, J.H. Brainard just didn't feel that this idea was viable. Perhaps a better idea would have been to just have a warehouse instead of an entire factory, but neither idea was used. Perhaps J.H. Brainard remembered how difficult the glass business could be in hard times and knew that the current prosperity couldn't last forever. Mr. Brainard was correct in his assumption, as 1957 was the last year of phenomenal profits.

The milk glass boom was over by 1958. Even though Westmoreland produced a large quantity of milk glass in the 1960's, they tried to produce crystal tableware as well as colored items. This for the most part was very unsuccessful. Most customers thought of Westmoreland as only making milk glass.

The company even received mail addressed to Westmoreland Milk Glass Company. Also, after 1957 the grinding and polishing of the glass appears to have ceased.

On April 12, 1962, Westmoreland started its on-site gift shop. This gift shop was the brainchild of Walter Brainard and Bob Rupp. J.H. Brainard was not wild about the idea of selling the product at the factory. J.H. figured that if they made more than $50 on the first day they would be doing great. The first day brought in $150.

The gift shop proved to be a good idea because so many people stopped throughout the year to take the plant tour. After the tour they were now able to take home a souvenir. The shop also turned out to be a great test-market site. If a new color, item, or hand painting was tried, Westmoreland would know very quickly whether or not it would sell. Clipboards were placed in various areas of the gift shop to solicit comments from shoppers. Sometimes the visitors were brutally honest!

Bob Rupp was in charge of the gift shop during the first few years. Helen Parker then ran the shop until Stella Brainard came in and started to run it in the late 1970's. Stella enjoyed this job as much as J.H. enjoyed running the company. She continued on in the gift shop until the company was sold.

Shortly after the shop opened, Westmoreland started selling its seconds. Seconds are slightly imperfect pieces, but totally usable. Up until this point Westmoreland would always break every piece that didn't meet its high standards of quality. The seconds were cheaper in price, but most customers had a difficult time finding a flaw. This proved to be a major money-saving idea. Sometimes the flaws would not appear until the final firing, so the cost of the material, heating, and hand painting would be totally wasted if the piece were broken because it wasn't absolutely perfect.

The 1960's brought the introduction of color. Even colored milk glass, such as Mint Green, Almond and Antique Blue, was tried at this time. Antique Blue was the best selling color, but none really took off as anticipated. Antique Blue had been produced in the 1950's as well, but the color was a few shades darker then. Golden Sunset, Laurel Green and Brandywine Blue were introduced in 1964. The Golden Sunset was a dark amber which some customers referred to as "beer bottle amber." None of these colors caught on either. Westmoreland basically kept its head above water by appealing to the bridal trade. This was done through advertising in many of the bridal magazines, as well as in publications such as Better Homes and Gardens.

Handmade glass is very labor intensive. Therefore, most of the cost of the glass came from paying employees. In the 1970's several different methods were utilized to try to cut costs and thereby cut the price of the final product. At this time, some decals were introduced. It was much easier to put a colorful decal on an item than it was to pay an artist to paint it. Some of the decals sold a fair amount, but some, even today, are not collected.

It was also at this time that officials at Westmoreland realized their products were competing against themselves. By producing two grape patterns (Paneled Grape and Beaded Grape), one pattern was taking customers away from the other pattern. One item that did sell during the downturn was the covered animals.

The Beginning of the End

In 1980, J.H. Brainard started searching for a buyer for the company, mostly because he was disheartened with the changes in the glass industry. A collection of six employees approached J.H. about buying the company and operating it as an employee-owned company. J.H. probably had instincts that told him the glass industry had changed so much that he did not want to burden close friends and co-workers with such a difficult future. So J.H. refused to sell it to these men. Instead, an outside individual, David Grossman, was approached with the suggestion that he buy Westmoreland. David Grossman is a St. Louis-based distributor and importer, most famous for his Norman Rockwell Collectibles series.

The deal was struck and Westmoreland became a Grossman enterprise in March of 1981. The employees saw this deal as adding years to their jobs, so the union also approved. Bob Rupp became president and general manager. For 15 months there were no changes in staff or organization. After Mr. Rupp left, along with a few other valued employees, things were never the same. Line numbers were changed and very old molds were brought out of storage and placed back into production. Mr. Grossman must be given credit for trying, quite a few different color effects were attained. He also tried a limited edition series. This worked with the Norman Rockwells, but it didn't with glass.

The end came early in 1984. Production ceased after the close of business on January 8, 1984, and only those items already in stock were sold. The auctions soon started. Although there are still quite a few molds as well as other items left in the buildings, a great number of molds, glass, historic information, furniture, and catalogs were sold at these auctions. There were employees still working as late as 1985.

Currently, there are plans in the making to turn the factory into an artist colony or cultural center. Jim Miller is in charge of this operation along with owner George Snyder, and he has applied to the state for historical landmark status of the site so that it may be preserved for generations to come. This new life for the factory is called the Mainline Works Corporation.

EMPLOYEE FOCUS

Part of the success of Westmoreland was due to the dedicated employees who were employed there. During the lean years employees would work with only the promise of payment. I imagine having the promise of a paycheck was better than being entirely out or work.

Although the work was very tedious and repetitious, the employees continously came up with creative ideas. Whether it was to crimp the edge of an item a different way or a new format for hand painting, the management usually listened and encouraged employee participation. The feeling was that someone who did a certain job day in and day out would certainly know more about that job than someone sitting in an office.

The following brochure shows how each job was done. This brochure focuses on the manufacture of a large Dolphin compote from start to finish.

1. *Making the Mold.* As the Artist paints on canvas, the Mason carves in stone, and the Engraver etches on copper, so does the Mold Maker sculpture out with fine tools on the inside of a rough iron casting the pattern to be impressed in glass. Here the Mold Maker is sculpturing a Westmoreland Reproduction of the Dolphin Shell Compote.

2. *Gathering the Metal.* The required amount of molten glass to make the Dolphin Compote is gathered from the pot of glass on a punty rod by the Gatherer. This is then carried to the readied mold.

4. *Resetting the Mold.* After the Dolphin Compote has been pressed and removed from the mold, the Presser resets the mold while the Gatherer collects another gather on his punty. The Compote is now ready to "warm in."

3. *Molding the Glass.* The gather of molten glass is raised above the open mold where the Presser cuts off the exact amount necessary to fill the open Dolphin Compote mold. Then he presses it by hand.

5. *The Glory Hole.* The molded Compote is carried to the Glory Hole where it is subjected to an intense temperature of 1500°. Here it takes on a glaze and is reduced to a semi-molten state for finishing.

6. *Hand Finishing, first operation.* From the Glory Hole the Compote is given to the first Finisher. With special tools he shapes, by hand, the lip and neck. The Compote is then returned to the Glory Hole.

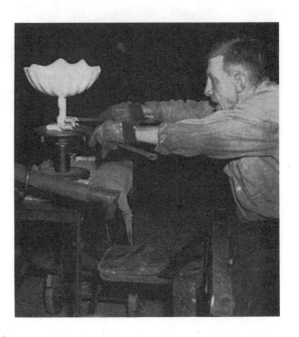

8. *Hand Finishing, third operation.* The still pliable Dolphin Compote is removed from the snap for the third finishing operation. Now the foot is shaped and the piece is carefully inspected before going into the annealing lehr.

7. *Hand Finishing, second operation.* After being reheated the Dolphin Compote is brought to the second Finisher, where it is squared up, and the Bowl is shaped, top and bottom, then again returned to the Glory Hole.

9. *Fifth Inspection.* The finished Bowl has been inspected by the Presser and the three Finishers before making a ten hour trip through the annealing lehrs. Now it is again carefully inspected before being labeled.

10. *Final Inspection and Packing.* The finished Dolphin Compote that has passed all previous inspections finds its way to the Packer who again carefully examines it for the slightest defect. If it passes approval it is then carefully packed to assure safe delivery.

Besides the skilled laborers there were many other employees who helped Westmoreland turn out a quality product.

Bob Rupp started in 1950 as a timekeeper and an industrial engineer trainee. At the time Mr. Rupp started, Westmoreland had decided to revamp the furnace. This was done in part to conserve the ever-increasing use of gas. Westmoreland wanted to heat only eight of the 16 pots in the furnace at one time. This would save quite a bit of gas. While the eight pots were heating, the other eight pots would be cooling. These pots would switch every 20 minutes and thereby keep a constant temperature. Mr. Rupp was assigned to the clerical end of this job. He worked in conjunction with the Frasier Simplex Company.

After this major accomplishment, Mr. Rupp worked in advertising, met with the sales representatives, and was the personnel manager. Mr. Rupp referred to this time as "getting his feet wet."

In 1961 Mr. Rupp became the general manager. This was a position which was directly under J.H. Brainard. Both gentlemen respected each other, and it was a benifical working arrangement. Mr. Rupp continued in this capacity until Westmoreland was sold to David Grossman in 1981. In 1981 Mr. Rupp was named president and general manager and continued on for a period of 15 months.

After Mr. Rupp parted company with Westmoreland, he tried other forms of employment, but none seemed as satisfactory as working in the glass industry. In June of 1982 Bob Rupp began Treasured Editions Limited. This is a small company whose employees are all ex-Westmoreland workers. Treasured Editions Limited holds the exclusive rights to the large Wedding Bowl (Line#1874). All pieces which are hand painted by this small firm are signed by the artist and dated with the current year. Although one could say that these pieces are reproductions of original Westmoreland items, the items pose no threat to any collectors, because if original colors are used, as in the Wedding Bowl, the pieces are signed and dated. The primary colors used at the time of the writing of this book are crystal with either a cranberry flashing, ruby flashing or light blue flashing. Most of these pieces are hand painted after the stain is applied.

One of Mr. Rupp's employees is Ernest Brown. Ernest Brown started working at Westmoreland April 1, 1960. After working as a decorator and designing quite a few decorations, Mr. Brown became the head decorator in May of 1971. Mr. Brown was responsible for decorations such as Almond Rose, which is a shaded brown rose on almond milk glass. Mr. Brown continued to work for Westmoreland until August 1982, when he switched over to Treasured Editions Limited.

Another Westmoreland employee who was highly valued was Dwight Johnson. Mr. Johnson started with Westmoreland in 1944. His first position was that of traffic manager and apprentice glassmaker. Dwight was directly under Sam Guy, who for years was the head chemist at Westmoreland. In 1955, J.H. Brainard realized that it was time to have a person who could take over for Sam Guy when the time came. J.H. had Dwight Johnson attend the McKeesport campus of Pennsylvania State University. He studied at night school so that he could still learn about the industry firsthand during the day, and also so that Sam Guy wouldn't get wind of the operation. If Sam Guy had found out, Westmoreland could very well have been without a chemist.

Dwight Johnson also studied under Harry Blau, who was an expert in the field of glass as well as ceramics. After Mr. Johnson's studies were complete, he did become the head chemist. He turned out to be an excellent choice for the job. He had quite an eye for good color. Anyone who collects any of Westmoreland's colors holds a piece of Mr. Johnson's very capable work.

These are just a few of the faithful employees who made Westmoreland such a success for so many years. From the employees I talked with I got a sense that they enjoyed working for Westmoreland and cared about the quality of the product. This is rare in today's world, and is, perhaps, another reason why Westmoreland could not exist any longer. With today's fast-paced society, we tend to overlook quality for speed and ease. Maybe we could all learn a lesson from this.

MARKINGS "OLD" AND "NEW"

The first Westmoreland mark seems to have appeared on its Keystone lines produced around 1910. The mark was a keystone symbol (which is the Pennsylvania state symbol which is found on all road signs), with a "W" in the centers (see fig. 1). This mark will be found on lines such as #1776 Colonial and others of that time. Some pieces which were produced in the 1970's will still bear the Keystone marking because Westmoreland liked to promote the fact that original molds were being used, and this was a way of proving it.

The Keystone mark was discontinued before the onset of the Depression. Not all pieces of the 1910 period were marked.

Please do not get confused with the new reproduction markings which at a quick glance bear a striking resemblance to the Keystone mark. Plum's marking consists of the Keystone symbol with a large "P" and a smaller "G" next to the "P" (see fig. 2). The other original Westmoreland markings will not be removed. If a piece has two parts, such as a lid and bottom, usually only the bottom will be marked with the "new" marking. These "new" marks are also very difficult to find at times. Plum Glass, which owns several original Westmoreland molds, is usually quite conscientious about marking their products.

The other "new" mark which utilizes the Keystone symbol contains an "R" in the center (see fig. 3). This mark was not placed on very many pieces, but it is a mark that everyone should be aware of. This mark represents Rosso Wholesale Glass Dealers. This is a company which is run by Phil and Helen Rosso. They don't produce the glass, but have several companies who will manufacture so that they may sell.

In the late 1940's, Westmoreland started marking their glass with a "W" with a "G" on top of the "W" (see fig. 4). In a catalog from the 1960's, J.H. Brainard wrote a letter explaining why the company was marking its wares. It basically was due to finding

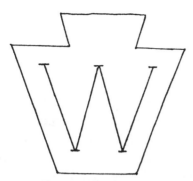

Fig. 1 Original Westmoreland Mark Circa 1910
Used Basically on Keystone lines only.

Fig. 2 New mark by Plum Glass. Pieces may still
have a "WG" mark also. Lids may not be marked
with this new mark.

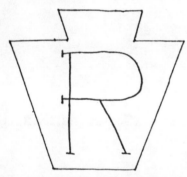

Fig. 3 New mark used by Rosso Wholesale Glass
dealers. Not many pieces carry this mark.

currently produced items being portrayed as antique glass in the area's antique shops.

Most pieces that are found today bear the "W" under "G" mark. I do know collectors who will not buy a piece that is not marked. The mark only dates the piece to the last 40 years of production and does not verify that it is not a reproduction. So don't pass a good deal just because a mark is not present. Again, not all Westmoreland pieces were marked.

As stated before, when David Grossman took over the company in 1981, the changes didn't start for about a year and a half. Then, even the Westmoreland mark was changed. The last marking was 'WEST-MORELAND" spelled out in circular fashion with a very odd type "W" in the center. The "W" looks more like three fat lines than a "W" (see fig. 5).

I would like to caution all collectors and dealers that this mark seems to be appearing more and more on all reproduction pieces.

Another mark which appears on glass is a "W" in a circle. THIS MARK IS NOT WESTMORELAND. This mark is found on only a few items which were produced by L.G. Wright (see fig. 6).

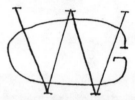

Fig. 4 Original Westmoreland mark used after late 1940's Most pieces bear this mark but all pieces were not marked.

Fig. 5 This mark was used by David Grossman when he owned Westmoreland. Reproductions may also bear this mark.

Fig. 6 Not Westmoreland

STICKERS

Westmoreland did use paper labels on most of its wares. There are several different variations in design to be found.

Fig. 7 This type of sticker will be found on items made before the early 1960's.

Fig. 8 This sticker was used from the early 1960's through closing. Larry Hamby was responsible for this redesign.

Fig. 9 This sticker was used only on milk glass items.

I would caution collectors and dealers not to rely on a sticker for confirmation of authenticity. When I was at the Westmoreland factory in September of 1985, a roll of 1,000 stickers was selling for $10. I have found many reproductions with original stickers taped to them. I have also found Fenton and Kemple items with Westmoreland stickers; so know what you are buying. Luckily most stickers must be taped because new glass in general is very oily or slimy to the touch and the glue on the sticker will not stick!

REPRODUCTIONS, REISSUES, OR NEW GLASS FROM WESTMORELAND MOLDS

I suppose imitation is the sincerest form of flattery, but this doesn't seem to extend to the glass industry. Although Westmoreland did its share of copying from other companies, it did not intend to misrepresent its glass as being something it was not.

I don't think the fault lies with the manufacturers entirely. They have no control over unscrupulous dealers who intend to cheat the public. My only complaint is that each and every piece should carry a mark of the producing company. I would think the manufacturers would be proud enough of their work that they would want everyone to know who made a particular piece.

18

Several different companies and individuals own Westmoreland molds. A few of these companies are:

DALZELL/VIKING GLASS CO.
ROSSO WHOLESALE GLASS
  DEALERS
SUMMIT ART GLASS
PLUM GLASS
TREASURED EDITIONS LIMITED
FENTON

As I stated before in the chapter on markings, some of these companies are marking their glass. But not all pieces will be so marked.

The bulk of the reissued glass seems to be found in cobalt. Cobalt is very easily and cheaply manufactured. Some milk glass will be found to be reproduced, but I have been told by several companies that milk glass will no longer be made. Milk glass is very corrosive to the day tanks, so these tanks must be replaced often. Day tanks are not cheap to replace. The milk glass which was produced by Plum Glass was of extremely good quality due in part to Plum's use of the original Westmoreland cullet. Cullet is glass shards and pieces which help melt the chemicals needed to make glass. Without cullet the glass would not be easily controlled and would appear burnt.

Besides cobalt and milk glass there are several other colors being made. Ruby, crystal, mother of pearl (or carnival) on any color of glass, light blue, alexandrite (light lilac), as well as any type of hand painting, can be found.

In each description of each item in this book I will attempt to list any and all colors currently being reissued. Since these above mentioned companies, as well as other companies who haven't as yet used the molds which they purchased, are still producing, this will be an ongoing task. The best advice I can give collectors and dealers is to know from whom you are buying and what you are buying.

CARE AND FEEDING OF WESTMORELAND GLASS

It should be noted that Westmoreland glass has some special concerns when it comes to washing and otherwise caring for it.

The first point is NEVER WASH ANY WESTMORELAND IN A DISHWASHER, ESPECIALLY MILK GLASS. You may open the dishwasher after the cycle to find shards of a once beautiful piece. Milk glass, especially, cannot stand any variation in temperature. This problem plagued Westmoreland for years.

Westmoreland received many letters with stories of cups exploding, punch bowls shattering, and plates cracking in half. Westmoreland always replaced the broken item. Since it no longer exists, it may be difficult, if not impossible, to replace an item. One suggestion Westmoreland gave to customers was to place a spoon in a coffee cup before putting any hot liquid into it. Supposedly, this took the heat away from the glass and concentrated it onto the spoon. This does not always work. Westmoreland got to the point that enough complaints were being received that it started dunking some milk glass items into a boiling water bath before shipping. They figured if the milk glass didn't crack then, it might hold together for their customers.

When buying milk glass in the winter in cold climates, be sure to let the glass warm up to room temperature very slowly. The same thing applies in the summer: If your glass has baked in a hot trunk for hours, it is not wise to put it in any water until it cools down.

A different problem arises with any of the frosted glass colors. Many dealers wrap their glass in newspaper. With Westmoreland's frosted or mist colors this newsprint does not always come off of the piece. Excessive scrubbing on mist pieces will get you a shiny spot. The only way to tell if the newsprint will be easily removed is to wet the piece and rub lightly with a finger. If this takes off most of the newsprint, the rest should come off when the piece is bathed.

There are many items which are difficult to clean because of their patterns. English Hobnail and Old Quilt are about the worst if they are found with years of built-up grease and dirt. A soft-bristle toothbrush is best for dealing with these types of patterns. If the item is frosted, be careful not to rub in one place for an extended period of time.

Price stickers, especially the non-removable type, pose problems also. Sometimes a dab of nail polish remover will help rid your prized possession of its price. In some of the secondhand stores, as well as in flea markets in my area, prices are placed on items with a magic marker. This will come off if the item is not frosted. If the piece is frosted, the price may be a permanent fixture. I have found no product which removes magic marker from a frosted piece.

Storing Westmoreland is another problem. Maybe other collectors either have bigger homes or less in their collections than I do, but be sure all shelves holding Westmoreland are very securely anchored to the studs in your walls. I had a shelf take a diving leap off of a wall. Oddly enough the items that fell 7 feet did not break, the items that fell 6 inches did break. I would also advise checking any cabinet shelves. I am especially wary of those that have little pin-type arrangements holding up the shelves in antique cabinets. The holes that these pins fit into may, over time and with excessive weight, enlarge the holes and cause the entire shelf to crash into the next shelf. When one shelf falls, it is a sure bet that the shelves underneath it will also fall.

Washing a treasure that has a Westmoreland sticker is easily done by holding a finger over the sticker and bathing the rest of the piece. Items with stickers should be wiped dry immediately. If any moisture does get on to or under the sticker, place a towel over the sticker and press with your thumb; this should help the sticker stay in place. I have noticed that earlier stickers tend to stay in place better than the stickers from the Grossman era.

Beaded Bouquet items were originally painted with shards of broken glass in the paint mixture to build up the flower petals. These parts will often retain newsprint as well as other dirt. Newsprint may not come off. Other dirt can be removed with mild soap on a soft-bristle tooth brush. Remember to scrub very lightly.

PATTERN SECTION

American Hobnail (Line #77)

Westmoreland joined quite a few other glass manufacturers in making a "Hobnail Pattern." American Hobnail is discussed in Ruth Webb Lee's "Antique Fakes and Reproductions." Mrs. Lee stated that she had found this pattern in a department store in 1933, and that an entire dinnerware set was available at that time.

Westmoreland did produce American Hobnail on and off for quite a few years. Not all pieces were produced at all times. Occasionally, a few pieces would be produced in new colors to test the market.

American Hobnail did not have a dinner plate, but used either a Beaded Edge (Line #22) dinner plate or a Line #1901 dinner plate, which is a plain plate with a scalloped edge. Saucers and all other plates will be found in either of these "go-with" styles.

The bulk of the milk glass production of this pattern was done in the milk glass heyday of the 1950's. This pattern, even then, did not sell very well in milk glass. For this reason some pieces are very difficult to find. These include the 1/2-gallon pitcher, grapefruit bowl, double egg cup, sherberts, and large bowls. The items most commonly found are the candlesticks, puff box, cruets, cheese dish, and water goblets.

In 1971, American Hobnail was shown in Candlelight, which is a crystal color with opalescent edges, and a Brandywine Blue Opalescent. These were referred to as Moonstone, more because of the coloring than the pattern. These colors had a very limited production run and, therefore, will be more difficult to find than a milk glass piece.

American Hobnail will also be found in Golden Sunset (dark amber), Brandywine Blue, and Laurel Green. Only water goblets were produced in these colors. These goblets were made to match china patterns which Westmoreland hoped would spur sales. Although it was a good idea, it didn't seem to work.

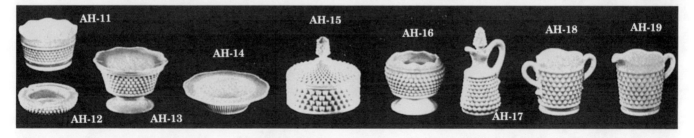

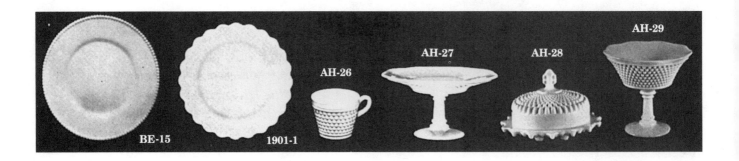

BE-15   1901-1   AH-26   AH-27   AH-28   AH-29

Ashburton (Line #1855)

The Ashburton line is another line which was produced by many companies. The first company believed to have made an Ashburton pattern was the Boston and Sandwich Glass Company. This original Ashburton dates back to the 1850's.

Westmoreland produced Ashburton in the 1940's as well as the 1950's. During this same period Fostoria had good success with its Argus pattern, which is very similar in shape. Perhaps this added competition was one of the reasons that the Westmoreland version of Ashburton did not sell well.

In the 1970's Ashburton was attempted again, but it had the same poor sales record. Hence this pattern will be slightly difficult to find. The only item in the line which did sell well was the rocks tumbler.

This line was basically a barware type pattern. A dinner plate was produced which was used with Ashburton as well as the Colonial line (#1776). Other occasional pieces, such as a cake salver, compote, and sugar and creamer were also produced, although not in any great quantity.

Ashburton was produced in Bermuda Blue, Olive Green, Amber, Crystal, Crystal with Ruby accents, Crystal with Platinum accents, green marble, purple marble, Pink, Brown, Milk Glass, Milk Glass with Roses and Bows Decoration, and Crystal Mist. Not all pieces were produced in all colors.

Scarce pieces would include the pitcher, cake salver, and compote with ruffled rim. Common pieces include goblets and the sugar with lid, although none of this line seems easily found.

AB/CO-15

AB-2   AB-1   AB-6   AB-3   AB-4   AB-5

AB-11   AB-12   AB-13   AB-11   AB-14

AB-7

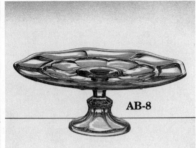

AB-8

AB-9   AB-10   AB-9

Beaded Edge (Line #22)

Beaded Edge appears to have been Westmoreland's own creation. Beaded Edge was introduced in the milk glass craze of the late 1940's to early 1950's. This line will be found in plain milk glass as well as several decorations which were hand painted.

The most popular hand painted decoration then and now is the #64-2 Fruit decoration. There are eight different fruits represented in this decoration: Pears, Apples, Strawberries, Plums, Grapes, Cherries, Peaches, and Blackberries. Items with these fruit decorations will be more difficult to find than just plain milk glass.

Another decoration featured coral red beads around the edge of each item. This decoration was referred to as decoration #A-28. In one of Westmoreland's brochures it states that by special order, a hand painted Holly and Berries decoration could be added to the Coral Red Beading. This Holly

decoration was referred to as decoration #37. Since the Holly items had to be special-ordered they are extremely scarce today.

Birds also appeared on Beaded Edge. Birds, however, will mainly be found on 7"

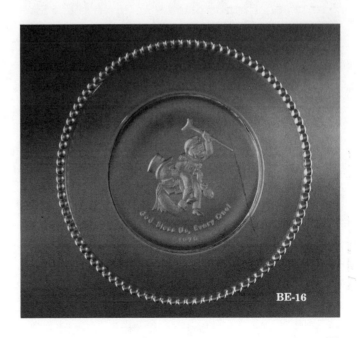

BE-16

croup salad plates, although the catalogs state that a complete dinnerware service was available. The dinnerware service with the birds would have been a special order, hence it is very scarce today. Incidentally, croup-shaped plates are slightly curved upward around the rim, and have a flat middle section, whereas the regular dinnerware plates have a slightly depressed center with a wide rim.

Eight birds were available. These included a Bluebird, Scarlet Tananger, Goldfinch, Mocking Bird, Cardinal, Titmouse, Chickadee, and Yellow Warbler. The Bird decoration is referred to as decoration #70.

A flower series is also available on Beaded

Edge and is referred to as decoration #4. The eight different flowers include a Violet, Apple Blossom, Pansy, Tulip, Yellow Daisy, Morning Glory, Poinsettia, and Poppy. Again, as with the other decoration, mainly croup salad plates will be found. A 15" torte plate is also occasionally found with either a fruit or a flower decoration. Most of these torte plates have the impressed signs of the zodiac on the bottom side of the plate. The flower decoration was available in a full dinnerware set, but only by special order.

Although most of the production in Beaded Edge consisted of milk glass, some items may be found in crystal. In 1970 a Bob Cratchet plate was issued for the Christmas trade. The center has a frosted picture of Bob Cratchet and states "God bless us, every one!" and "1970". I have only found these on regular-style plates with the depressed center and wide rim. These plates were produced for a few years.

Another decoration on milk glass is referred to as the Poultry series, decoration #74. This decoration consists of roosters and chickens, which include a White Leghorn Hen, White Leghorn Rooster, Colored Leghorn Hen, Colored Leghorn Rooster, Rhode Island Red Hen, Rhode Island Rooster, Two Chicks, and Two Chicks with Eggshell. These decorations may be found in a complete breakfast set, as well as a dinnerware set. Most commonly found are the 7" croup-shaped plates, but even these are scarce. A full set would be an extremely fortunate find.

Even though Beaded Edge has its own creamer and sugar, Westmoreland often paired the #108 Grape & Cherry creamer and sugar with Beaded Edge. The #108 creamer and sugar both have lids and can be found hand painted on milk glass, plain milk glass, crystal, and crystal with hand painting. The crystal versions of these are more scarce than the milk glass versions.

American Hobnail (Line #77) was also pictured often with Beaded Edge. Westmoreland may have helped failing lines in this manner by picturing a good selling line with a few pieces of a slow selling line. Beaded Edge dinner plates were also shown with the American Hobnail line, so both of these lines are very much interchangeable.

Beaded Grape (Line #1884)

Beaded Grape was originally designed to take over the selling limelight when Paneled Grape stopped being popular with the public. Beaded Grape combined two popular selling patterns, Paneled Grape and Beaded Edge.

Beaded Grape was designed and first marketed in the 1950's but it came into prominence in the 1960's. Quite a bit of money was put into making the molds for this pattern. I would suspect most of the buying public just thought this pattern was an addition to Paneled Grape. Customers did purchase a few pieces to blend with the Paneled Grape line, but since Paneled Grape didn't seem to wane, it tended to hurt the sales of Beaded Grape.

Beaded Grape has its origins in the Pattern Glass era. According to Heacock &

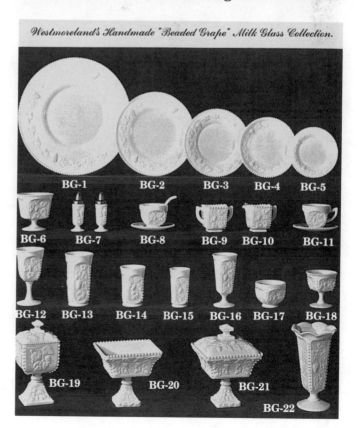

25

Bickenheuser's "Book 5, U.S. Glass from A to Z," the United States Glass Company produced a similar pattern which it referred to as "California." This very old pattern was produced in crystal and emerald green. Westmoreland never made its version in these colors. Also the U.S. Glass line did not have quite as many pieces.

Colors produced by Westmoreland include Brandywine Blue, Golden Sunset, and Laurel Green. Milk glass made up the bulk of the production in this pattern. Several decorations may be found on Beaded Grape. Roses and Bows (dec. #32) on milk glass, Crystal Mist with Roses and Bows (dec. #32-1) 22 kt. Gold (dec. #915) on milk glass, and green leaves with 22kt. gold grapes (dec. #86) on milk glass, and a pastel hand painting (dec. #85) which includes pink grapes and green, buff and gray leaves on milk glass are just a few of the variations. There may be an entire dinner set of Beaded Grape in the Roses and Bows decoration. This would have been a special order and not commercially available. If anyone finds such a set it would definitely be a very rare find.

Two different types of plates were produced in Beaded Grape. The round plates which are shown here were the most commonly

BG-40

produced. Square plates (which are shown in the Color Section) were also produced. The square plates were very difficult to make in milk glass. Milk glass is very hard but brittle at the same time. When the square plates were manufactured, the center of the plate would keep its high temperature, but the square ends would tend to cool very quickly. Consequently when the plates were placed in the lehr they would reheat again and cracks would appear. This was not a problem with the Golden Sunset. Any of the square plates would be an extremely good find in today's market due to their limited production.

This pattern has many pieces which would be considered either scarce or rare. The cake salver, any goblets, any tumblers, all plates square or round, and vases would be included in the category.

The commonly found pieces would include the honey and cover, which is low-footed, and the 4" square box with lid. Ashtrays are also found frequently.

Be aware that this pattern is being heavily reproduced or reissued. Most of the production is being done by Plum Glass which does mark most pieces. Reproductions will be found in milk glass, black glass, cobalt, and pink, as well as other colors. See the individual codes to find out what is currently being reproduced.

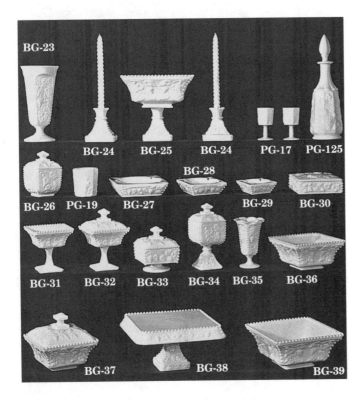
BG-23
BG-24   BG-25   BG-24   PG-17   PG-125
BG-28
BG-26   PG-19   BG-27   BG-29   BG-30
BG-31   BG-32   BG-33   BG-34   BG-35   BG-36
BG-37   BG-38   BG-39

Cherry Pattern (Line #109)

The Cherry pattern was introduced about 1960. Most of these pieces were made in very limited quantities. The best-selling items were creamer and sugar sets. All of the large footed pieces were very difficult to make, hence they were very expensive and did not sell well.

The footed cookie jar was probably the most difficult piece to manufacture. Westmoreland tried to mate a candlestick bottom to a cookie jar by using a glob of glass. This process was aborted due to cracking of the foot during the annealing process. The cookie jar top would keep its heat much longer and more intensely than the smaller candlestick foot. Westmoreland finally resorted to gluing the base to the top after both pieces had cooled. This was also done on all of the other footed pieces in this pattern.

The honey and cover may be found with two different lids. It was originally made with a lid that just had the thumbprint type

CH-1 CH-2 CH-3 CH-4 CG-2 CG-2 CH-7 CH-6 CH-5 CH-8 CH-9 CH-10 CH-11 CH-12

pattern that is on the bottom, but someone at Westmoreland realized that it did not have cherries in its motif, so a new lid was designed to have cherries. The thumbprint will be more difficult to find than the cherry lid.

The bulk of the production in this pattern was milk glass. Some pieces were produced in carnival colors. These colors would have been by special request of a client, usually Levay Distributing Company.

This entire pattern is classified as scarce to rare. The only available pieces are the creamer and sugar. Although these are not found every day either.

The hand painted examples which exist are even more difficult to find than plain milk glass. The hand painted examples had the cherries and leaves outlined in color, with the balance of the piece being plain.

In my travels I have found many miniature versions of this cherry pattern. The pieces include a miniature pitcher set. The tumblers in this set are about the size of a shot glass and the pitcher looks like a tall creamer. A butter dish, cracker jar and a spooner will also be found. NONE OF THESE MINIATURE PIECES WERE PRODUCED BY WESTMORELAND. These pieces are currently being produced in crystal, chocolate type glass, crystal with hand painted cherries and leaves, and purple carnival.

Colonial (Line #1776)

The Colonial pattern originally dates from the 1910-1920 period. This pattern was originally part of the Keystone lines. Most of these original pieces will bear the Keystone "W" marking. A few of the pieces produced from 1950 through the 1980's will still bear this marking, although most will have the "W" with the superimposed "G" mark.

In the 1950-1980's period, not all pieces of the original line were produced. The most produced and best selling piece was the high-footed, two-handled sweetmeat. This sweetmeat was manufactured in a myriad of colors. The other pieces which were produced in the Colonial pattern were more of the barware type items. The dinner plate, which is a go-with piece, is line #1855 (AB/CO-15). This same dinner plate was also used with the Ashburton line.

Colonial was produced in crystal, flame, green marble, mint green, purple marble, Bermuda Blue, Golden Sunset, Laurel Green, moss green, brown, apricot mist, brown marble, brown mist, dark blue mist, pink, green mist, pink mist, yellow mist, antique blue mist, blue carnival, milk glass, milk glass with decorations and ruby. Not all pieces were produced in all colors. The colored pieces did not sell well, so they may be a bit difficult to find today.

Scarce items would include the pitcher, tall candlesticks, and compote or fruit bowl.

CO-1   CO-2   CO-3   CO-4   CO-5   CO-6

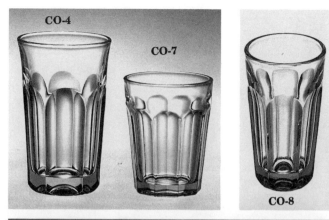

CO-4

CO-7

CO-8

AB/CO-1

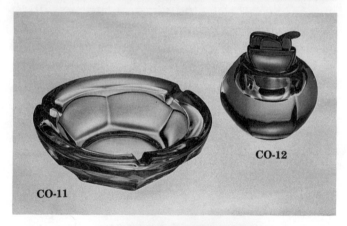

CO-9

CO-10

CO-9

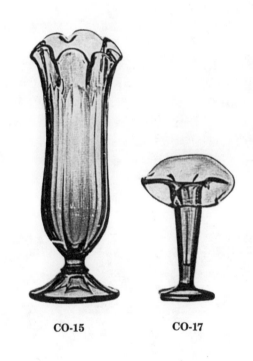

CO-15

CO-17

CO-11

CO-12

CO-13

CO-16

Della Robbia (Line #1058)

Della Robbia was manufactured on and off from the Depression Era to the late 1970's. This was a good-selling pattern for Westmoreland. Most of the dinnerware items were produced in the 40's and 50's. In the 1950's, since milk glass items were in such great demand, several items of Della Robbia were produced in milk glass. These items were mostly stemware and a few occasional items like the domed candy dish.

The most collected items in Della Robbia are crystal with dark luster colors, which were hand applied. The colors in the luster consisted of red apples, yellow pears and red or purple grapes. Another pastel stain is much harder to find than the dark stain. I have only pointed out pieces in this stain that I have actually seen, there may be others available that I have not listed. Other colors which Della Robbia made in are Roselin (Westmoreland's name for pink), green and amber, any pieces found in these colors would be considered rare finds. Plain crystal was also produced.

Items with the stain colors and crystal can, with much searching, be collected in a full dinnerware set. All other colors will only be

"Della Robbia" Pattern in Crystal with Applied Lustre Colors.

DR-2, DR-3, DR-4, DR-5, DR-6, DR-7, DR-1, DR-8, DR-9, DR-10, DR-11, DR-12, DR-13, DR-14, "Della Robbia" DR-16, DR-17, DR-18, DR-15, DR-15 "Zodiac" Plate, DR-19, DR-20, BE-13

found in occasional pieces. Some pieces of Della Robbia will have a Roses and Bows hand painted decoration. This occurs mostly on milk glass but may be found on crystal mist. The domed candy dish is the piece most often found in this manner.

Goblets in Della Robbia may also be found in milk glass with a gold banding near the rim or in Antique Blue, which is a blue milk glass. The latter would have been produced in the 1950's when this color was most popular.

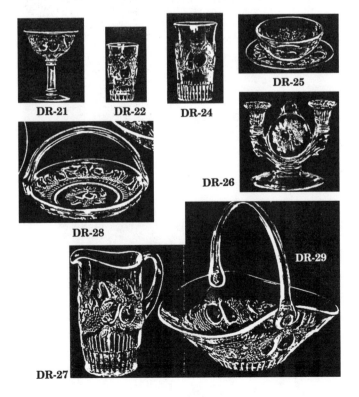

DR-21, DR-22, DR-24, DR-25, DR-26, DR-28, DR-29, DR-27

Doric (Line #3)

The Doric pattern was in general a good seller for Westmoreland. Even though these pieces are intricate, they were amazingly easy to produce. In fact, when the workers came in on Saturdays for overtime, one of the pieces that would be made was the oval 12" crimped bowl. Workers were paid hourly

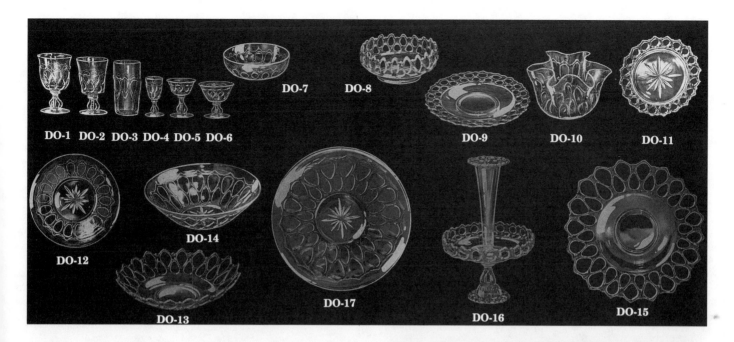

DO-1 DO-2 DO-3 DO-4 DO-5 DO-6   DO-7   DO-8   DO-9   DO-10   DO-11

DO-12   DO-14   DO-13   DO-17   DO-16   DO-15

wages but would be paid extra if they surpassed the set piece-rate for the day. On this crimped bowl this was easily done, so the employees were happy and the company was happy also!

In the late 40's or early 50's, Westmoreland made a crystal version of this pattern and called it "Crystal Lace." The line number for this pattern was #3/1. Quite a few of these pieces did not have the intricate lacy edging but would incorporate the lacy pattern on the side or bottom of the pieces. These pieces are not easily found today. The Crystal Lace was not made in any great quantity.

In the 1970's, the water goblet was made into a sweetmeat by pulling the top outward and crimping the rim. This was made in just about every color and decoration combination that Westmoreland ever produced. Please see the Color section for an example of this piece (DO-34).

All of the footed items have candlestick bottoms. These bottoms were fused to their tops with a glob of glass. This worked better with this pattern than it did with the #109 Cherry pattern. Doric pieces are not as thick or as heavy, therefore the cooling problems didn't occur with this pattern as it did with the Cherry pattern.

When searching for pieces in this pattern, great attention must be given to pieces which have the lacy edges. These edges can

crack very easily since they are so thin. The best way to check for cracks is to hold the item up to a light. Cracks will appear very easily under strong light.

Most pieces can be found in Doric. Scarce items include 10" high compote with lid, 6-1/2" flared rose bowl, as well as any of the Crystal Lace items. The Crystal Lace items are code numbers DO-1 through DO-18.

DO-30

DO-31

DO-32

DO-33

Westmoreland's Line No. 3. "Doric" Border Lacy-Edge Items

DO-18
DO-19 DO-20
DO-21
DO-22
DO-23
DO-24
DO-25
DO-26
DO-27 DO-28
DO-29

Note: The footed items, shown above, except Compote
and Cover, and 10½" Footed, Crimped Bowl, are packed
in individual cartons to assure safe delivery.

English Hobnail (Line #555)

English Hobnail was Westmoreland's best-selling line. Even today, English Hobnail still continues to sell. The #555 line was originally produced in the early-to-middle 1920's. The first production was in crystal, but soon various colors and treatments were added to this line.

A full set can, with diligent searching, be accumulated in crystal. English Hobnail was also manufactured in turquoise, cobalt (very few pieces in cobalt), light green, pink, milk glass, blue mist, Golden Sunset, Lilac Pastel, Blue Pastel, ruby, pink mist, Brandywine Blue, Laurel Green, Purple Marble, moss green, antique blue milk, black milk glass, crystal with black flashed bases, and crystal with red flashing.

There are three different variations of English Hobnail. Line #555 will have round-bottomed pieces with round plates. The plates will either have a plain edge or a pointed edge. Line #555/2 will have square bases and the plates will be square. Line #555/3 is mostly stemware and will be barrel shaped. All of these lines blend with each other extremely well.

With all of these different-shaped lines Westmoreland invested quite a lot of money into molds. It seems to have paid off though, because this pattern alone kept the company going for many years. The stemware and dinnerware always sold well, but there were

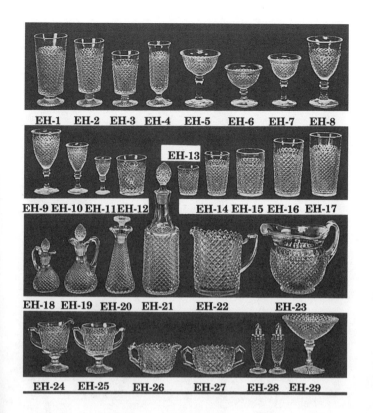

EH-1   EH-2   EH-3   EH-4   EH-5   EH-6   EH-7   EH-8

EH-13

EH-9   EH-10   EH-11   EH-12   EH-14   EH-15   EH-16   EH-17

EH-18   EH-19   EH-20   EH-21   EH-22   EH-23

EH-24   EH-25   EH-26   EH-27   EH-28   EH-29

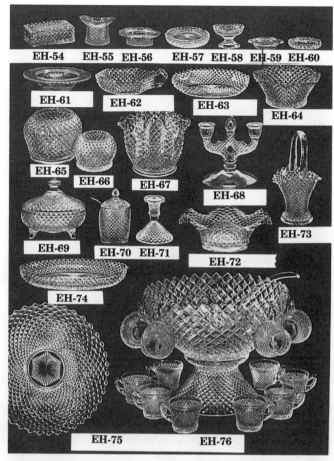

EH-54   EH-55   EH-56   EH-57   EH-58   EH-59   EH-60

EH-61   EH-62   EH-63   EH-64

EH-65   EH-66   EH-67   EH-68   EH-73

EH-69   EH-70   EH-71   EH-72

EH-74

EH-75   EH-76

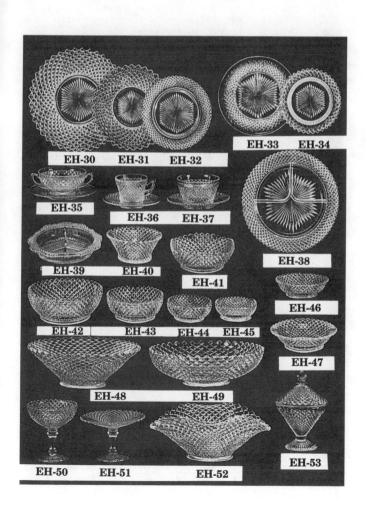

EH-33   EH-34

EH-30   EH-31   EH-32

EH-35   EH-36   EH-37   EH-38

EH-39   EH-40   EH-41

EH-42   EH-43   EH-44   EH-45   EH-46

EH-47

EH-48   EH-49

EH-50   EH-51   EH-52   EH-53

EH-77   EH-78   EH-79   EH-80   EH-81   EH-82   EH-83   EH-84

EH-85   EH-86   EH-87   EH-88   EH-89   EH-90   EH-91

EH-92   EH-93   EH-94   EH-95   EH-96

EH-99   EH-97

EH-100   EH-101

EH-98   EH-102

EH-103   EH-104   EH-105   EH-106

EH-107 EH-108 EH-109   EH-110 EH-111 EH-112

EH-113 EH-114   EH-115   EH-116 EH-117

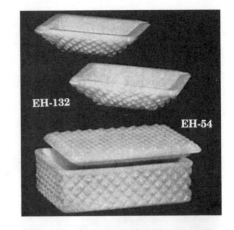

EH-132

EH-54

EH-118

EH-119

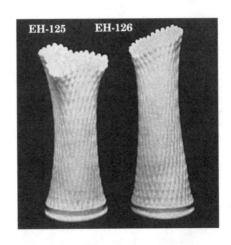

EH-120

EH-121

EH-123

EH-122

EH-124

EH-125   EH-126

EH-127

EH-129

EH-130

EH-128

EH-131

34

EH-56
EH-55
EH-133
EH-58
EH-28

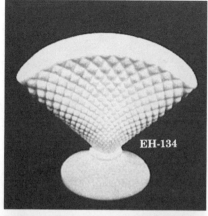

EH-134

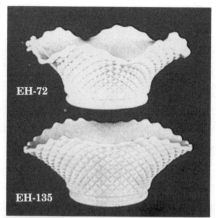

EH-72
EH-135

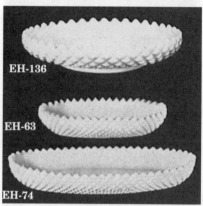

EH-136
EH-63
EH-74

EH-138
EH-40

EH-139

a few pieces that did not catch the consumers' eyes. These pieces today are naturally the ones to watch for! The canister sets did not sell well perhaps because they did not seal out moisture or bugs. The lid just sat on top. These pieces today are extremely rare. The punch bowl sets did not do well either. These sets are very breathtaking in color. Decanters, Pitchers, large plates and dinner plates, 2-lite candelabras, cheese and butter dishes, and the urn and cover are among the very scarce items.

Black-trimmed items were only produced during the 1929-1931 period. These are also extremely difficult to find. It is possible to gather a luncheon set in black trim, but a collector must be willing to be patient.

In the code section I will only attempt to list those colors which would have been manufactured during the 1950-1984 period, or items which are shown in this book. One entire book could be done on English Hobnail alone. Prices in the price guide will also only reflect the aforementioned period.

Please note that the item coded EH-139 is not English Hobnail, but Line #300. These are very similar to English Hobnail, so they were included here due to space restrictions.

EH-140   EH-68   EH-141   EH-70
EH-142   EH-143   EH-45   EH-144
EH-103-back
EH-99-front
EH-81   EH-99
EH-139   EH-146   EH-55
EH-145

Lattice Edge (Line #1890)

Lattice Edge was produced at the height of the milk-glass era from the 1950's until about 1968. Most of the production of Lattice Edge consisted of milk glass but some plates were manufactured in black milk glass and dark blue mist.

The plates were almost always hand painted, which added quite a bit to the retail cost of each piece. These plates even in the 1950's retailed for about $15 to $18. Adjusting for inflation since then, one can see this was expensive. The decorations would either have flowers, birds, ducks, or a Mary Gregory design. The game birds came in a set of eight. The game birds were listed as decoration #2, which consisted of a wild turkey, bob white, pheasant, grouse, snipe, woodcock, blue jay, and redbird. The flower cluster was decoration #18 and was a large bouquet of flowers. Decoration #360 was a large rose with gold leaves. Decorations 1A and 1B were the mallard ducks which

depicted a male mallard, baby mallard, and a female mallard.

The plates were especially difficult to make in milk glass. The plates had to be poured into a bowl mold and later reheated and flattened, because when poured flat as a plate the lacy edge tended to crack when the hand painting was fired.

All footed items have a candlestick as a base attached to the top with a glob of glass.

The hand painted plates are the most difficult items in this line to find but even the plain items are not common.

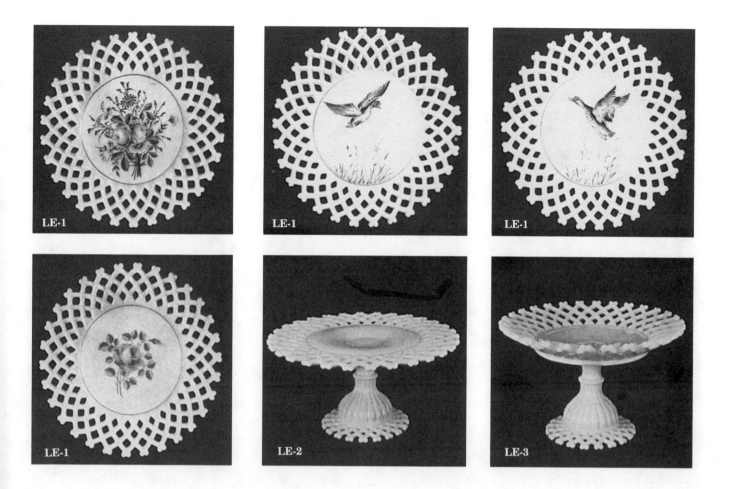

LE-1   LE-1   LE-1

LE-1   LE-2   LE-3

Lotus (Line #1921)

The Lotus line was originally produced in the 1920's and was an extensive line during that period. During the 1950's to the closing of Westmoreland, less of this pattern was produced.

In the late 50's to early 60's Westmoreland made Lotus in crystal with every other panel hand painted with a ruby stain. This treatment did not sell very well. Later on, when a new color would be introduced, a few pieces of Lotus would always be produced.

The ruffled candlestick (LO-10), which was made from a mint dish which was flattened, ruffled, and had a candleholder added to the middle, may be found in an orange color called "Flame." Westmoreland copied a color that Viking was having great success with and called "Persimmon." These candlesticks in this color were not made in any great quantity.

LO-7

LO-8

The three-piece mayonnaise set was made for Barber Brothers, a New York company. It was made in a variety of colors. Sometimes these would be hand painted with a rose decoration.

Items LO-7, LO-8, and LO-9 are Line #1933, not the Lotus pattern. These items blend very well with the Lotus line, which is

why they are included here. The cornucopia vase sold very well, but the other two vases were very limited in production and are very scarce in today's market.

In 1984, David Grossman reissued quite a few pieces in Lotus. Most of these items will be found in Pink opalescent. Mr. Grossman also re-formed old pieces into new pieces by crimping or pulling the edges. All of these pieces date from the 1984 catalog.

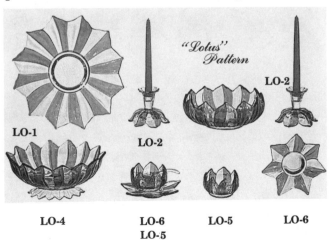

LO-1

LO-2

LO-4   LO-6   LO-5   LO-6
            LO-5

Maple Leaf or Bramble (Line #1928)

When Line #1928 was first introduced in the 1920's, it was called Bramble. Several items were available in the line during this era. In the milk glass heyday of the 1950's, the #1928 line was reintroduced as Maple Leaf and basic production was in milk glass.

When Bob Rupp visited the Westmoreland representative in Canada, he took all of the Maple Leaf pattern along with him. He thought that since the maple leaf was the Canadian national symbol, there would be a good market for such a pattern in Canada. Mr. Rupp was told by the representative that he didn't feel this pattern would sell because the Canadian public didn't seem as patriotic as the Americans. Not only was the representative correct on the Canadian connection, but this pattern did not sell well in the States either. Maple Leaf was introduced at a time when the buying public seemed to want to escape from heavily patterned glass and preferred simple, clean lines and thinner glassware. Because of its bad sales record Maple Leaf was not produced in large quantities or for a prolonged period of time.

The third attempt at Maple Leaf came after David Grossman owned Westmoreland. Mr. Grossman got the molds out and started producing them in Blue Pastel, which is a light turquoise color, Lilac Opalescent, Ruby, and Pink Pastel. The Blue Pastel is found more frequently than any of the other colors. The explanation is that the blue is a beautiful color, and because of this probably sold better originally.

Common items include sugars and creamers, and the six-pointed rose bowl all in milk glass. Scarce items include the cookie jar, with or without the lid, and any smaller bowls.

Plum Glass now owns most of the Maple Leaf molds. They have been producing this pattern mostly in black milk glass. Most items are marked with the Keystone "P" marking, but this mark is very difficult to find due to the heavy pattern. Some items will also be found in cobalt.

Also keep in mind that one mold can be made into several different types of pieces. Plum has made plates, banana bowls, and large baskets out of the 10" bowl.

ML-18

ML-17

Old Quilt (Line #500)

The Old Quilt line dates back to early in this century. Examples of Old Quilt were shown in a 1910 Butler Brothers Catalog. These items were available in crystal or crystal with gold hand-painted accents around each rim and in-between the square quilt blocks. Items shown included the large creamer, spooner, covered sugar or candy, 4-3/4" bell berry bowl, 9" bell bowl, cheese dish, 1/2-gal. pitcher and water tumblers. The entire set was priced at 75 cents. This catalog also mentions that the tumblers had ground bottoms. Another Butler Brothers catalog from 1925 showed more Old Quilt, but it was only available in crystal. Most of these early examples were produced in crystal. Examples of this early Old Quilt can still be found today. It appears that the older items have very sharp edges, whereas the pieces made in crystal in later years have a softer edge. Usually the older crystal item will be chipped due to the sawtooth type edging.

Old Quilt was also called "Checkerboard" in some of Westmoreland's catalogs, but since the 1940's it has always been referred to as Old Quilt. The 1940's saw a resurgence of Old Quilt, primarily in milk glass. Quite a bit of this pattern was produced during that time, but because of the popularity of Paneled Grape, Old Quilt did not enjoy the same fantastic sales.

Westmoreland invested quite a large sum of money into molds for Old Quilt, which may have hurt them in the long haul. In the 1970's when the gas crisis was at its peak, Westmoreland did not have the capital to invest a gas-recuperation system which would have drastically decreased the cost of production. This lack of capital was a direct result of pouring money into molds and

ignoring all else. Even the office facilities were not updated. Of course, Westmoreland utilized the Old Quilt molds from earlier in the century, but a mold cannot be expected to last forever and must be replaced.

Because of its original poor sales record, Old Quilt is quite a bit more difficult to find today than Paneled Grape. Scarce items include the complete perfume/puff set with tray, batter and syrup set, dinner plates, cups and saucers, bowls in any size, flat tumblers, punch set, and any goblet except the water-sized goblet.

Common pieces, although few, include 6" octagon footed compote, water goblet and fan vase.

Old Quilt will be found with several different types of hand paintings. One of these hand painted effects was done by Phillip Brainard's wife. Mrs. Brainard would visit the factory every so often to paint Old Quilt items with alternating squares in black and gold. She would then give these items as gifts to her friends. Westmoreland did produce a very limited amount of this type of hand painting, but it was very expensive due to the time involved and the cost of gold-leaf paint. Since these items were not shown in any catalogs, just about any piece could show up with this gold and black decoration.

Other decorations include a Forget-me-not decoration, which is five dots of blue around one dot of yellow. Forget-me-not will usually have gold trim. Decoration #32, Roses and Bows was applied to various items in milk glass, and Decoration #32-1 will appear on crystal mist items.

Old Quilt, besides being produced mainly in milk glass, will appear in several limited-edition colors. Antique Blue, Antique Blue Mist, Ice Blue Carnival, Ruby Carnival, Purple Marble, Honey Carnival, Cobalt Carnival, and Mint Green are just a few of the colors to be found. Golden Sunset, Brandywine Blue, and Laurel Green will also be found, but very rarely and usually only in the water goblet.

Most of the carnival colors listed were produced in very limited quantities for Levay. Today these colors are eagerly sought and usually very scarce.

Paneled Grape (Line #1881)

Paneled Grape has been and still is the most popular pattern throughout Westmoreland's history. It is the pattern most associated with Westmoreland's name.

Paneled Grape does not appear to be Westmoreland's original idea. According to James Measell's article accompanying the catalog reprint of the "D.C. Jenkins Glass Co. Catalog," Kokomo Glass Company of Kokomo, Indiana, appears to have been the originator of Paneled Grape. Kokomo's Paneled Grape was designed by Auburn Long (who was head moldmaker at Kokomo Glass, according to Mr. Measell) and was produced around the turn of the century. It appears to have been produced as late as 1903. Kokomo produced its Paneled Grape in crystal, and crystal with gilded colors applied to the grapes. I have been fortunate enough to have seen some of these early

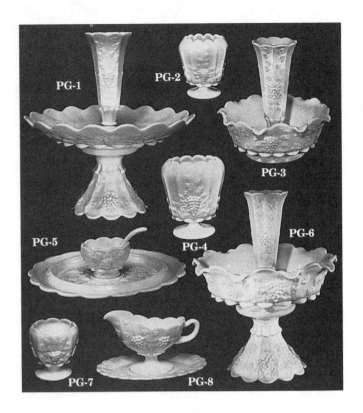

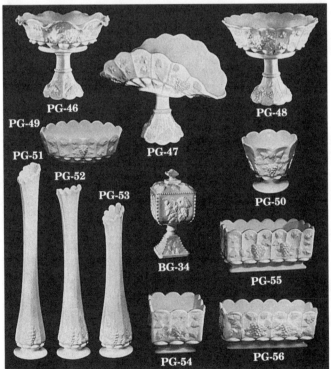

pieces, and the colorings are mostly dark in color. I don't believe Kokomo took the extra step of firing its pieces after hand painting, as Westmoreland did, because usually the painting is very badly worn. Kokomo Glass Company was destroyed by a fire in 1905. The company was rebuilt the next year and assumed the D.C. Jenkins Glass Company name.

It is not clear whether Westmoreland purchased molds from either of the above companies, or simply made its own molds. Whatever the case, Westmoreland found its niche in the glass industry with the addition of Paneled Grape.

Paneled Grape was produced in milk glass from the 1940's until the factory's closing. During this time many different items were

made. Complete dinner and luncheon sets were available. Because Paneled Grape was produced in such quantity a collector might be led to believe that it will be easily found. Not really! Some items such as the small creamer & sugar, water goblets, skirted candlesticks, both pitchers, cruets, bud vases, and the oval basket with split handles may be found with little difficulty. All of the

other items in this line will take an abundance of patience to acquire. A few pieces such as the three-branch candelabra, punch bowl sets, wall pocket vases, pickle jar vase, and dinner plates will command immediate attention when found for sale.

Westmoreland produced Paneled Grape in several different colors and applied several different decorations. Colors include crystal,

43

PG-11 BG-19 PG-27 BG-29 BG-30
BG-26 PG-83
PG-20 BG-33 PG-95

Not all items have been reproduced, but the ones that have will be found in several color variations. See each individual code for reproduction information.

PG-97 PG-98 PG-99 PG-100
PG-37 PG-18 PG-19 PG-28 PG-101 PG-102
PG-103 PG-104 BG-42 PG-105
PG-49 PG-106 PG-107 PG-60

antique blue, antique blue mist, blue mist, brown mist, almond, dark blue mist, green mist, honey carnival, ice blue carnival, purple carnival, mint green, mint green mist, pink mist, yellow mist, Golden Sunset, amber, brown marble, crystal velvet, Brandywine Blue, Laurel Green, Red Carnival, lilac pastel, blue pastel, pink pastel, brown marble, and green marble. Decorations include Roses and Bows, ruby stain on crystal, pastel leaves and grapes, 22kt. gold, daisy decals, rose decoration on almond and pansy decoration. All pieces in the line will not be available in all colors or decorations.

In most instances, the red Paneled Grape being found today was not manufactured by Westmoreland. The red was produced by, or actually for, L.G. Wright. See page 79, for a detailed comparison.

Most tumblers and plates in Paneled Grape will have ground bottoms. This was done during the time when more milk glass was sold than produced. In subsequent years when times were tough, the bottoms were not ground. If an item does not have a ground bottom, this does not mean it is a reproduction. It just means that it was produced after Westmoreland stopped the grinding operation.

Because Paneled Grape was and is popular, it has fallen prey to reproductions.

Paneled Grape Complete Canister Set

PG-96-C
PG-96-B
PG-96-A

PG-136

Princess Feather (Line #201)

Princess Feather made its first appearance in the 1920's, according to Mrs. Weatherman in her "Colored Glassware of the Depression Era 2." During this period and on into the 1950's, Line #201 was produced in crystal, crystal with ruby hand painted accents, blue, pink and green. Some items were also available in milk glass, although only occasional pieces and not a dinner service.

With the advent of the 1960's, Princess Feather was produced in Golden Sunset. This was an effort by Westmoreland to capture the color market that had escaped it up until this point. The colors of the sixties were golds, avocados and oranges. Westmoreland attempted to capture the market with its addition of Golden Sunset. Sadly, it did not work. Even though Princess Feather was produced in quantity in Golden Sunset, very little of it is being found today.

Westmoreland aggressively advertised Princess Feather in this new color. A complete set of Princess Feather was given away on a game show. The woman who was lucky enough to win this set did not want it and attempted to cash it in for the dollar value. If the woman had only known how valuable the set would become in the future, I am sure she would have kept it.

PF-26

PF-27

PF-28

PF-29

Princess Feather is often confused with other "Sandwich" type patterns, especially Duncan & Miller's Sandwich. When two pieces are side by side, the differences become apparent.

On flat pieces, such as dinner plates, etc., Duncan's Sandwich has a flower motif in the center of the plate. This flower on Duncan's plate does not extend the entire width of the circle the way Westmoreland's does. Please note that different-sized Westmoreland plates will have different numbers of flower petals.

On items which have sides, or on the rim of plates, both Duncan and Westmoreland

45

"*Princess Feather*"

PF-1 PF-2 PF-3 PF-4 PF-5

PF-6 PF-7 PF-8 PF-9

PF-10 PF-11 PF-12 PF-13

PF-14 PF-15 PF-16 PF-17 PF-18

PF-19 PF-20 PF-21 PF-22 PF-23 PF-24 PF-25

PF-26 PF-27 PF-28 PF-29

have scrolled areas which look like the letter "H". In Duncan's Sandwich, when the "H" starts curving a small flower can be found in each curve. Westmoreland's Princess Feather has no such flower in the curved areas.

The third difference also occurs on the rims. In between the scrolled "H" on both Duncan and Westmoreland there is a rosette. Duncan's rosette is rounded and Westmoreland's rosette is oblong, longer than it is wide. Shapes of the pieces in the Westmoreland version are also quite different than that of the Duncan.

PF-30

Ring & Petal (Line #1875)

Ring and Petal was most likely copied by Westmoreland from old Atterbury molds. Several examples of the Atterbury versions can be found in pattern-glass or milk-glass books.

Most of the production of Ring and Petal occurred from the 1950's to the company's closing. Milk glass versions are found most often, but all kinds of colors were produced. All pieces were not produced in color.

The 8" plate will be occasionally found with a hand painted motif in the center of the plate. The most commonly found painting is that of birds, although others were surely produced.

Most items can be found with variations of crimping or ruffling. Some round bowls were squared off to produce a slightly different effect. Banana bowls and cake plates may be found with either a candlestick base or a low ribbed foot. The candlestick was used as a base on other patterns as well as Ring and Petal, although the Doric candlestick was more commonly used.

RP-1   RP-2   RP-3

RP-4   RP-5   RP-4

RP-6   RP-7

RP-16

RP-17

RP-8

RP-9

RP-10

RP-11

RP-12

RP-13

RP-14

RP-15

Rose or Rose & Lattice (Line #1967)

The only reference to a name for Line #1967 is in a 1970 catalog which refers to it as "Rose." Most collectors and dealers refer to it as "Rose & Lattice," which may be a more appropriate title.

Line #1967 was introduced in the late 1960's. Only one or two items per year were marketed. This line has very few pieces and most pieces served double duty. A bowl would be made into a basket, or crimped a different way to form a myriad of different items.

Most of the production consisted of milk glass, but some pieces will be found in color. Decoration #33 will be found hand painted on some of Line #1967. This is a pastel color and basically enhances the pattern already in the glass.

Collectors must be careful when buying items in Line #1967, as it has been reproduced quite extensively. Most reproductions will be found in cobalt blue, which Westmoreland never made in this pattern.

RL-1

RL-2

RL-3

RL-4

48

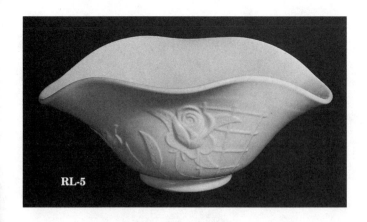

RL-5

Sawtooth (Line #556)

The design of Sawtooth seems to date back to the 1860's era. Just about every company making glass during that era had a similar pattern. These older pieced will not have the quality or sheen that Westmoreland pieces will have.

Westmoreland made Sawtooth during the 1950's when milk glass was so very popular. During the color splurge in the 1960's and beyond, Sawtooth was also made in various colors. Sawtooth was produced even during the Grossman era, although Grossman appears to have used molds that had not been used for quite a number of years.

The 14" tall bowl with lid was made into a lamp. The base of the bowl was drilled out to accept a lamp cord. This proved very expensive as most drill bits were dulled rather quickly by the thick glass in this part of the piece. The normal finial on the top was replaced with a metal eagle. Not many examples of these lamps exist today. Most of these lamps were in the Golden Sunset color. The light bulb was housed inside the covered bowl part and it illuminated the Golden Sunset color quite well.

Quite often at antiques shows examples of Sawtooth will be found at exorbitant prices. I assume dealers who price them that way believe these pieces to be of an older vintage than they actually are. Most of the colors will date from 1960 through 1984. The colors are very scarce but surely do not command some of the prices that have been attached to them!

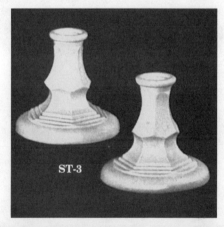

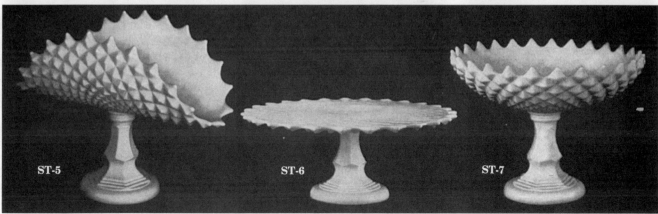

Swirl & Ball (Line #1842)

Swirl and Ball was a line which was introduced in the early 1940's. Its roots actually go back even further. This pattern originated as Line #1710, which Mrs. Weatherman calls "Wagner" in her "Colored Glassware of the Depression Era." According to Bob Rupp, when this line was reissued in the 1940's the balls were added by the moldmaker by scooping them out on the original molds. This is one of the few times that Westmoreland used a line that was already at its disposal instead of creating an entirely new line. I would imagine this saved quite a large sum of money.

Since the bulk of production occurred in the 1940's, most of the pieces which are found today are in crystal. A few pieces will be found in milk glass. Some crystal pieces will have hand painted stain colors applied. Some of these stain pieces will only have ruby, others will have ruby, blue and yellow.

In the 1960's and later, select pieces of Swirl and Ball were produced. These were only occasional pieces, but they will be found in several colors. Some carnival colors will also be found, usually in water sets.

SB-1

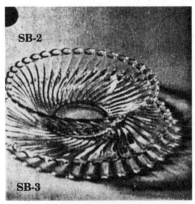

SB-2
SB-3

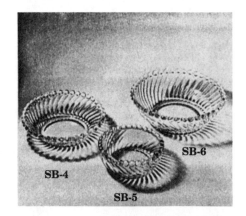

SB-4
SB-5
SB-6

SB-7
SB-8
SB-9
SB-10

SB-11
SB-12

SB-13
SB-14

SB-15
SB-16

SB-17 SB-18 SB-19 SB-20 SB-21 SB-22 SB-23

SB-25
SB-24 SB-26 SB-27 SB-28 SB-29

SB-30 SB-31 SB-3 SB-32 SB-33 SB-34

SB-35 SB-36 SB-37 SB-38 SB-39 SB-40

51

Thousand Eye (Line #1000)

Thousand Eye was another pattern that Westmoreland copied from older pattern glass. Most of the older versions, however, will be slightly different.

According to Charles West-Wilson, Thousand Eye was introduced some time in 1934 and continued sporadically until the milk glass surge of the 1950's, although a complete dinner set was still available through the 1955 catalog. Basically a crystal production, a complete set could, with great difficulty, be collected in crystal with hand-painted stain colors. The colors of the stain include ruby, yellow and blue. In some pieces the colors appear darker than others.

The turtle cigarette box was one of the best sellers in this pattern. Because it still continues to be a widely collected piece, it has fallen prey to reproductions. However, so far, it is the only piece in this pattern to have been reproduced.

In 1977 when Westmoreland appeared to enter into the lamp business, Thousand Eye fairy lamps were produced. These can be found in many colors and stain variations. There are footed and flat versions of the fairy lamps.

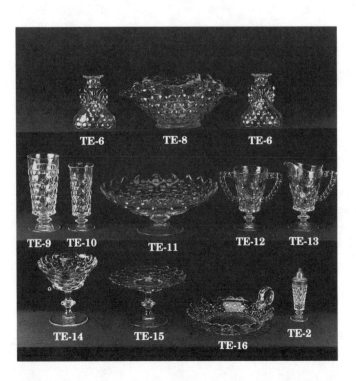

Waterford or Irish Waterford (Line #1932)

Westmoreland seems to have had a dilemma deciding what to call the 1932 line. In the 1950's it was referred to as Irish Waterford. Later in the 1960's and 1970's it was called Waterford.

This pattern appears to have been made to compete with the influx of foreign-made crystal. It is of the finest quality, and when the ruby stain is applied it bears a striking resemblance to Bohemian glass.

Waterford was made early on only in crystal. Production continued sporadically until the company closed. It seems the most varied production occurred in the 1960's and 1970's. This is when most of the ruby stain

WF-1 WF-2 WF-3 WF-4 WF-5 WF-6 WF-7 WF-8 WF-9 WF-10 WF-11 WF-12 WF-13

WF-15 WF-17

WF-14 WF-16 WF-18 WF-19 WF-20 WF-21 WF-22

WF-23 WF-24 WF-25 WF-26 WF-27

items seem to have been produced in the largest quantity. Westmoreland did save some money on molds with this pattern because by crimping or ruffling a piece in a different way an entirely new item was born. The iced tea tumbler was made into a crimped rim vase; the footed finger bowl was crimped and marketed as a candy and later used as the base for the fairy lamps. The only item which I wish Westmoreland had made from these molds is a bell. With the quality of the glass, a bell would have looked beautiful and also had a wonderful tone.

A full luncheon set is possible to collect with the exception of cups and saucers, which, although they have not appeared in any catalog, were produced, according to Bob Rupp.

The manner that this pattern was marketed seems to show that customers did not purchase this line in a set. Instead, customers used Waterford to accent what they already owned. For instance, numerous goblets and tumblers were produced, but no pitchers or decanters seem to exist. Perhaps this was a less expensive alternative to the imported glass.

Wedding Bowl (Line #1874)

The Wedding Bowl line is a copy of a very old pattern glass pattern from the mid-to-late 1800's. The pattern glass version will be found mostly in crystal and has a large number of very impressive pieces.

Westmoreland chose to copy only four pieces from this extensive line. The Wedding Bowls got their name from use at weddings. See the reprint of a Westmoreland brochure which accompanied the Wedding Bowls.

The most popular items in this line are any of the hand painted Roses and Bows (dec #32) items. Although there are other hand paintings such as the Grapes and Leaves decoration (dec #36), and crystal with ruby stain. The ruby stain items may also have white roses hand painted on top of the stain.

The hard to find items are the 6" wedding bowl which is low footed and the candlesticks. Neither of these pieces sold very well. The other two sizes of bowls will be found, perhaps not when you need to find one, but, nonetheless, they are available.

Several other companies manufactured similar wedding bowls. Jeannette Glass

Company, which was located close to Westmoreland, produced two sizes of wedding bowls in the Shell Pink color. Shell Pink was a pink opaque or milk glass. These wedding bowls are 8" and 6-1/2" tall, and they are not decorated. Production of these wedding bowls occurred in the late 1950's. Pictures of these items can be found in Hazel Marie Weatherman's "Colored Glassware of the Depression Era."

Duncan Glass also produced three sizes of wedding bowls. Duncan's sizes are 6" square and 12" high, 5" square and 10" high, and 4" square and 6-1/2" high. The latter was marketed as a cigarette box. Pictures of these items can be found in Fred Bickenheuser's "Tiffin Glassmasters, Book III."

WB-1 · WB-2

WB-3

WB-1 · WB-2

WB-4

Wildflower & Lace (Line #999)

Wildflower & Lace is a pattern that was resurrected by David Grossman in 1983. Previously, this pattern had not been produced since the 1920's or early 1930's.

Hazel Marie Weatherman shows this line in her "Colored Glassware of the Depression Era 2" book. There is no reference as to the color of the line. Most of these older pieces will be differently shaped or slightly different in size when compared to the new versions.

The colors that David Grossman chose for this pattern seem to enhance the pieces. Most pieces will be found in crystal or pastel colors, with some having a mother-of-pearl or carnival treatment.

Since the Grossman colors were produced very late in Westmoreland's history, items should be easily found in the general area near the factory. In other areas which are farther away, they may not be found at all. Most of the dealers who attended the company auctions will own some pieces of this pattern. I have not found too many examples at antiques shops or flea markets as yet.

Wildflower and Lace Pattern Mother of Pearl

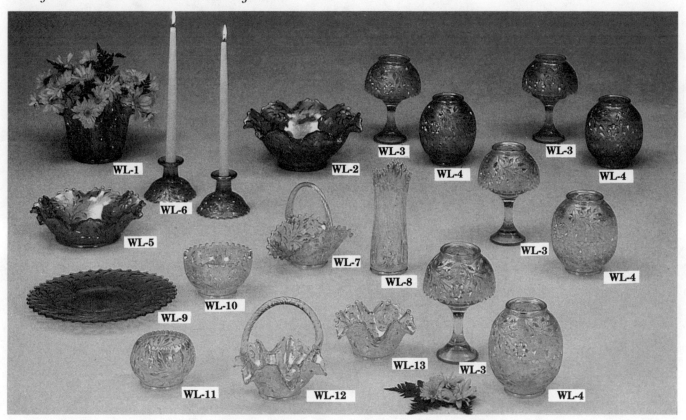

WL-8

WL-3

WL-14

WL-15

WL-3

WL-3

WL-3

WL-3

WL-12

WL-4

WL-3

WL-4

WL-4

WL-16

WL-7

WL-12

WL-4

WL-4

WL-11

WL-11

WL-17

Other Patterns in Milk Glass

RL-6   LO-26   PF-10   SW-1 SW-2   1940-1

LO-9   OQ-64

324-1   FR-1   LO-15

229-1   1800-5   229-2

56

COLORS IN WESTMORELAND

Almond, Almond Mist, Coral, Coraline, Coraline Soft Mist and Soft Mist Coral

When Westmoreland entered the 1970's it found itself struggling more than ever. It decided to come up with a variety of new and different colors that would help Westmoreland enjoy the same profits as it had during the milk glass rage of the 1950's.

In 1973 Dwight Johnson, who was the master chemist at the time, developed the color Coraline. This was a tan opaque (or milk glass) color.

The same color in 1978 was called Coral. In 1980 the name was changed for the last time to Almond. There are slight differences in the colors which are more due to heating differences than changes in the formula.

In certain lighting Almond will appear almost pinkish. J.H. Brainard had also seen the pinkish cast to this color and did not especially like it because of the pink cast.

The Almond was combined with brown hand painting to create Almond rose. The dark brown of the hand painting compliments the light color of the glass very well. Beaded Bouquet will also be found on some pieces in this tan opaque color.

Of all of the opaque colors, Almond ,Coral, or Coraline (whichever you prefer) seemed to sell the best, but it still was not a runaway bestseller. The hand painted items most likely drew the most attention because of their beauty, but the added expense of hand painting made these items more expensive. One problem that tended to crop up on all of the opaque colors was a light-colored or almost white line. This line would appear usually in the center of the piece. It made the piece look like the batch of glass was not mixed properly. Westmoreland could never solve this pesky problem, so instead of solving the problem it covered it with hand painting. The hand painting tended to hide the white line.

I have been told by several high-ranking employees of Westmoreland that a complete dinner or luncheon set in Paneled Grape was not produced in Almond or Mint Green because of the aforementioned white line and the color differences resulting from heat differences. Although I have never found a cup and saucer, I have found dinner plates, luncheon plates, and bowls that look like a puff-box bottom. The two sizes of plates, although found rarely, were most likely made to become a two-tier server. These servers, or tidbit trays, have holes drilled in the centers of the plates to accommodate the metal center handle. Perhaps these tidbit trays did not sell well, and the plates were sold without the holes in order to get rid of old stock.

Items in Almond will be more difficult to find than the same item in milk glass. Hand painted items will even be more difficult. Shortly after Westmoreland closed, almond items—plain or hand painted—seemed to be all over the area, but the supply seems to have vanished in recent years.

Almond Mist or Coraline Soft Mist first appeared in the 1973 catalog. (Basically, any mist color is achieved by dipping a piece of glass in an acid bath after it has been molded and cooled.) The next appearance of this color was in the 1979 catalog. At this time Westmoreland referred to it as Soft Mist Coral. A variety of occasional pieces were available in these coral mist colors.

The 1979 catalog was the last one to show any opaque mist items. With such a relatively short life, these items may be a little more difficult to find than the regular shiny version.

Amber or Soft Gold

Amber was introduced in the 1974 catalog supplement. The printing company that printed this catalog had listed this color as Soft Gold. This color is more of a yellow color. This color is much softer than that of the Golden Sunset. The Golden Sunset appears more orange in color when compared to the amber.

Also for the 1974 supplement, the amber or soft gold pieces were frosted to create Yellow Mist. It appears that more items were made in the Yellow Mist than that of the amber. Perhaps at this time the mist colors sold better for Westmoreland.

Only 12 items were shown in amber. More may exist but this, like other colors, appeared to be very short-lived.

Antique Blue and Antique Blue Mist

Antique Blue is a robin's-egg-blue opaque color which was produced as early as 1950. In the 1950 catalog only seven items were shown. They included a #7 Robin on Nest, #115 Swan vase, #115 Swan toothpick holder, #1 Covered Hen on lacy oval base (only part of the hen was antique blue, the head and base were milk glass), #757 Pansy basket, #2 medium Hen on oval basketweave base (all blue), and #3 Toy-chick dish (all blue). These items were even shown in color in the catalog, which for that era was rare.

The next time Antique Blue was shown in a catalog was 1952. The line was expanded to include the previously mentioned items and a pitcher set in Old Quilt, a low footed compote in Old Quilt, Forget-me-not plates, the Swan covered creamer and covered sugar, an 8" Dolphin compote as well as the #6 Standing Rooster (available with a milk glass head or all blue).

The next appearance did not occur until 1977-78. The 1977 version was mostly the frosted version called Antique Blue Mist. This was the same color with a matte finish. In 1978 Antique Blue was shown with Beaded Bouquet hand painted in white. Some of the animal kingdom was also produced during these few years, but most will be found in the Antique Blue Mist rather than the plain Antique Blue.

In the 1978 and 1979 catalogs, the Shell collection was produced in Antique Blue and Antique Blue Mist. This included all dolphin items as well as the Starfish candlesticks, the #1 Shell bowl, and Dolphin and Shell covered candy. Also in the 1979 catalog, the Beaded Bouquet items appeared again, but this time dark blue leaves were used to accent the white flowers.

Since both attempts at this color did not last for any length of time, it may not have sold as well as Westmoreland had hoped.

Also in the 1950's version, although not shown in any catalog that I have seen, Westmoreland produced some pieces in English Hobnail. The colors on the 1950's version will vary widely from a very dark opaque to a light sky blue. Please take a look at the photo on page 88 titled "Blues & Lilacs," for the color comparisons on the top row.

Apricot Mist

Apricot Mist was born out of Westmoreland's desire to be able to market some of the vast quantities of Golden Sunset that did not readily sell. Simply stated, Apricot Mist is Golden Sunset with a frosted or mist finish. Westmoreland's plan worked fairly well because the Apricot Mist pieces did enjoy a fair amount of sales. Even though it did do well, production did not last any extended length of time, and, therefore, items in this color will be difficult to find.

Apricot Mist first appeared in the 1971 catalog. Very few items were shown in Apricot Mist, but any item that was produced in Golden Sunset could be found in Apricot Mist.

Bermuda Blue

Bermuda Blue is a dark almost teal color which was introduced in the 1967 catalog. This color is very similar to Brandywine

Blue except that the Bermuda Blue is much darker.

Bermuda Blue was a short-lived color, but quite a number of items were available. The colors which were marketed along with Bermuda Blue in 1967 were Olive Green and Golden Sunset. Several pieces from the Colonial, Lotus, and Ashburton lines were available in any of the three colors. Covered animals such as the #20 Lovebirds, #2 Hen, and #7 Robin were also available in all three colors.

Bermuda Blue seems to have been only marketed in the one catalog. After this catalog it just disappears. For this reason Bermuda Blue will be scarce, especially in the animals.

Black Opaque or Black Milk Glass

Black opaque glass was produced by Westmoreland throughout its history. The most commonly produced item was the Forget-me-not border plate with the Mary Gregory-style white hand painting. These

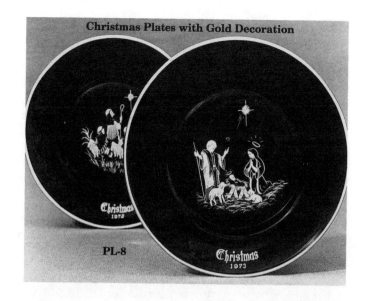

Christmas Plates with Gold Decoration

PL-8

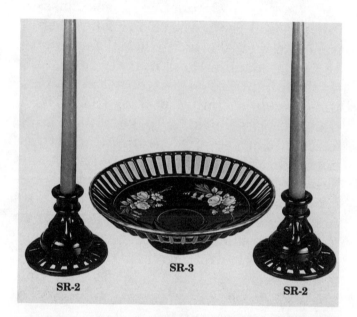

SR-3

SR-2   SR-2

Black Milk Glass

PL-1

1902-6 1902-4 1902-6
Tray 1902-7

PL-3

LO-28   SP-2   RV-1

PG-34   PG-28

IR-1

PL-4

PL-6

PL-5

TE-21

PL-7

PL-8

PL-9

plates were produced from the early 1950's.

Other items which may be found are Turtle cigarette boxes and ashtrays; Dolphin candlesticks, and some covered animals, as well as a very plain #1801 and #1802 line. This line consisted of a small dinner set. This set did not sell well in the midwest. In New York City and Los Angeles this set sold the best.

Another item produced in black glass was the small Bulldog and the Bulldog door stop. The small Bulldog will be found today with only a little difficulty. But the door stop Bulldog is extremely rare. The door stop is solid glass and is very heavy. This dog was very limited in production. Black glass in this size and volume tended to melt when it was placed in the lehr. Special machinery had to be manufactured in order to prevent this melting. Also be aware that Tiffin/U.S. Glass made a similar bulldog (See "Tiffin Glassmasters Book II," page 159). I have been told by several people that Tiffin borrowed Westmoreland's mold for the bulldog in order to make its Bulldog for a special order. I have no documentation to confirm or deny this. But it is suspicious that quite a few of Tiffin's items bear a striking resemblance to Westmoreland's. Since all of the glass companies tended to copy one another's work, I have always wondered if this was the case with the Bulldog.

Also be aware that the large Bulldog has been reproduced. As the maker (Summit Art Glass in conjunction with Rosso Wholesale Glass Dealers) soon found out, these are very difficult to make, even in cobalt. The new

versions will be found in cobalt as well as milk glass. These reproductions were not made for an extended length of time and are not found much today. In some cases, even these reproductions are being sought because the originals are so elusive.

Other items in black glass have also been reproduced. Please see the specific items in the code section, to determine which ones have been reproduced.

In the Grossman years, specifically 1984, black glass was also produced, although it

BL-1

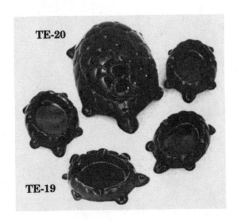
BD-2

PL-10

PL-5

RWS-1

TE-20

TE-19

never appeared in any of the catalogs. When I visited the factory in September of 1985, there were several pallets of black glass. These pallets contained either lids or bottoms. It appeared that production ceased before the companion pieces to either the lids or bottoms could be produced. I suspect that if Westmoreland had continued, these items would have been shown in a 1985 catalog. In future years this may drive collectors crazy as they look for either a lid or a bottom.

Several complete items were also produced during this time in black glass. Most often, these items were in Paneled Grape. These items will bear the last mark, which is the "Westmoreland" in a circle.

Black Milk Glass

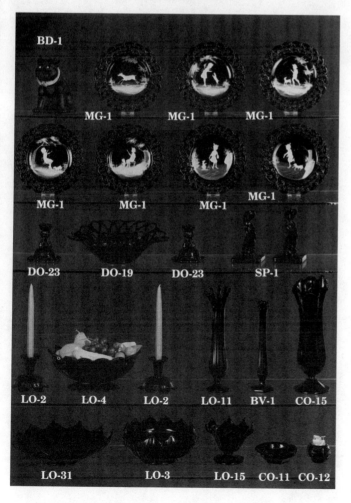

Blue Pastel

Blue Pastel is a Grossman product first introduced in a July 1, 1981, catalog supplement. This is an aqua color.

Although Westmoreland did produce a turquoise or aqua color during the depression era, the comparison to the Grossman color is easily made. Grossman's color is a darker color, whereas the Depression Era turquoise is a very light color. Also the items that Grossman chose to manufacture in this color were not produced in the Depression Era turquoise.

Very few items were produced in this color. Patterns include Maple Leaf, English Hobnail, Doric, and Paneled Grape, as well as several occasional items in other patterns. The Maple Leaf 14" basket is beautiful in the Blue Pastel. Please be aware that this basket has been reproduced, although not in this color as yet (see the code section under each individual piece for reproduction information).

In the same 1981 supplement, Grossman produced a frosted version of Blue Pastel, which I have called Light Blue Mist. Animal items made include the large oval Covered Duck, Raised-wing Swan, small Butterfly, and small Wren. Pattern pieces produced are the same as those produced for Blue Pastel.

In 1984 Grossman chose to use the same Blue Pastel with the Wildflower and Lace line. Some of the Wildflower and Lace pieces will have a carnival or mother-of-pearl finish.

Blue Mist, Light and Dark

The first blue mist to appear was the lighter variety. This Light Blue Mist was first produced in the late 1960's. Only a few items were produced in Light Blue Mist. Doric, Colonial, and Lotus occasional pieces, as well as a few animals, lamps, and candlesticks, were manufactured in this color.

This light blue is the same shade as the

later color which Grossman produced.

The Dark Blue Mist first appeared in 1971. Perhaps this version was a much better seller for Westmoreland because it had a sustained life until about 1978. The first items produced were mostly of the plain lines such as the 1902 line. These were often hand painted with the daisy decoration. Later a daisy decal was used on these same pieces. A variety of items were manufactured without decorations as well. These include items in Doric, Ring and Petal, Lotus and Colonial. Some of the animals were also produced in the dark blue mist.

In 1974 quite a few more items were added in Dark Blue Mist. These include items in Paneled Grape and Rose and Lattice. 1974 seemed to be the year that the mist colors were marketed the most. This was also the year of the dark colors such as Brown Mist, and Green Mist.

Mary Gregory-style plates are also available in Dark Blue Mist. The dark blue shows off the white hand painting exquisitely.

The Dark Blue Mist was made by taking Brandywine Blue and dipping it in an acid bath to create a frosted appearance.

Brandywine Blue

Brandywine Blue was introduced in 1964 along with Golden Sunset and Laurel Green. Brandywine Blue is a vibrant azure-blue color.

Several patterns were produced in this color which include a luncheon set in Paneled Grape, as well as English Hobnail, Sawtooth, Old Quilt and Beaded Grape occasional pieces.

Goblets were also produced in patterns such as Princess Feather, Old Quilt, Swirl and Ball, and American Hobnail. These goblets were primarily manufactured to blend with china patterns of the early 1960's era. Although this was a good idea, it just did not sell well. These goblets today are very scarce.

Westmoreland kept Brandywine Blue in its line for quite a few years. During this time different pieces were produced each year, and when these items did not sell, the company would frost the items (see Blue Mist). The mist colors for some reason sold better than the regular colors. An opalescent version was also produced, which can be found under Brandywine Blue Opalescent in this section.

Brandywine Blue has a companion color in Bermuda Blue. Bermuda Blue is a much darker color than Brandywine Blue.

Brandywine Blue Opalescent & Candlelight

Brandywine Blue Opalescent was a short-lived color produced in 1971 only. It, however, was revived in 1976-1978 for production for Levay. This is basically Brandywine Blue with a phosphorus compound added so that when heated a white accent appears in various places on each piece.

The only pattern that was attempted in this color was American Hobnail. Only 13 pieces were ever produced for regular sale. See the Levay Colors section for other pieces. Westmoreland referred to the color process as "Moonstone". This process does remind one of several other companies who manufactured large quantities of the same type of ware. Most of these other companies manufactured these items with clear or crystal glass with white accents. Westmoreland was very creative to imagine a color with the white accents.

According to Bob Rupp, this color process was also done in a green color with white accents. I have not found any evidence of this in any catalog, nor have I ever found an actual piece to confirm this fact.

Westmoreland also made this in the crystal with white accents and called it Candlelight. The same pieces in American Hobnail were produced for the same length of time.

Both Brandywine Blue Opalescent and Candlelight are extremely hard to find today. If there is a common piece it would be the puff box in Brandywine Blue Opalescent, but even this is more often than not elusive.

A few items in Brandywine Blue Opalescent were also produced for an A.A. Importing Co. catalog in the 1970's.

Brown and Brown Mist

Brown and Brown Mist appeared in catalogs from 1975 through 1980. The first appearance of Brown in 1975 included a goblet assortment in Ashburton and Colonial. This color appears to have been a poor seller, which is odd considering that other companies were having good success with their brown colors.

Brown Mist also appeared for the first time in the 1975 catalog. Items included Mary Gregory-style hand painting on the #30 Wicket Border plate, as well as plain pieces in Rose and Lattice, Paneled Grape and Colonial. Another grouping of brown mist items were shown with a daisy decal. At this time the daisy decal must have been a very popular decoration. Quite a number of items were produced with daisies.

In the 1977-78 catalog the Floral Bouquet decoration was introduced on Brown Mist. Westmoreland also carried the daisy decal in this catalog. Other plain pieces of Brown Mist were added at this time. These include some items in Old Quilt as well as some covered animals.

In the 1980 catalog the production of Brown Mist seems to have slowed considerably. Only nine items were shown at this time and all had the daisy decal.

Crystal

Crystal was produced continuously throughout Westmoreland's long history. The premier era for crystal was during the 1940's. During this time patterns such as English Hobnail, Princess Feather, Waterford and others were produced in crystal for the bridal trade. It was very much in vogue to have at least one glass table setting in crystal. This crystal production kept the company in business during the 1940's. Other companies also centered their efforts on crystalware and many beautiful etched lines were produced during this era. This is one area of endeavor that Westmoreland never entered. During the early part of this century Westmoreland did engraving work as well as wheel cutwork, but they never did etchings of any type.

When Westmoreland entered the milk glass era of the 1950's crystal production was drastically reduced, but it never ceased altogether.

In the late 1950's and early 1960's Westmoreland started producing Paneled Grape in crystal. The Paneled Grape that

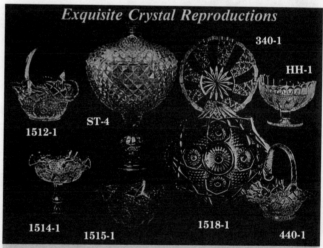

Exquisite Crystal Reproductions

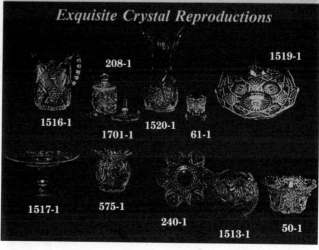

Exquisite Crystal Reproductions

Westmoreland Crystal Reproductions

Westmoreland produced was a very clear type crystal. I have found some items in what appear to be Paneled Grape that have a yellowish cast. These pieces may have been produced by the original manufacturer of Paneled Grape, Kokomo Glass Company of Indiana.

Westmoreland produced almost every piece of Paneled Grape in crystal. Certain items like the canister set, shallow bowl, and epergnes were not produced in crystal. But, certainly, a dinnerware or luncheon set was available. Even a punch set and a decanter set were available in crystal.

Some items of crystal such as the Waterford line and Wedding Bowl line were hand painted with a ruby stain. Paneled Grape also was made in a ruby-stain version with only the grapes and leaves painted and the rest crystal. This was a labor-intensive process which in turn made these pieces expensive to the retail public.

When David Grossman took over at Westmoreland, crystal was still produced. During Grossman's tenure some of the turn-of-the-century molds were pulled from storage and produced again in crystal.

Even though crystal was produced for such a great length of time in some patterns, the crystal versions are more difficult to find than the milk glass versions. This fact may not be readily noticed, since collectors do not seem to search out the crystal versions as much as they do the milk glass versions.

Crystal Mist

Crystal Mist was introduced in 1969. Quite a number of items are available in Crystal Mist. These include items in Colonial, Lotus, and Doric, as well as other occasional pieces and some covered animals.

Crystal Mist was the base color for some of the decals that were introduced in the 1970's and 1980's. Decals like China Rose, Strawberry, Andrea West Rooster, and Andrea West Country Floral. Anniversary decorations and Roses and Bows were also shown on Crystal Mist, and were hand painted.

All of the Dolphin series is available in Crystal Mist, as well as the Starfish candleholders, Shell bowl and Argonaut Shell covered candy.

Some of the later examples in the 1980's with the aforementioned decals were not produced by Westmoreland. Canisters and such were produced by Anchor Hocking. This was an attempt to bring down costs and give the public inexpensive ware that was enhanced by Westmoreland's decals.

Few examples of Crystal Mist are found in today's marketplace. Since some items in this color are more recent in manufacture, perhaps they have not reached the point of being on the secondary market as yet.

Flame and Flame Mist

Flame was introduced in January of 1967. This was a very difficult color to manufacture. According to Bob Rupp, very high temperatures were needed to melt the selenium in this color. The batches often melted unevenly and blisters could be found in some of the pieces due to the high temperatures. With such a high content of selenium, this was also a very expensive color to manufacture.

Flame was basically made to compete with Viking's Persimmon color. At the time Persimmon was one of the hottest colors in the glass industry.

With all of the problems in the melting of Flame, other problems developed later in the process. This color is what is referred to in the glass industry as a "struck color." This means that the final color does not appear until after the newly formed pieces are placed in the glory hole on a punty rod. This is when most of the piece will turn a reddish orange. Some parts of the piece will remain a yellowish orange. This was a very crucial part of the process. Too much heat would tend to make the pattern fade away, which is why no animals were ever produced in the Flame color. Too little heat would prevent the correct color from appearing.

Since this was a very labor-intensive color to make, the retail price was high. The lack of a wide variety of pieces and the price most likely contributed to the slow sales in this color. Because of the slow sales, Flame was produced in 1967 only. Only 15 items were shown in this color and most of those were either in the Lotus or Colonial patterns.

Since Flame was so limited in production and duration, any examples will be very scarce or rare.

Flame Mist is a frosted version of Flame. It appears to be a dark red with yellow tinges at the ends of each piece. Flame Mist was not shown in any catalog and is a very rare find today.

Golden Sunset

Golden Sunset was introduced in 1964 along with Laurel Green and Brandywine Blue. This was the year that Westmoreland decided to jump on the color bandwagon.

Golden Sunset is an orange-amber color. It has been described as a "beer bottle amber" by some of the former Westmoreland employees and customers.

Quite a number of different patterns can be found in the Golden Sunset color. Princess Feather and Paneled Grape are among the more well-known examples. Some of the covered animal dishes were also produced in this color.

In the early 1960's Westmoreland's manufacturer's representatives approached the management at the plant with the idea of producing goblets to match china patterns being produced during this time. It sounded like a fine idea at the time, hence several goblets can be found in Golden Sunset. Unfortunately, the buying public did not agree with this new strategy. Most often, when customers purchased a new china pattern, a stemware pattern would be shown with the china set. Most of the stemware that was matched with these china patterns were of the plain-patterned type. Westmoreland came along with a heavily patterned, thick stemware and the public simply did not favor this type of glass. Fostoria and Imperial did have success with this type of arrangement. In fact, Imperial oversold its stemware lines to the point that Westmoreland was asked to help Imperial meet its commitments by manufacturing glass for it. By today's standards it may see odd for competing companies to help one another out, but this was done quite a lot by the glass companies.

When Westmoreland realized that this new color was not going to sell, it tried frosting the pieces. Thus, Apricot Mist was born. Apricot Mist items did sell a bit better.

Because of the lack of sales in Golden Sunset, it does not appear frequently today. It was made in enough quantity that it should be easily found, but this is not the case. Items in Golden Sunset will range from very difficult to scarce.

Green Mist

Green Mist was first introduced in the 1968 catalog. This first Green Mist appeared to be a very mossy-colored green, a dull sort of color. It most likely did not sell very well, because in the 1969 catalog the Green Mist color appears to have a brighter cast and is more of a yellowish green.

The 1969 version of Green Mist did last for quite a number of years. The last appearance in any catalog occurred in 1977. During most of the production of this color the items were kept plain. In the middle seventies the daisy decoration was added to green mist. This combination was a popular seller.

Most of the items which were produced in Green Mist were occasional items. These included items in Doric, Colonial, Paneled Grape, Beaded Grape, and Rose and Lattice. Dinnerware sets were not produced in this color. As each year progressed, more items were added.

Usually, Green Mist items will be available to the collector. The items with decals will perhaps be a little difficult in some areas, but, in general, will also be available.

Honey Carnival and Ice Blue Carnival

Honey Carnival was introduced in the 1976 catalog. Only nine pieces appear to have been produced for the regular Westmoreland line during this year. Other items will be found, but they may have been produced for Levay. (See the Colors for Levay section for more information.)

The items produced include: #81 Fruits 15-piece punch set, #500 Old Quilt 3-pint pitcher and water tumbler, #1048 Shell candy, #1881 Paneled Grape lacy (crimped and ruffled) candy, #1881 handled nut basket, #1884 Beaded Grape covered low-footed honey, #500 Old Quilt celery vase, #1900 Slipper, and #303 Fan and File child's punch set.

None of these items for the regular line were produced in limited editions.

Honey Carnival is a light amber color with a carnival or mother-of-pearl finish applied.

Ice Blue Carnival was introduced in the same 1976 catalog. The same nine pieces were produced in Ice Blue Carnival and Honey Carnival for the regular line. Other items will be found, but they were produced for Levay. (See the Colors for Levay section for more information.)

None of the above items were limited editions, although large amounts were not produced. In 1980, however, Westmoreland did produce a #81 Fruits punch bowl for Levay in a Turquoise Carnival. This color is slightly darker than Ice Blue Carnival, but it is such a slight difference that a difference in temperature could be the primary cause. This production for Levay was limited to 400 sets.

Ice Blue Carnival is a light aqua color with a carnival finish applied. Any carnival color will be found only with great difficulty.

Laurel Green

Laurel Green was introduced in 1964 along with Brandywine Blue and Golden Sunset. Laurel Green is a lovely Kelly green.

Several items were produced in Laurel Green. A complete luncheon set is available in Paneled Grape. Several different patterns of goblets were produced to match china patterns of the day. Sawtooth, Old Quilt, and Beaded Grape, as well as some covered animals were produced in Laurel Green.

The Colonial or Keystone lines were also produced in Laurel Green. Most of these items will bear the Keystone "W" marking, as Westmoreland did not remove old markings because it felt this added to, rather

than detracted from, the collectibility of the piece.

Laurel Green items will not be found easily.

Lilac and Lilac Mist

Lilac is a dark purple color which was produced during 1973 only. During the same year some of the Lilac items were frosted and made into Lilac Mist. More items were made in the Lilac Mist than Lilac. Some of the Lilac Mist items were hand painted with a Daisy decoration. These hand painted items include #750 small basket, #275 square jewel box, #1902 heart-shaped trinket box, #1902 footed bud vase, #1902 dresser set with two perfume bottles, one puff box and one oval tray (the tray will be void of decoration), and #1700 covered candy with lid.

Although this is a lovely color, it most likely was too dark to attract the public's attention. It was only produced for one year. In today's market, Lilac and Lilac Mist are extremely scarce, and items with the Daisy decoration are almost rare.

Marble Colors

Marble creations appeared in 1972. The first two colors were Purple and Green Marble. Most of the other glass manufacturers called this process "slag glass," but Westmoreland chose to be different and called it "marble."

Marble glass takes a bit of planning in order to find two compatible glass types to combine. Both the white base and the color must melt at approximately the same temperature and not separate during the molding process. This takes knowledge of chemical properties and experience. This was an area in which Westmoreland was very capable. Both master chemists, Sam Guy and, later, Dwight Johnson, were very capable and dedicated craftsmen.

In 1975, Brown Marble was added to the marble pallet. The Brown Marble looks like a chocolate sundae which has been stirred up. This particular color did not sell as well as the Purple and Green Marble versions.

The rarest examples of any of the marble glass would be the Paneled Grape canisters. These items are impossible to find in milk glass and even more impossible to find in Green and Purple Marble. These were not marketed as canisters. The large canister was marketed as a cookie jar, and the small version was labeled as a covered jar. I don't believe this helped sales at all. These items again suffered from the fact that the lids did not seal out moisture.

The most commonly found item in marble is the spiral candlesticks. These are available in all three colors of marble. The Brown Marble spiral candlesticks may be a little more difficult to find than ones of Purple and Green Marble.

Other patterns produced in marble include Colonial, Doric, Lotus, and Paneled Grape, as well as some covered animals.

In 1978, Purple Marble was produced for Levay. Several different patterns were utilized. In the same year, the Purple Marble had a carnival or mother-of-pearl finish applied. Levay marketed this as Purple Slag Carnival. All of these carnival examples were done in very limited editions and are very rare in today's market. See the Colors for Levay section for more information on the carnival colors.

Milk Glass Mother-of-Pearl

Mother-of-Pearl is a carnival type finish which is applied to any color piece after the item has been molded and cooled. Westmoreland introduced this process on milk glass in its 1973 catalog. In its 1980 catalog it described Mother-of-Pearl in this way: "Have you ever turned a sea shell over and looked at the inside—the pearly-white side? Did you notice how the sun's rays reflected on the shell's surface and seem to burst into a dozen different hues of purples and pinks and blues? Our Mother-of-Pearl gifts have a finish just like the inside of that sea shell, soft, subtle, and lustrous." This description is better than any I could attempt.

Mother-of-Pearl was produced in a variety of items in Paneled Grape as well as in many other patterns, even animals. For the most part, these items are found either hand painted with the Roses & Bows decoration or the Anniversary decorations. Another decoration used occasionally was Decoration #85 which consists of pastel colors highlighting the raised pattern parts of the pattern with pastel colors. The patterns on which this was done were Paneled Grape, Della Robbia, and #1048 Shell bowl. Quite a few items were produced without any decoration.

The last catalog which shows Mother-of-Pearl was the 1981 catalog. Even though this treatment had a sustained life of about eight years, it is not easily found today. The items which were decorated along with the Mother-of-Pearl treatment are even more elusive.

Mint Green and Mint Green Mist

Mint Green and Mint Green Mist were introduced in 1979. The mist version was dropped from the 1980 catalog, but the regular Mint Green was shown in 1980. This is an appropriately named color because it closely resembles the color of green centers of chocolate mints.

The 1979 catalog was not the first showing of a green opaque color. In 1970 a much darker version called Antique Green was produced. The color was darker and had a severe problem with white rings appearing in various areas of the glass. Neither the 1970 version nor the 1979-80 version sold very well. Perhaps by this time homemakers were tired of green. (Remember all of the avocado appliances?) Attempts were made to decorate the Mint Green with a Beaded

Bouquet design. This had a dual purpose. It most likely appealed more to consumers, and it tended to hide the white rings which appeared on Mint Green. The rings were less severe on Mint Green than on Antique Green, because of the lighter color, but they still appeared.

I have been told by several company employees who should know, that no dinnerware was ever produced in Mint Green. However, I keep finding plates in Paneled Grape. I suspect that since the only items I find could belong to the two-tier snack server (8-1/2" luncheon plate & 10-1/2" dinner plate) these employees could be correct. If a dinner service had been produced in Paneled Grape it would have been for a special order and not available to the general public. I have also found bowls which closely resemble the puff-box bottom. If a cup and saucer are found in Mint Green, perhaps we will have a more complete picture.

Items in Mint Green abound. Patterns include Doric, Paneled Grape, Beaded Grape, Cherry, Ring and Petal, and some covered animals.

Moss Green and Olive Green

Olive Green first appeared in 1967. Colonial and Ashburton were the major patterns shown in this olive color. Pitchers, goblets, tumblers, compotes, and candle-holders were available in both patterns. This color continued in production until the 1974 catalog. In most of the catalogs after 1967 only stemware and barware were available.

Moss Green was introduced in the 1969 catalog. This color is very similar to Olive Green but appears to have more yellow tones. Colonial and Ashburton items were also produced in Moss Green.

For a time these colors may have sold fairly well, but in today's market they are not easily found or sought.

Westmoreland did find some success when they frosted these colors. (See Green Mist.) Westmoreland is one of the few companies that can claim success with frosted glass. It more than likely came from the ingenious base colors and the decorations when applied.

Pink Pastel and Pink Mist

Westmoreland first produced pink glass during the color explosion of the Depression Era and called it Roselin. The patterns which were produced in this color were English Hobnail and Princess Feather, among many others.

The next time pink appeared in a Westmoreland line was in 1981. This was during the Grossman years, and this pink, called Pink Pastel, is a much lighter pink than the early Depression Era version. The bulk of the Pink Pastel was centered on English Hobnail, with old molds being used to create new and different pieces. Bowls were crimped or ruffled in a different manner, and handles were added to bowls to produce baskets. Other lines in Pink Pastel include Maple Leaf, Doric, and Paneled Grape.

Pink Mist, on the other hand, appeared in the 1969 catalog. This, according to Bob Rupp, was one of the prettiest colors that Dwight Johnson ever produced. Mr. Rupp also stated that this was a good-selling color. Items were produced in Paneled Grape, Doric, Ring & Petal, and Old Quilt, as well as many others.

In 1973 a Dogwood decal was added to very plain pink mist items. This is also a very pretty combination. This decoration is listed as Decoration #70.

On some of the Pink Mist items a finial or foot would be in clear glass and the rest of the piece would be frosted. This provided an interesting contrast. I find it interesting that Westmoreland produced Pink Mist during the 1970's but did not produce a plain clear pink at the same time.

Pink Mist items will be more difficult to find than Pink Pastel. The Pink Pastel seems to have been available in bulk quantity at the Westmoreland auctions.

Ruby and Ruby Stain

Ruby was produced by Westmoreland starting with the 1979 catalog. The bulk of the production during that year consisted of hand painted items. A floral decoration called Ruby Floral was hand painted in white tones which really accented the ruby background. Mary Gregory-style hand painting and Anniversary decorations as well as cameo decorations were also shown on ruby glass in this catalog. During the Grossman years, Ruby was also produced for Levay (see Levay colors).

When David Grossman took over Westmoreland he began producing quite a large line in Ruby. English Hobnail, Maple Leaf, Doric, and Paneled Grape pieces were available in Ruby. Grossman continued some of the Floral decorations in the line a well as adding a decal called Snow Flower. Grossman also produced a few Hens and Roosters in the ruby color.

Ruby Stain items started appearing in the 1967 catalog. This was not a new process for Westmoreland. During the 1930's and 1940's Westmoreland was painting stain colors on Della Robbia and Thousand Eye pieces. This is very tedious work and was probably discontinued because it is very labor intensive.

In 1967, items in Paneled Grape were stained. All of the leaves and grapes were painted and the rest of the piece was crystal. When finding these pieces one will notice the gold content in the painting. This is a very elegant looking treatment.

The #1932 Waterford pattern was also treated with a ruby stain. Often people seem to think that these pieces are either Bohemian or some other foreign manufacturer. Obviously this was the look that Westmoreland was attempting! Oft times these items will appear at the more elegant antiques shows and the prices will be extremely high.

The #1874 Wedding Bowl and #1943 Urn, made in crystal and stained in ruby, were favorites of Westmoreland. These may also be found with or without hand painting on top of the ruby stain.

The staining technique continued on into the Grossman era and for a time was even produced for Levay.

Yellow Mist

Yellow Mist appeared in the 1974 catalog supplement. This color is the Soft Gold or amber color with a mist finish. The last catalog in which Yellow Mist appeared was the 1975 catalog.

Several patterns can be found in Yellow Mist. Paneled Grape, Colonial, Doric, and Ring and Petal, as well as other occasional items, will be found. Animals such as the #1 Camel, #1 Owl, #10 Owl, #20 Love Birds and #5/1 Wren will also be found in Yellow Mist.

Some of the plain patterns such as the #1902 line were produced in Yellow Mist with a Daisy decal. Most often on items such as puff boxes and perfume bottles, the knobs on lids or stoppers will be clear and the rest of the pieces will be frosted.

Since the span of production of Yellow Mist was very short, items in this color will be difficult to find. Decorated examples will be even more difficult.

COLORS FOR LEVAY

In an attempt to build clientele, Westmoreland actively sought out companies that marketed glass and other novelties. Levay Distributing Company was just the right company. Levay is a family-run operation owned by Gary Levi and located in Edwardsville, Illinois.

According to the article "Levay Glass" by Paul Oard & Lee Wilkerson (Glass Review, Feb. 1981), in 1971 Gary Levi started a mail-order giftware business. He primarily wanted to stick with limited editions. He loved antiques and wanted to use old molds and produce them in colors which were not originally made. By using existing molds and having the company who produced the product ship directly to the dealer, the costs were kept to a minimum.

Bob Rupp stated that the relationship between Westmoreland and Levay began in 1973 with the Fan and File child's set in crystal. It must have been a good relationship for both parties inasmuch as it continued until Westmoreland closed its doors.

A Levay catalog states that limited edition pieces produced after January 1, 1978, will be signed Levay and dated. They will also have consecutive numbers denoting what number the piece is in the total run of the limited edition. Before the above date, items in limited edition series may have been signed sporadically, because many of the order forms indicated it was up to the dealer who placed the order to say whether or not the items were to be signed. Those that are signed were done so with an etching tool.

Most, if not all, colors produced for Levay can be traced back to similar base colors in Westmoreland's line. The names were sometimes changed or a carnival finish or opalescent accent added.

The following colors have been assembled from many sources. I would like to thank Gerry Gentry and Ray Reichard who freely loaned reams of Levay catalogs and brochures. This section could not have been written without their help.

Aquamarine/Teal

Aquamarine is listed as a blue-green color. The description of this color closely matches that of Laurel Green. I do not have any information as to when this was produced. The only items which I have found produced in this color are all cheese or butter dishes, although others may have been produced. The patterns include American Hobnail, Colonial, High Hob, Old Quilt, Paneled Grape, and Sawtooth. The Sawtooth piece is a covered flat box. These items were not limited in production to a specific number, but it does not appear that any great number of items in this color were produced. Items in this color would be considered scarce.

Aurora Blue Carnival, Cobalt, Cobalt Carnival and Royal Blue

Aurora Blue Carnival is a cobalt-blue base glass with a carnival finish applied. This color was introduced in December of 1980 and was available until mid-1981. Very old molds were used in the manufacture of items of this color. The largest amount of production occurred in the #550 High Hob line. This was originally produced circa 1910, according to a Glass Research Press reprint of the 1910 catalog. All items produced in Aurora Blue Carnival were limited editions. Items produced include a 4" spooner (1,000 made), 5-1/4" sugar (1,000 made), 4" creamer (1,000 made), 7" butter or cheese dish (2,500 made), 8" pitcher (800 made), 5-1/2" water goblet (1,800 made), 4" tumbler (3,000 made), 6" cruet (1,000 made), 6-1/2" celery vase (1,000 made), and 6-1/2" oval footed candy or compote (1,000 made). The only examples of this pattern shown in this book are the pitcher, tumbler and, oval footed candy.

A Paneled Grape pitcher set was also produced in this color and was limited to 50 sets (50 pitchers, 300 tumblers).

Another pattern which was utilized was

called Fine Cut Diamonds and Hob Star in a Levay brochure. Only five items were produced in Aurora Blue Carnival. These items were limited in production to 50 sets. A dealer had to purchase all five items at once. These items include: 6" spitoon, 5" rose bowl (see 1513-1 in crystal section), 9" oval basket (see 1512-1 in crystal section), 7-1/2" flared bowl, and 8-1/2" crimped bowl (see 1515-1 in crystal section). When a dealer ordered one of these sets he could then purchase the rose bowl and oval basket separately. Therefore, the rose bowl and oval basket were probably made in a larger quantity than the original limited amount of 50.

Other items produced in Aurora Blue Carnival include a Fan & File mini-punch set, and the 8" oval covered Duck. The Duck was limited to 150.

Cobalt and Cobalt Carnival were produced by Westmoreland for Levay in 1978. Items produced in Cobalt include a mini- or child's pitcher set in #304 Flute (or "Lil Jo" as Mrs. Weatherman calls it in her Book 2), High Hob 7" cheese/butter dish, Old Quilt cheese dish, large pitcher, and water tumbler, and Paneled Grape cheese dish. These cobalt items are of extremely good quality. The reproductions which are inundating the market today are slimy and tend to have lots of extraneous debris inside the glass. None of the cobalt items produced for Levay were limited in production.

Cobalt Carnival items include a Della Robbia 8" pitcher and 4" tumbler set, limited to 150 sets. A #81 Fruits punch set was also produced in Cobalt Carnival and limited to 100 sets. Covered animals were also made in Cobalt Carnival. Cobalt Carnival is the same color as Aurora Blue Carnival. The difference appears to be in production dates. Cobalt Carnival was produced in 1978 and Aurora Blue Carnival in 1980. Different items were produced in each color.

Royal Blue is the same as Cobalt and was produced in December of 1980. Royal Blue was marketed in the #550 High Hob pattern only. Items produced in Royal Blue are the same as those produced in Aurora Blue Carnival. The Royal Blue production was not a limited edition.

Blue Carnival, Electric Blue Carnival, Turquoise Carnival, Ice Blue Carnival and Electric Blue Opalescent Carnival

There are five different light-blue carnival colors which were produced for Levay.

Blue Carnival is actually Brandywine Blue with a carnival finish applied. The Electric Blue Carnival is the same color as Blue Carnival. Both colors are a medium-blue color which is quite attractive with the carnival finish. Several limited editions exist in both colors. One such example is the #1776 Colonial pitcher and tumbler set. This was limited to 100 sets and is listed in Blue Carnival. This color was produced from 1976 through 1978. Covered animals and the Fan & File punch set can also be found in Blue Carnival. One example in Electric Blue Carnival is a Paneled Grape banana bowl. This item was limited to 300 pieces and was produced in 1978. Covered animals were also produced in Electric Blue Carnival.

Turquoise Carnival and Ice Blue Carnival appear to be the same color, but when compared side by side the Turquoise Carnival appears slightly darker, but this difference could be due to temperature differences during the manufacturing process. Turquoise and Ice Blue Carnival are described in the same manner in both the Levay catalogs and the Westmoreland catalogs. Both are described as light aqua colors with an iridescent finish. The Ice Blue Carnival was one of two carnival or mother-of-pearl colors which Westmoreland marketed in its catalogs (Honey Amber Carnival was the other). The only difference between the two colors is that of production dates. Ice Blue Carnival appeared on the Levay scene in 1975 and in the 1976 Westmoreland catalog supplement. Turquoise Carnival appeared in 1980. The items produced in the 1980 series are somewhat limited in quantity. A #1058 Della Robbia pitcher and 4" tumbler were produced in the 1980 Turquoise Carnival and were limited to 400 sets. The #81 Fruits punch set was limited to 100 sets in the 1980 Turquoise Carnival. This is somewhat misleading though, because in 1975 when this same punch set was produced in the Ice Blue Carnival color, it was not limited in production.

Electric Blue Opalescent Carnival was produced from 1976-1978. This color is actually Westmoreland's Brandywine Blue Opalescent with a carnival finish. Westmoreland produced an Electric Blue Opalescent without a carnival finish during this time also. Most items produced for Levay in either color were limited editions. The patterns produced range from High Hob, Old Quilt, and Paneled Grape to the Lily of the Valley vase.

In Heacock's "Opalescent Glass Book from A to Z," he states that the 9" Dolphin candlesticks and the Peacock creamer and sugar were produced in a color similar to Electric Blue Opalescent. These items, Heacock states, were made by Westmoreland for A.A. Importing Company, Inc. of St. Louis, Missouri. Bob Rupp confirmed that they were indeed produced for A.A. Importing and that the color may have been called "Antique Blue." This is not to be confused with Westmoreland's opaque blue glass of the same name.

Mr. Rupp confirmed that Westmoreland produced glass for A.A. Importing from approximately 1973 through 1975. After that, it seems that A.A. Importing decided to have its wares produced more inexpensively overseas.

Butterscotch, Butterscotch Carnival and Butterscotch Opalescent

Butterscotch Carnival is described by a Levay ad as a "Beautiful Honey Lemon Color with a lovely iridescent finish." This same

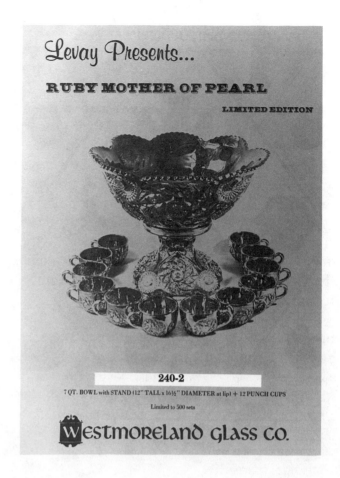
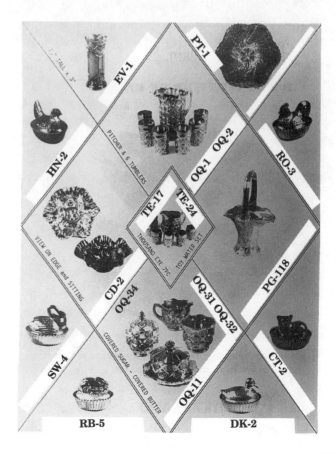

73

description could be applied to Honey Amber Carnival. Butterscotch Carnival was produced for Levay in late 1980. Only three items were known. These items were the #20 Love Bird covered dish (400 made), #750 7" basket (400 made), and #1048 Argonaut Shell bowl w/lid (400 made).

The Butterscotch color without any opalescence or carnival finish was only produced in the #550 High Hob pattern. Items include the cheese/butter dish, creamer, 8" pitcher, 4" spooner, sugar w/lid, and 4" tumbler. All were limited to 50 except the pitcher and tumbler which were limited to 55 sets.

Butterscotch Opalescent appears to have been produced in the Buzz Star 7-1/2" oval basket (1512-1, see code section). This piece was produced in 1983 and doesn't appear to have been a limited edition, though it was not produced for an extended amount of time.

Chocolate

Chocolate glass was produced for Levay in 1982 by Westmoreland. Although it was not a limited edition per se, not many examples of this color were produced. The items produced in this color include a #109 Cherry cookie jar, 8" Eagle covered dish, 8" covered Fox, 8" covered Hen, 8" covered Rabbit, and 8" covered Rooster. Chocolate describes the color of this glass perfectly. It is a brown opaque color.

Crystal and Crystal with Ruby Stain

Westmoreland produced some plain crystal items for Levay. Most of these were items which were in Westmoreland's regular line throughout the years and were not limited editions.

Some of the Crystal with Ruby Stain items which were made for Levay, such as the #1932 Waterford line, were also in Westmoreland's regular production and were not limited editions.

A limited edition of Crystal with Ruby Stain was produced in the #550 High Hob pattern. Items produced in this color include a butter/cheese dish, creamer, spooner or open sugar, and a sugar with a lid. All of these pieces were limited to 1,500 pieces produced in 1978.

Westmoreland also produced Old Quilt in Crystal with Ruby Stain. These were also produced in 1978 but were not limited in production. Old Quilt items include the cheese dish, large creamer, cruet, 8 oz. footed water goblet, large pitcher, spooner or open sugar, sugar or candy with lid, and the 6-1/2" sweetmeat with lid.

Emerald Green Opalescent and Emerald Green Carnival

Emerald Green Opalescent was a very limited-edition color. This color appears to be Laurel Green with opalescent accents. Line #550 High Hob was produced in this color. Items in High Hob include the butter/cheese dish (250 made), creamer (500 made), 1 quart pitcher (150 made), spooner or open sugar (500 made), sugar with lid (500 made) and 4" flat water tumbler (150 sets). Emerald Green Opalescent dates from approximately 1974-1976, according to Levay brochures. With such limited amounts of this color produced, any item in this color would be considered rare.

Another set which was produced in Emerald Green Opalescent is the #303 Fan & File child's punch set. In Heacock's "Opalescent Glass from A to Z," he states that this set was produced in 1975.

Emerald Green Carnival appears to have been produced during the same time period as that of the Emerald Green Opalescent. Emerald Green Carnival also appears to have its origin in Laurel Green. The #1 covered camel and #304 Flute or "Lil Jo" (as

Mrs. Weatherman named it) child's pitcher set will appear in Emerald Green Carnival. The Flute or "Lil Jo" set consists of a 4" pitcher and 2" flat tumblers which look like shot glasses. These were not produced in any great quantity but were not limited to a specific amount. One such set may be found with a white hand painted flower. This "Lil Jo" set will also be found in plain Emerald Green with no carnival or opalescent accents.

Lime Green Carnival

Lime Green Carnival is Moss Green with a carnival finish. This color was shown in Levay catalogs during the 1977-1978 period. Most items produced in this color were limited editions. Items produced in this color include the #500 Old Quilt water pitcher & tumblers (125 sets made), #1881 Paneled Grape: large footed creamer combined with whiskey tumblers to create a child's pitcher set (500 sets made), decanter with stopper & wine goblets (100 sets made), and water pitcher and water tumbler (250 sets made). Items found in this color are classified as scarce to rare.

Pastel Amethyst Opalescent and Pastel Amethyst Opalescent Carnival, Lilac Opalescent or Lilac Pastel

During the Grossman years Lilac Opalescent was a part of the regular production line. However, some items in Lilac Opalescent were made for Levay and called Pastel Amethyst Opalescent. Some of these Levay products were limited editions. The limited editions include the #109 Cherry cookie jar, #550 High Hob butter/cheese dish, creamer, spooner or open sugar, sugar with lid, #81 Fruits punch set (Note this punch set contains a bowl which is flared out instead of the usual cupped rim), #1881 Paneled Grape pitcher and water tumbler,

and #1875 Ring & Petal banana stand and cake plate. All of the above items were limited to 500 sets. Since they were so limited they are considered rare.

Pastel Amethyst Opalescent Carnival was also produced during the Grossman years for Levay. This color is one of the most limited colors produced for Levay. Limited pieces include the Carolina Dogwood basket: 8" double crimped (21 made), 8" bowl double crimped (33 made), and 10" plate (31 made); Daisy Wreath: 8" basket double crimped (12 made), 8" double crimped bowl (26 made), and 10" plate (27 made); Peacock Tail & Daisy: bowl 8" double crimped (19 made), 8" double crimped bowl (27 made), 10" plate (25 made); #999 Wildflower & Lace: 6" oval basket (46 made), 8" star crimped basket (20 made), 8" star crimped bowl (32 made), rose bowl 5" ball shape (100 made), and handkerchief vase 7" (17 made).

Other items produced in Pastel Amethyst Opalescent Carnival which were not limited editions include the English Hobnail 9" basket and Paneled Grape water pitcher & water tumbler set. The English Hobnail basket will be found faster than the Paneled Grape pitcher set, but neither of these is common.

Pink, Pink Carnival and Pink Opalescent or Pink Pastel

The pink color which was produced for Levay was Grossman's Pink Pastel. Several regular production items in pink were produced for Levay and were not limited in production.

Pink Carnival appears to have been produced for Levay from 1978 through the closing of Westmoreland. For the most part Pink Carnival was a limited-edition color. Items produced in Pink Carnival include the Robin on three-footed twig nest (160 made), #1058 Della Robbia domed candy with lid (500 made), #1048 Argonaut Shell candy, all pieces in the Fan & File child's sized set (not limited), #550 High Hob butter/cheese dish (not limited) and pitcher & water tumbler (200 sets made), Love Birds covered dish (500 made), and #1967 Rose & Trellis footed candy w/lid (500 made). The most limited item appears to have been the #556 Sawtooth 14" grandfather's bowl with lid; the Levay brochure states that only 40 of these were produced.

Another item which appears to have been severely limited is the Raised Wing Swan. An advertisement by Elemar Glass in November of 1977 stated that less than 25 complete swans existed. This, the ad said, was due to production problems. In November of 1977 these were selling for any bid over $55, and only six were offered. A Levay catalog labeled this Swan as experimental and offered it for $100. (It did not indicate whether this price was wholesale or retail.)

Pink Opalescent or Pink Pastel was a Grossman product mostly produced during the 1983 season. All items which were produced for Levay were also in Westmoreland's regular line.

Purple, Purple Carnival, Purple Slag and Purple Slag Carnival

Purple was produced for Levay by Westmoreland from 1974 through 1976. This color is called Lilac in 1973 Westmoreland catalogs. Since production was started for Levay in 1974, this could be the reason it was dropped from the regular Westmoreland line. All of the items below were limited to 300 sets. Items include the #550 High Hob water pitcher and water tumblers and the Paneled Grape juice pitcher and juice tumblers. Both pitcher sets are a very rare find today.

Please note that L.G. Wright also produced a purple color in its "Panel Grape." In its master catalog (which is shown in this section under L.G. Wright) the pitcher is only shown in crystal and ruby.

Purple Carnival was produced from 1974 on and off through 1980. Although 1978 appears to have been when the bulk of Purple Carnival was produced. Most items in Purple Carnival were limited in production. Items in Purple Carnival include the #304 Flute or "Lil Jo" child's pitcher and small tumblers (500 sets in 1977), #300 Fan & File child's creamer, open sugar and butter (1000 sets made), 7-12/" George Washington plate (5000 made), Indian plate (in 1978 5000 made), Three Kittens plate (in 1978, 5000 made), Three Owls plate (5000 made), #77 Tomahawk 6" (350 made, not shown in this book), #6 Strutting Peacock creamer and sugar both lidded (in 1974, 900 made), and Old Quilt cup and saucer (400 sets made). Other major patterns include the #550 High Hob: butter/cheese dish (500 made), creamer (500 made), 1 quart water pitcher and 4" flat water tumbler (300 sets made), open sugar or spooner (450 made), and sugar w/lid (500 made). In #1928 Maple Leaf, 200 of each of the following items were produced: 11-1/2" banana bowl, deep crimped 10" bowl, cookie or cracker jar w/lid, 5" rose bowl and 7" footed crimped sweetmeat. Princess Feather items include the 9" tall pitcher & 4-3/4" tumbler (165 sets made) and a 14-piece punch set (100 sets made). More punch cups may be available than punch sets since, after ordering a complete punch set, dealers were allowed to order extra cups. Both of these Princess Feather sets were produced in the latter part of 1980.

Purple Slag or Purple Marble, as Westmoreland called it, was a product during the 1978 season. All of the Purple Slag items which were produced for Levay were in Westmoreland's regular production line and were not limited editions.

Purple Slag Carnival was also produced in 1978 and all items were limited editions. Animal items include the covered Cat (500 made), Spread-wing Eagle dish (160 made), 8" covered Fox (200 made), 5-1/2" Hen on Basket (500 made), Rabbit 2/eggs dish (150 made), Rooster 5-1/2" long (500 made), and 8" covered Rooster (115 made).

Patterns in Purple Slag Carnival include the #109 Cherry cookie/cracker jar (200 made), #550 High Hob butter/cheese dish (500 made) and pitcher and water tumbler set (76 sets made), #500 Old Quilt cheese dish (500 made) and water pitcher and tumbler set (150 sets made), and #1881 Paneled Grape cheese dish (500 made). All of these Carnival Slag items would be a rare find in today's market.

Ruby or Cerise, Crimson Mother of Pearl and Ruby Slag

Ruby was produced in large quantities for Levay. Most of the Ruby was in Westmoreland's regular product line. One of the largest assortments in Ruby was produced in #555 English Hobnail. Ruby was produced for Levay as late as 1983.

Levay advertisements in 1979 called the new ruby color "Cerise." Items produced in Cerise include the #6 Peacock rose bowl (made by cupping the rim of a sugar bowl), #6 Peacock creamer and sugar (both with lids), #7 Robin on twig next, #10 Owl on books paperweight, #109 Cherry cookie jar, #303 Fan & File Child's punch set, #500 Old Quilt cruet, #1058 Della Robbia stemmed rose bowl, and #1842 Swirl & Ball pitcher & tumblers. All of the items in Ruby/Cerise will be extremely hard to find but do not appear to have been limited to a certain number.

Crimson Mother of Pearl appears to have been quite a large line for Levay. I have found several brochures which show a large and varied number of pieces and patterns. Crimson Mother of Pearl was produced as early as 1979 and as late as 1983. In the 1983 version this red carnival color was called Ruby Mother of Pearl, according to the Levay brochure. All of the Crimson Mother of Pearl and Ruby Mother of Pearl lines were limited editions. Patterns which can be found in Crimson Mother of Pearl include Swirl & Ball, Old Quilt Paneled Grape,

English Hobnail, and Buzz Star (in a punch set which had severe production problems and was limited to approximately 140 complete sets according to an article in the "Towne Crier Newsletter"), as well as various covered animals, plus much more. All items in Crimson Mother of Pearl are considered a rare find. In the code section of this book, since so many names were attached to this color, I have referred to it as Ruby or Red Carnival to alleviate any confusion, I hope!

Ruby Slag was a 1982 product for Levay. Although none of the brochures indicate any limited amounts, I suspect that not many items were produced in Ruby Slag. Items which may, with great difficulty, be found in Ruby Slag include the #109 Cherry cookie/cracker jar, spread-wing Eagle dish, 9" English Hobnail basket, 8" covered Fox, 8" covered Hen, 8" covered Rooster and 8" Rabbit w/eggs dish.

Vaseline and Vaseline Carnival

Vaseline is a yellowish color that appears that it could glow in the dark. Several companies had great success with their Vaseline lines, but it appears that the Westmoreland/Levay issues did not do as well. Any item in Vaseline could be considered very scarce to rare. Items produced in Vaseline include the Robin on nest, 5-1/2" Hen on nest, 7" Love Birds covered dish, Paneled Grape 1/4-lb. butter dish, and Paneled Grape cheese dish. These items appear to have been produced during 1979 through 1980. The Love Birds were limited to 400 pieces and the Paneled Grape butter dish was limited to 500 pieces.

Vaseline Carnival was also very limited in production. Items produced in this color include the Fan and File child's set which includes creamer, sugar, spooner, butter and punch set. I have not found any figures on how many of these were produced, but it does appear that very few were manufactured.

White or Crystal Carnival

White Carnival was featured by Levay in a spring 1979 brochure. White Carnival is simply crystal glass with a carnival finish. This was the year that the bulk of the production in this color occurred. Only one item appears to have been produced previously and that was the #241 Lily of the Valley vase which was made as early as 1975. This vase was limited to 400 pieces. Most other items in White Carnival were limited to 1,500 pieces or sets.

Items produced in White Carnival include the Child's Chick mug, Chick on egg pile, Chicken egg cup, Hatching Chicks plate, Chicks 4" x 5" small tray, 8" oval covered Duck, Duck salt dip, 8" covered Hen, 5-1/2" Hen on basket, Old Quilt water pitcher and tumblers set, Rabbit & Horseshoe plate, oval Rabbit covered dish, Rabbit on picket-fence dish, 8" covered Rooster, and Fan and File toy punch set (which was limited to 500 sets).

The #1700 Flute or Arch pitcher set was also produced in White Carnival. Some of these sets had a cardinal decal on them. Each set, whether plain or decorated was limited to 300 sets.

Other Levay Colors Which May Be Found

Other colors which have been found in Levay brochures include Amberina Carnival, Black Carnival, Orange Carnival, Marigold Carnival, and Smoke Carnival.

The Amberina Carnival could have been a factory error. Amberina usually results from unevenly heating ruby glass which tends to leave yellowish accents in the glass.

Black Carnival was an experimental color according to Ted Gasowski, who had a beautiful Buzz Star punch set at the 1990 Westmoreland Convention in Pittsburgh, Pennsylvania. Mr. Gasowski stated that the punch set was one of approximately 31 complete sets which were produced. Mr. Gasowski said that Black Carnival was produced in 1984 before the company closed and was severely limited. The Black Carnival items will be very shiny on the plain parts of any piece. These plain parts will almost appear mirror-like. A Black Carnival Paneled Grape basket is shown on the top row of one of the Limited Edition Colors photos in this section of the book. Other items available in Black Carnival include the Elf stein (EF-1), Lovers stein, Peacock Tail & Daisy plate (PT-1), Carolina & Dogwood bowl, and some of the 5-1/2" covered animals.

Orange and Marigold Carnival most likely are two names for the same color. I have found Fan and File child's items, especially the butter dish, in an orange flashed-on color. The pieces I found appeared to be crystal with a rusty looking carnival on the top of the piece. According to Levay brochures the only item produced in either Orange or Marigold Carnival was the Fan and File child's set.

Smoke Carnival appears to have been a factory error. The color will appear brownish purple in color, but you can see straight through the piece. The only item shown in this book in Smoke Carnival is a Paneled Grape large basket (see Limited Edition Colors, top row, far left). With photography lights it may appear quite different in the photo than it does in actuality.

L.G. Wright "Panel Grape" vs. Westmoreland's "Panel Grape" (Line #1881)

The L.G. Wright Company was a distributor of all types of glass products. According to Bob Rupp, L.G. Wright never manufactured its own glass; it had several different companies manufacture their glass with L.G. Wright molds and formulas.

Westmoreland did quite a bit of work for L.G. Wright in the 1970's, when Westmoreland was struggling to stay alive financially. This proved to be a worthwhile venture for both companies. And although Westmoreland did produce some items (according to Mr. Rupp quite a few covered animals were produced), Westmoreland did not make the Panel Grape which L.G. Wright produced.

The basic difference that can be seen between the Westmoreland and Wright examples, is that of color. The L.G. Wright colors consist of Amethyst, Blue, Crystal, Green, Amber, and Ruby. Of these colors the Ruby seems to be the most plentiful. Very few items of Westmoreland's Paneled Grape pattern were produced in Ruby.

The next difference is in the sizing and/or shaping of the items. Although L.G. Wright's examples are very close to Westmoreland's, when the two companies' wares are side by side the differences become apparent.

None of the L.G. Wright items will be marked with any kind of company logo.

LGW-1 water goblet, 6-7/8" tall, 3-1/4" diameter at rim, 9-5/8" circumference around bowl, 3-1/4" diameter of the foot.

The Westmoreland Paneled Grape water goblet (PG-14) measures 6-7/8" tall, 3-1/4" diameter at rim, 10" circumference around bowl, 3-1/8" diameter of the foot.

Both have essentially the same dimensions, the top rim of the Wright goblet will extend above the arched panels a bit more than the Westmoreland example. The Westmoreland rim will smoothly flow into the panels, whereas the Wright example will have a small lip before the arches of the panels. The leaves on the Wright example will have much less detail.

L.G. Wright colors: amethyst, blue, crystal, green, amber, and ruby.

LGW-2 wine goblet, footed. 4" tall, 2-1/8" diameter across top rim, 6-5/8" circumference around bowl. The stem measures 1-5/8" from bottom of bowl to top of foot. The foot is 2-1/8" in diameter.

The Paneled Grape wine goblet is 3-3/4" tall, 2-1/8" diameter across top rim, 6-3/4" circumference around bowl. The stem measures 1-1/2" from bottom of bowl to top of foot. The foot is 2" in diameter.

As you can see the difference is very slight. The leaves on the L.G. Wright wine are not as detailed as that of the Westmoreland Paneled Grape. The top rim of the L.G. Wright wine extends beyond the panels. Westmoreland's wine ends at the panels and has no extra glass above the arches.

L.G. Wright colors: amethyst, amber, green, blue, crystal, and ruby.

LGW-3 covered compote w/lid. The most obvious difference is that the bottom does not flare out on the Wright piece as much as the Westmoreland piece does. The Wright compote bottom is 3-5/8" in diameter and the Westmoreland bottom is 4-3/4". Both lid diameters match the bottom dimensions. The Wright bottom is 3-7/8" tall without lid and the Westmoreland bottom is 4-1/2" tall. The bottom of the compote is the same as the sherbert (LGW-6) in the Wright example.

L.G. Wright colors: amethyst, blue, green, ruby, amber, and milk glass.

LGW-4 sugar, indiv., footed, no lid. The Wright sugar is 3-1/4" tall, 2-9/16" in diameter, 8-1/8" in circumference.

The Westmoreland sugar is 3-1/4" tall, 2-3/4" in diameter, 9" in circumference.

The Westmoreland sugar lid will NOT fit the L.G.Wright sugar bottom.

L.G. Wright colors: amethyst, blue, green, and ruby.

LGW-5 creamer, indiv., footed. The Wright creamer is 3-3/16" tall, 2-9/16" in diameter, 8-1/4" in circumference.

The Westmoreland creamer is 3-5/8" tall, 2-13/16" in diameter, 9" in circumference.

The L.G. Wright creamer is much smaller around than the Westmoreland creamer. This is very noticeable.

L.G. Wright colors: amethyst, blue, green, and ruby.

LGW-7 plate, torte, 15". This plate is shown under the punch set (LGW-8). Westmoreland's torte plate measures 14-1/2". The pattern on the L.G. Wright plate is on the bottom of the plate, whereas Westmoreland's plate has the pattern on the top of the plate around the rim.

L.G. Wright colors: ruby, amber, possibly others, but not in milk glass.

LGW-8 punch set. Includes large straight-sided bowl, straight-sided cups, 15" plate & ladle. L.G. Wright punch cups look like a creamer without a spout. Westmoreland punch cups will have a plain band around the rim and will be more round than the L.G. Wright punch cups. The L.G. Wright punch bowl will be very straight sided and will not be scalloped as the Westmoreland punch bowl is. The Westmoreland bowl is also usually belled. The Westmoreland punch ladle has a cup-like bowl with a spout and ice lip, whereas the L.G. Wright ladle is a more bowl-like ladle.

L.G. Wright colors: ruby, amber, possibly others, but not in milk glass.

LGW-9 console bowl, crimped rim, 12" diameter. The pattern on this bowl is on the outside of the bowl. This bowl was no doubt made from the torte plate (LGW-7). Westmoreland did not make a bowl with these dimensions or this type of crimping.

L.G. Wright colors: ruby, amber, possibly others, but not in milk glass.

LGW-10 pitcher, 1 quart, footed. This pitcher is smaller in circumference than the Westmoreland pitcher.

L.G. Wright colors: crystal, ruby, possibly others, but not in milk glass.

LGW-11 lily bowl or torte plate, cupped rim, 12" diameter. The Westmoreland bowl which is shaped similiar to this bowl is 14" in diameter and the pattern is on the inside of the bowl, whereas the pattern on the L.G. Wright version is on the outside.

L.G. Wright colors: ruby, possibly others, but not in milk glass.

LGW-12 plate, 8". This plate has the pattern on the underside of the plate, whereas the Westmoreland version will have the pattern on the top side of the plate. Westmoreland's plate will measure 8-1/2".

L.G. Wright Colors: Ruby, possibly others, but not in milk glass.

LGW-13 cup & saucer. These cups are the same as the punch cups. Westmoreland's regular cups are belled. The L.G. Wright saucer will have the pattern on the bottom, and the pattern of the Westmoreland will be on the top of the saucer.

L.G. Wright colors: ruby, amber, possibly others, but not in milk glass.

LGW-14 plate, 10" dinner. Again, the pattern of the L.G. Wright plate will be on the bottom of the plate, whereas the Westmoreland plate will have the pattern on the top of the plate. The Westmoreland dinner plate will measure 10-1/2".

L.G. Wright colors: ruby, possibly others, but not in milk glass.

LGW-15 cake stand (shown in the misc. items photo, page 81). This cake stand measures 9-1/4" in diameter, 4" tall and is stem footed. None of Westmoreland's many cake plates are stem footed in this manner. Westmoreland cake plates will have a bell or skirted foot with the Grape pattern on this foot.

L.G. Wright colors: amber, possibly others, but not in milk glass.

L.G. Wright's "Panel Grape" vs. Westmoreland's "Paneled Grape"

LGW-1   LGW-1   PG-14

LGW-2   PG-17   LGW-3   PG-27

LGW-4   PG-92   LGW-5   PG-91

Misc. Items

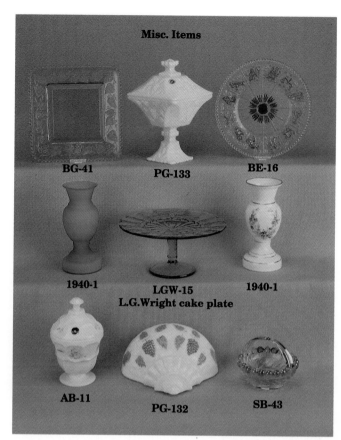

BG-41   PG-133   BE-16

1940-1   LGW-15   1940-1

L.G. Wright cake plate

AB-11   PG-132   SB-43

L.G. Wright Panel Grape

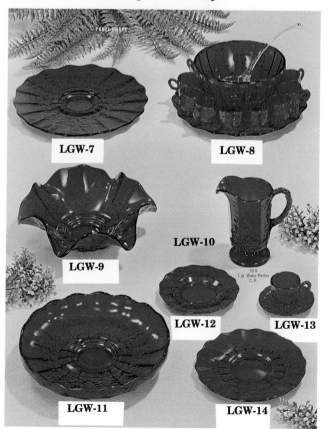

LGW-7   LGW-8

LGW-9   LGW-10

LGW-12   LGW-13

LGW-11   LGW-14

L.G. Wright Panel Grape

PANEL GRAPE

LGW-1   LGW-3

LGW-6

LGW-2

LGW-4   LGW-5

Almond or Coral Mist

DO-34 PG-112 AS-1 PG-10

DO-18 BV-1

DO-23 PB-1 SP-1 PG-113 SP-1

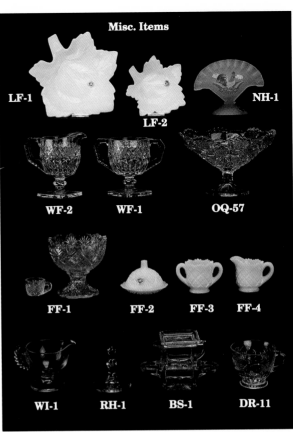

Misc. Items

LF-1 LF-2 NH-1

WF-2 WF-1 OQ-57

FF-1 FF-2 FF-3 FF-4

WI-1 RH-1 BS-1 DR-11

Colonial in Laurel Green

CO-18 CO-19 CO-14 CO-1

Lotus in Colors

LO-27 LO-2 LO-21 LO-28

LO-12 LO-29 LO-30

Depression Era Colors

Grossman Era Pink **Depression Era Pink**

EH-172 EH-148

EH-149 EH-150

"Woolworth" Line

WW-1 WW-2

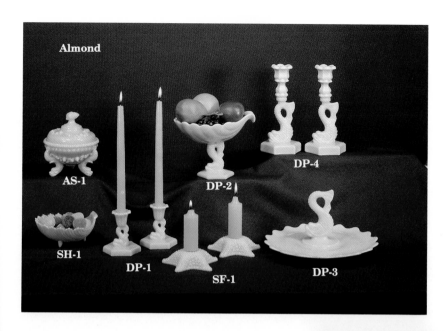

Almond

AS-1

SH-1

DP-1

DP-2

SF-1

DP-3

DP-4

PG-20

PG-1

PB-1

OQ-34

PG-112

AS-1

BG-33

PG-34

DH-1

DR-17

PG-113

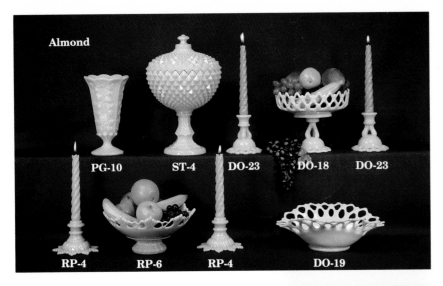

Almond

PG-10 ST-4 DO-23 DO-18 DO-23

RP-4 RP-6 RP-4 DO-19

Almond

PG-109 BV-1 CH-9 PG-110 SP-1

BG-24 BG-25 BG-24 DO-34 PG-111

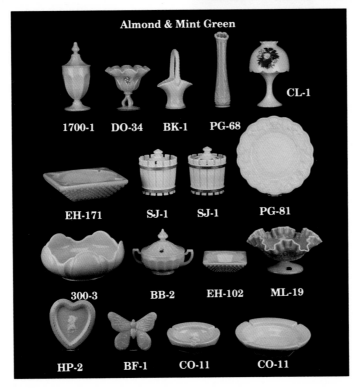

Almond & Mint Green

1700-1 DO-34 BK-1 PG-68 CL-1

EH-171 SJ-1 SJ-1 PG-81

300-3 BB-2 EH-102 ML-19

HP-2 BF-1 CO-11 CO-11

Antique Blue Dophin Items

DP-2
AS-1
DP-3
DP-4
SF-1
DP-1
SF-1
SH-1

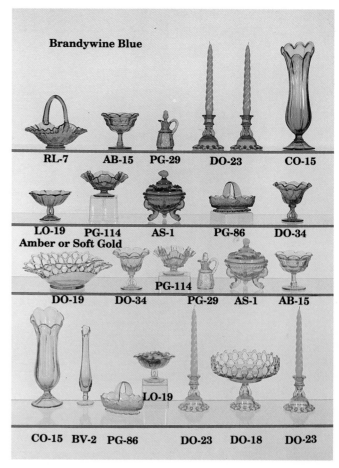

Brandywine Blue

| RL-7 | AB-15 | PG-29 | DO-23 | CO-15 |

| LO-19 | PG-114 | AS-1 | PG-86 | DO-34 |

Amber or Soft Gold

| DO-19 | DO-34 | PG-114 | AS-1 | AB-15 |
| | | PG-29 | | |

| CO-15 | BV-2 | PG-86 | LO-19 | DO-23 | DO-18 | DO-23 |

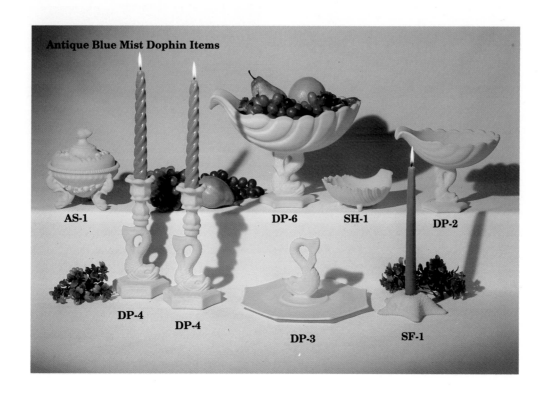

Antique Blue Mist Dophin Items

AS-1
DP-6
SH-1
DP-2
DP-4
DP-4
DP-3
SF-1

Soft Mist *Antique Blue*

DO-34

OQ-34

LF-2

1902-1

PG-112   BV-1   PG-113   BB-2   DO-18

Soft Mist *Antique Blue*

AS-1   1900-1   BK-1

RP-4   RP-6   PG-114

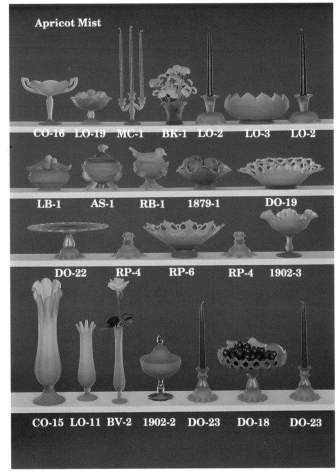

Apricot Mist

CO-16   LO-19   MC-1   BK-1   LO-2   LO-3   LO-2

LB-1   AS-1   RB-1   1879-1   DO-19

DO-22   RP-4   RP-6   RP-4   1902-3

CO-15   LO-11   BV-2   1902-2   DO-23   DO-18   DO-23

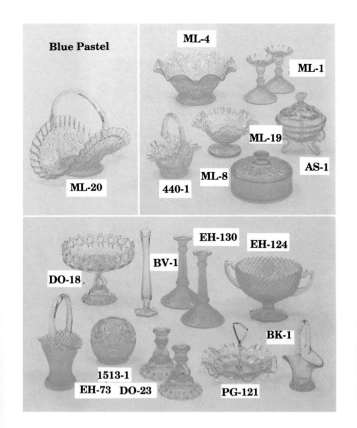

Blue Pastel

ML-4
ML-1
ML-20
440-1
ML-8
ML-19
AS-1

DO-18
BV-1
EH-130
EH-124
1513-1
EH-73   DO-23
PG-121
BK-1

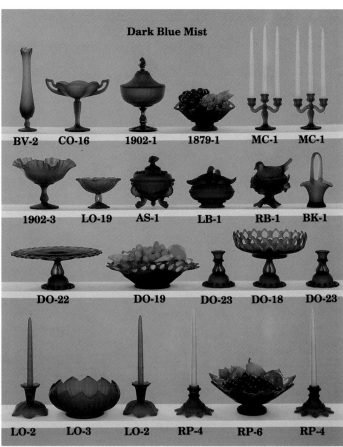

Dark Blue Mist

BV-2   CO-16   1902-1   1879-1   MC-1   MC-1

1902-3   LO-19   AS-1   LB-1   RB-1   BK-1

DO-22   DO-19   DO-23   DO-18   DO-23

LO-2   LO-3   LO-2   RP-4   RP-6   RP-4

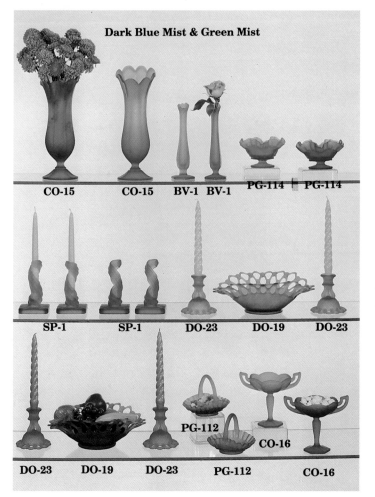

Dark Blue Mist & Green Mist

CO-15   CO-15   BV-1   BV-1   PG-114   PG-114

SP-1   SP-1   DO-23   DO-19   DO-23

DO-23   DO-19   DO-23   PG-112   CO-16

PG-112   CO-16

Light Blue Mist

RB-1

1902-2

BV-1

BK-1

BA-1   1879-1

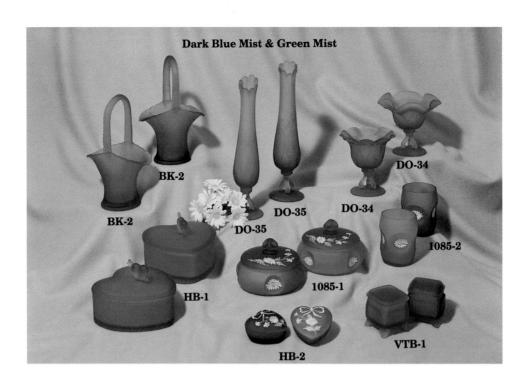

Dark Blue Mist & Green Mist

BK-2

BK-2

DO-35

DO-35

DO-34

DO-34

1085-2

1085-1

HB-1

HB-2

VTB-1

Brandywine Blue Opalescent or Moonstone

AH-31

AH-30

AH-9

AH-9

AH-4

AH-32

AH-15

AH-13

AH-10

AH-17

AH-18

AH-19

AH-20

AH-23

Blues & Lilacs

CO-17

EH-108

OQ-35

OQ-9

OQ-10

LO-15

DO-34

ML-19

PK-1

PK-2

LO-19

RL-7

EH-55

PG-115

BF-1

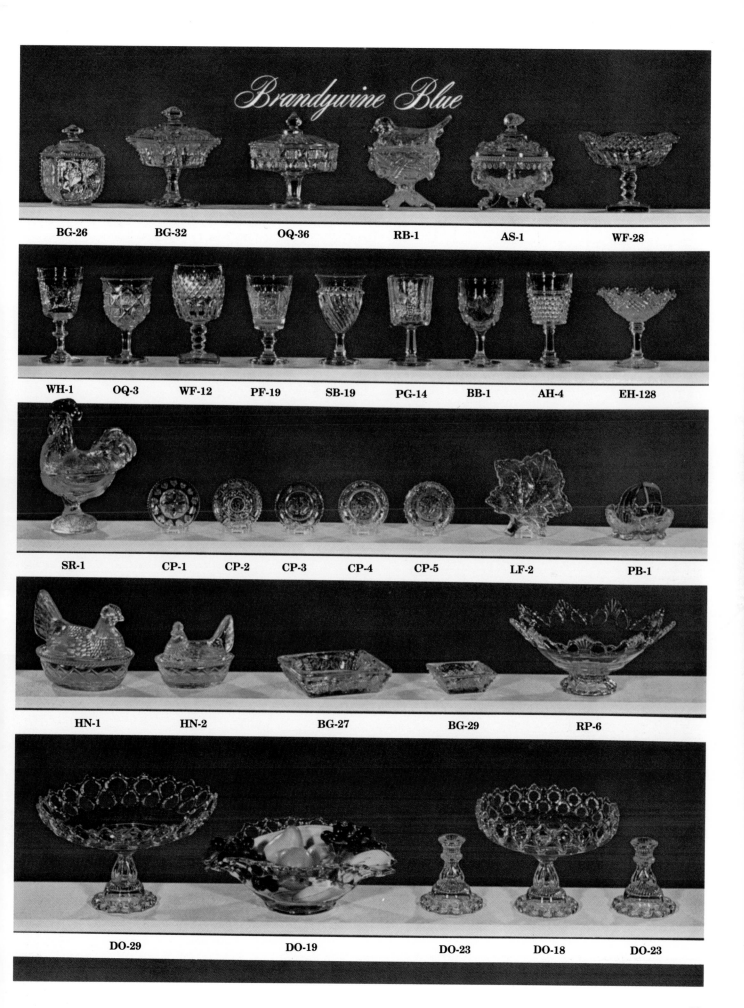

Brandywine Blue

BG-26   BG-32   OQ-36   RB-1   AS-1   WF-28

WH-1   OQ-3   WF-12   PF-19   SB-19   PG-14   BB-1   AH-4   EH-128

SR-1   CP-1   CP-2   CP-3   CP-4   CP-5   LF-2   PB-1

HN-1   HN-2   BG-27   BG-29   RP-6

DO-29   DO-19   DO-23   DO-18   DO-23

Brandywine Blue

BV-1   **PG-120**   **PG-10**   **PG-117**   **PG-97**   **PG-118**

PG-46   **PG-119**   **PG-20**   **PG-65**   **PG-20**   **PG-27**

PG-92   **PG-91**   **PG-28**   **PG-80**   **PG-87 & 88**   **PG-15**   **PG-14**   **PG-12**   **PG-13**

ST-7   **ST-4**   **EH-147**   **EH-126**

"Brown Mist"

A New Addition to our family of "Soft Mist" Colors. Extensive market testing during 1974 indicate this to be the color your customers will be asking for. It's Soft — It's Warm and It's a Money Maker. We plan to promote our "Mist" Colors in upcoming consumer advertising — so be prepared.

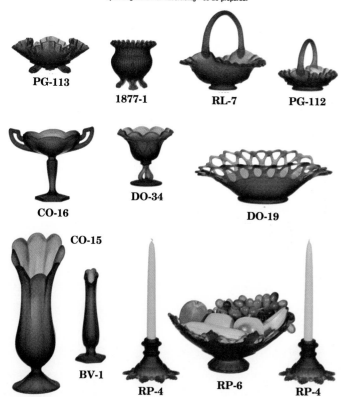

PG-113

1877-1

RL-7

PG-112

CO-16

DO-34

DO-19

CO-15

BV-1

RP-4

RP-6

RP-4

Moonstone or Candlelight

AH-30

AH-9

AH-23

AH-9

AH-4

AH-32

AH-13

AH-31

AH-15

AH-17

AH-18

AH-19

AH-21

AH-10

Crystal

ST-4

DR-19

PG-85

PG-125

PG-17

PG-12

PG-13

PG-28

PG-105

PG-71

PG-19

PG-30

PG-80

PG-14

Crystal

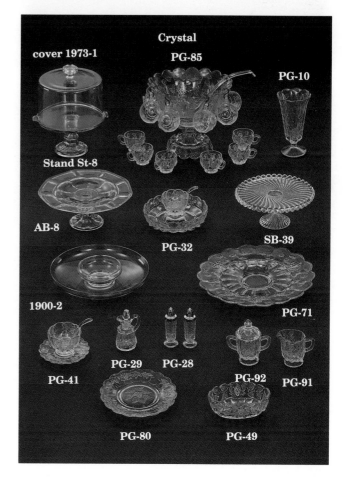

cover 1973-1

PG-85

PG-10

Stand St-8

AB-8

PG-32

SB-39

1900-2

PG-71

PG-41

PG-29

PG-28

PG-92

PG-91

PG-80

PG-49

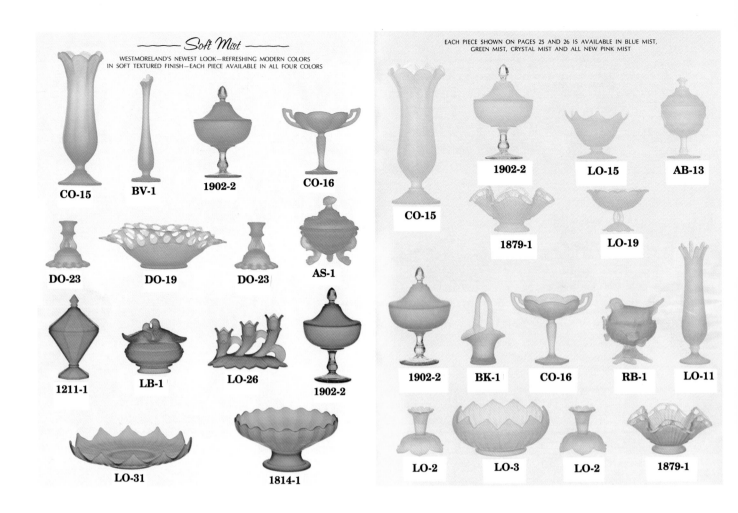

Soft Mist

WESTMORELAND'S NEWEST LOOK—REFRESHING MODERN COLORS
IN SOFT TEXTURED FINISH—EACH PIECE AVAILABLE IN ALL FOUR COLORS

CO-15

BV-1

1902-2

CO-16

DO-23

DO-19

DO-23

AS-1

1211-1

LB-1

LO-26

1902-2

LO-31

1814-1

EACH PIECE SHOWN ON PAGES 25 AND 26 IS AVAILABLE IN BLUE MIST,
GREEN MIST, CRYSTAL MIST AND ALL NEW PINK MIST

CO-15

1902-2

LO-15

AB-13

1879-1

LO-19

1902-2

BK-1

CO-16

RB-1

LO-11

LO-2

LO-3

LO-2

1879-1

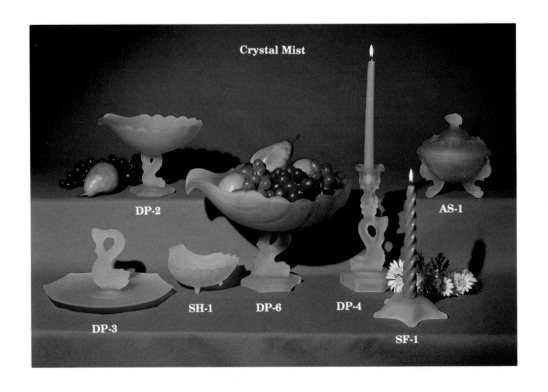

Crystal Mist

DP-2

AS-1

DP-3

SH-1

DP-6

DP-4

SF-1

Choice Pieces in popular "Flame"

CO-15　　CO-17　　LO-11　　BV-1　　AB-13

DO-19　　DO-23　　PB-1

LO-10　　LO-19　　CO-11　　LO-2

LO-3　　LO-31　　LO-15

Amber - An All Time Favorite
ITEMS SHOWN ON THIS PAGE ARE ALSO AVAILABLE IN MOSS GREEN

ST-4　　CH-12　　SP-1　　ST-7

DO-18　　RP-4　　RP-6　　RP-4　　PB-1

RL-8　　RL-4　　1877-2　　1814-2

TE-19　　TE-20　　RB-1　　RL-9　　1814-1　　RL-9

"Green Mist"

An Outstanding Decorating Color in versatile shapes and patterns. This color was in Our Original "Mist" Program and continues to be The Consumer's Favorite.

AS-1　　BG-33　　RL-7　　DO-34　　CO-16

PG-86　　PG-112　　DO-19　　PG-113　　1877-1

May we suggest you carry an ample stock of all "Soft Mist" Colors. Blend Colors with Milk Glass for an attractive display.

CO-15　　BV-1　　PG-10

RP-4　　RP-6　　RP-4

DO-23　　DO-18　　DO-23　　PG-114　　PG-56

Golden Sunset

BV-1   PG-120   PG-10   PG-117   PG-97   PG-118

PG-46   PG-119   PG-20   PG-65   PG-20   PG-27

PG-92   PG-91   PG-28   PG-80   PG-87&88   PG-15   PG-14   PG-12   PG-13

ST-7   ST-4   EH-147   EH-126

Golden Sunset

| BG-26 | BG-32 | OQ-36 | RB-1 | AS-1 | WF-28 |

| WH-1 | OQ-3 | WF-12 | PF-19 | SB-19 | PG-14 | BB-1 | AH-4 | EH-128 |

| SR-1 | CP-1 | CP-2 | CP-3 | CP-4 | CP-5 | LF-2 | PB-1 |

| HN-1 | HN-2 | BG-27 | BG-29 | RP-6 |

| DO-29 | DO-19 | DO-23 | DO-18 | DO-23 |

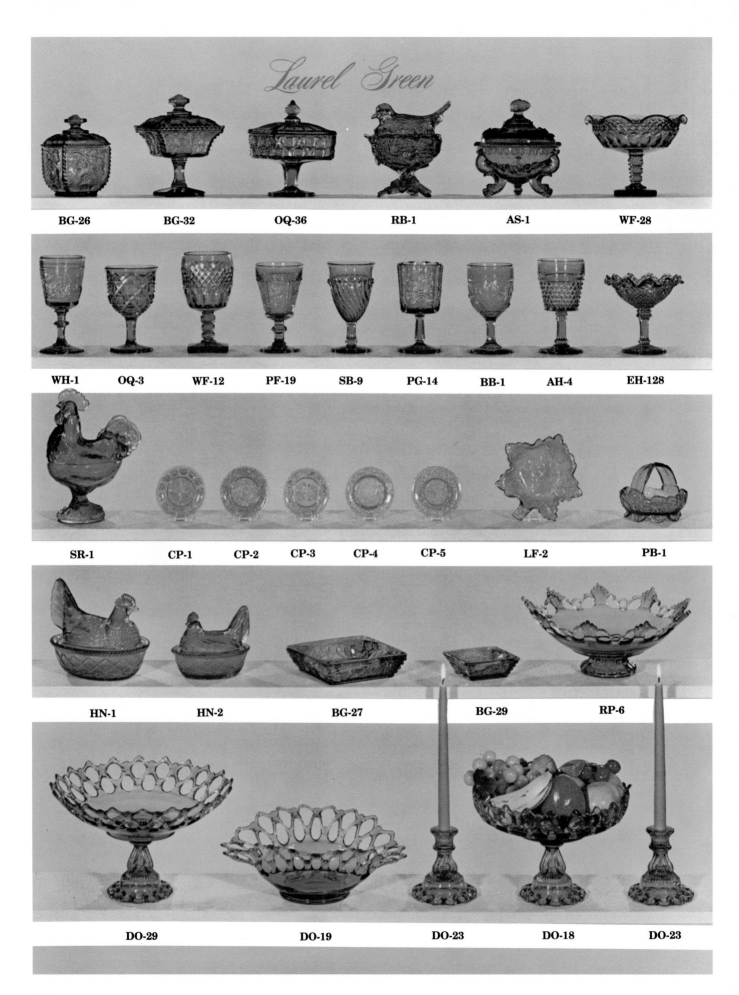

Laurel Green

BG-26 BG-32 OQ-36 RB-1 AS-1 WF-28

WH-1 OQ-3 WF-12 PF-19 SB-9 PG-14 BB-1 AH-4 EH-128

SR-1 CP-1 CP-2 CP-3 CP-4 CP-5 LF-2 PB-1

HN-1 HN-2 BG-27 BG-29 RP-6

DO-29 DO-19 DO-23 DO-18 DO-23

Laurel Green

BV-1   PG-120   PG-10   PG-117   PG-97   PG-118

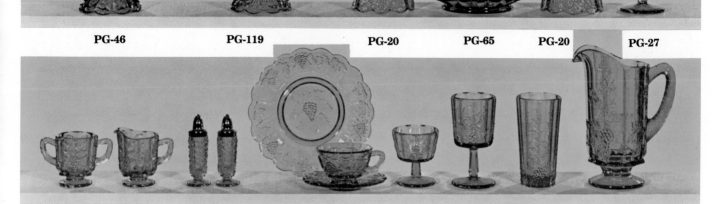

PG-46   PG-119   PG-20   PG-65   PG-20   PG-27

PG-92   PG-91   PG-28   PG-80   PG-87&88   PG-15   PG-14   PG-12   PG-13

ST-7   ST-4   EH-147   EH-126

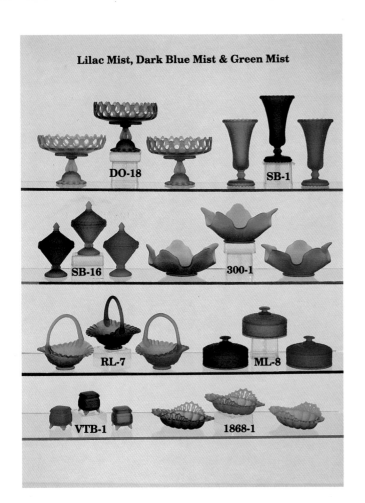

Lilac Mist, Dark Blue Mist & Green Mist

DO-18

SB-1

SB-16

300-1

RL-7

ML-8

VTB-1

1868-1

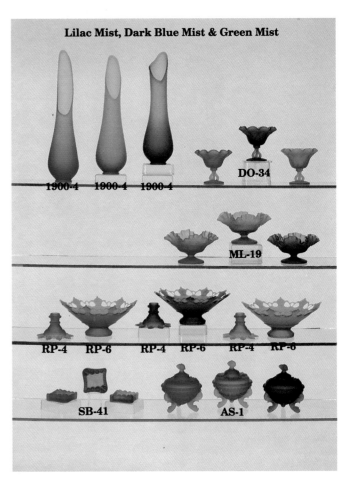

Lilac Mist, Dark Blue Mist & Green Mist

1900-4 1900-4 1900-4

DO-34

ML-19

RP-4 RP-6 RP-4 RP-6 RP-4 RP-6

SB-41

AS-1

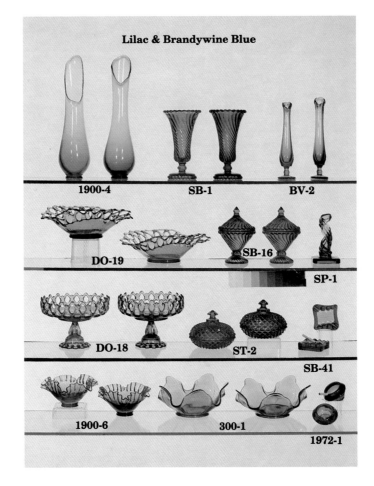

Lilac & Brandywine Blue

1900-4

SB-1

BV-2

DO-19

SB-16

SP-1

DO-18

ST-2

SB-41

1900-6

300-1

1972-1

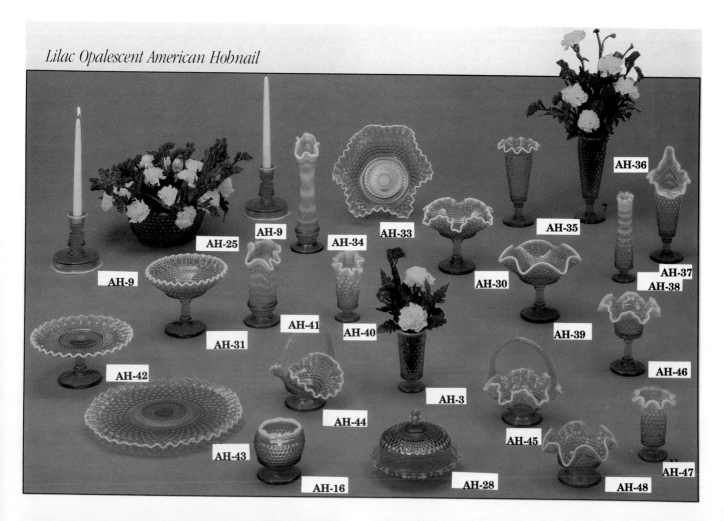

AH-36
AH-9
AH-25
AH-9
AH-34
AH-33
AH-35
AH-37
AH-38
AH-9
AH-30
AH-41
AH-40
AH-31
AH-39
AH-42
AH-3
AH-46
AH-44
AH-45
AH-43
AH-16
AH-28
AH-48
AH-47

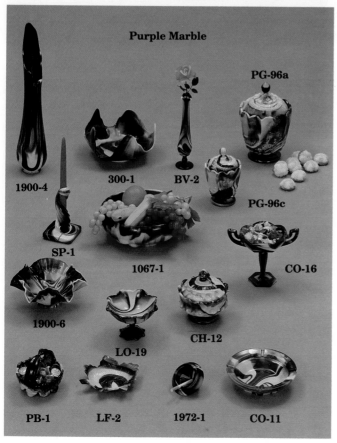

Purple Marble

PG-96a
1900-4
300-1
BV-2
PG-96c
SP-1
1067-1
CO-16
1900-6
LO-19
CH-12
PB-1
LF-2
1972-1
CO-11

ML-1
ML-4
AS-1
ML-19
ML-8
440-1

Lilac Pastel

ML-20

EH-124
BV-1
EH-130
EH-73
DO-18
BK-1
1513-1
PG-121
DO-23

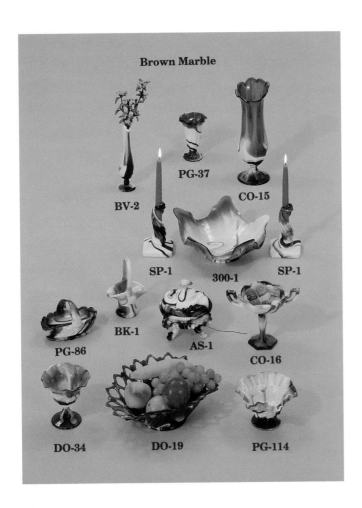

Brown Marble

BV-2

PG-37

CO-15

SP-1

300-1

SP-1

PG-86

BK-1

AS-1

CO-16

DO-34

DO-19

PG-114

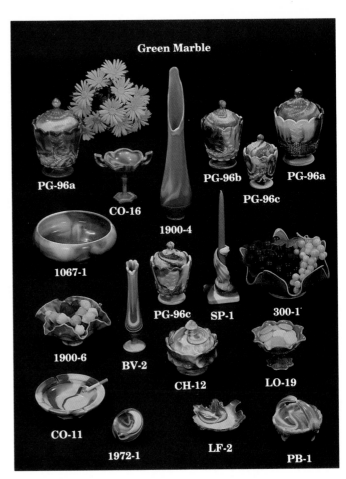

Green Marble

PG-96a

CO-16

PG-96b

PG-96a

PG-96c

1900-4

1067-1

PG-96c

SP-1

300-1

1900-6

BV-2

CH-12

LO-19

CO-11

1972-1

LF-2

PB-1

Purple & Green Marble

PG-114

1211-1

CO-15

AB-15

TE-22

CO-15

PG-34

PG-86

DO-19

DO-19

Green & Purple Marble

BV-2

DO-19

300-1

CO-15

1211-1

SB-1

AS-1

CO-16

PG-86

CO-11

PG-114

AB-15

ST-2

SP-1

PG-34

CL-1

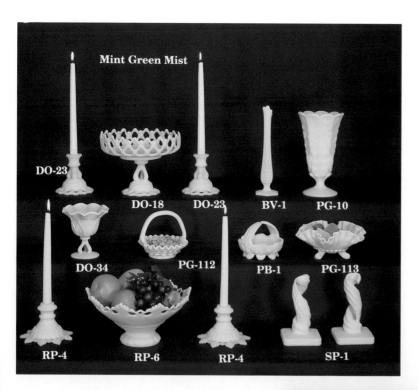

Mint Green Mist

DO-23

DO-18

DO-23

BV-1

PG-10

DO-34

PG-112

PB-1

PG-113

RP-4

RP-6

RP-4

SP-1

Mint Green

PG-34

DO-23

DO-18

DO-23

Mint Green

PG-10

SP-1

SP-1

DO-34

DR-17

BV-1

Ice Blue Carnival

ST-4
OQ-59
AS-1
SW-2
FR-1

OQ-34
OQ-31
OQ-9
OQ-10
PG-114
WF-38

ST-2
OQ-11
FF-1
OQ-16

Mint Green

PG-110
RP-4
RP-6
RP-4
PG-112
AS-1
PG-111
DO-19

Mint Green

PG-20
PG-109
PG-20
OQ-34
DH-1
BG-33
PB-1
PG-1
PG-113
CH-9

Honey Carnival

BG-33
PG-114
OQ-9
OQ-10
FR-1
AS-1
GS-1
OQ-59
PG-112
FF-1

Moss Green - A Fine New Decorator's Color

COMBINING POPULAR GREEN WITH A TINT OF GOLD.
ALL ITEMS ILLUSTRATED ARE ALSO AVAILABLE IN AMBER

BV-1
AB-13
LB-1
DO-21
ST-4

CO-16
LO-2
LO-3
LO-2
AB-15

ST-2
DO-23
DO-19
DO-23
DR-17

AB-9
AB-7
AB-9
BL-1
FMN-1

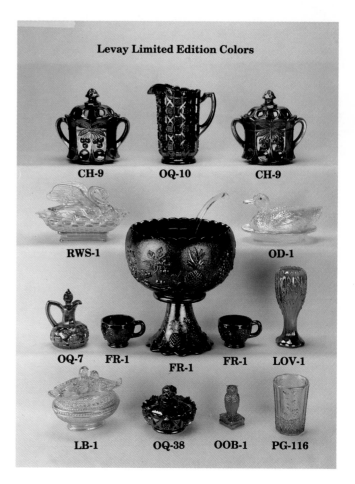

Levay Limited Edition Colors

CH-9
OQ-10
CH-9

RWS-1
OD-1

OQ-7
FR-1
FR-1
FR-1
LOV-1

LB-1
OQ-38
OOB-1
PG-116

Levay Limited Edition Colors

PG-118 PT-1 PT-1 PG-118

PG-116

PG-13 PG-116 PG-13 CO-7 CO-6 OQ-9 OQ-10

OQ-9 OQ-10 HH-3 FL-1 OQ-10

HH-2 OQ-9

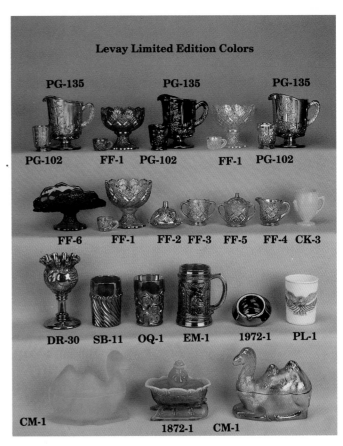

Levay Limited Edition Colors

PG-135 PG-135 PG-135

PG-102 FF-1 PG-102 FF-1 PG-102

FF-6 FF-1 FF-2 FF-3 FF-5 FF-4 CK-3

DR-30 SB-11 OQ-1 EM-1 1972-1 PL-1

CM-1 1872-1 CM-1

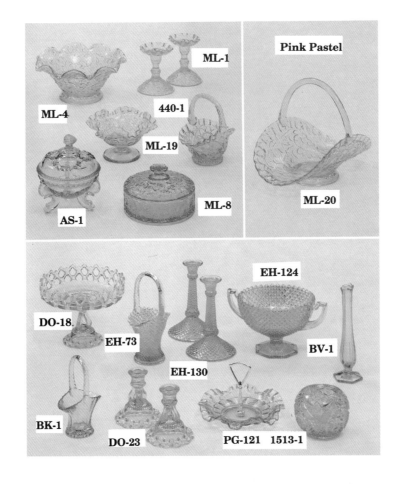

ML-1

ML-4 440-1

ML-19

AS-1 ML-8

Pink Pastel

ML-20

DO-18 EH-124

EH-73

EH-130 BV-1

BK-1

DO-23 PG-121 1513-1

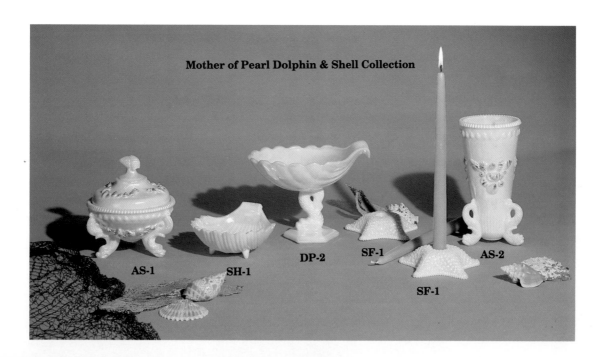

Mother of Pearl Dolphin & Shell Collection

AS-1 SH-1 DP-2 SF-1 SF-1 AS-2

Milk Glass Mother of Pearl

PG-65

AS-1 HB-2 PG-20 PG-20

BV-1 LB-1 OQ-34 DR-17

PB-1 SP-1 PG-113 300-3

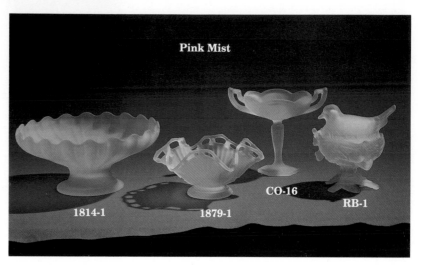

Pink Mist

1814-1 1879-1 CO-16 RB-1

EH-42
EH-25
EH-153
EH-154
EH-67
6
EH-124
EH-130
8
EH-71
EH-71
EH-152
4
5
EH-130
EH-155
EH-72
EH-156
EH-50
EH-158
EH-40
EH-159
EH-157
EH-128
EH-73
EH-69
EH-166
EH-160
EH-161
EH-165
EH-162
EH-28
EH-24
EH-168
EH-66
EH-163
EH-167
EH-169
EH-170
EH-164

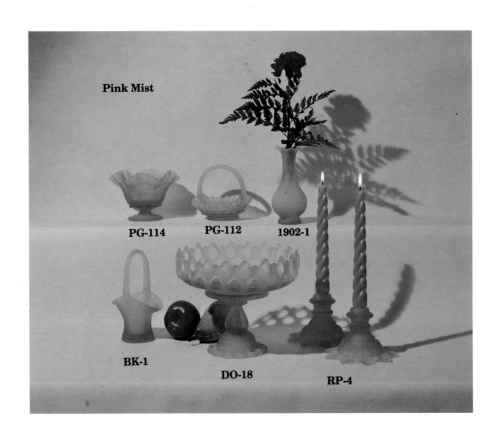

Pink Mist

PG-114
PG-112
1902-1

BK-1
DO-18
RP-4

Ruby Stained Ashburton

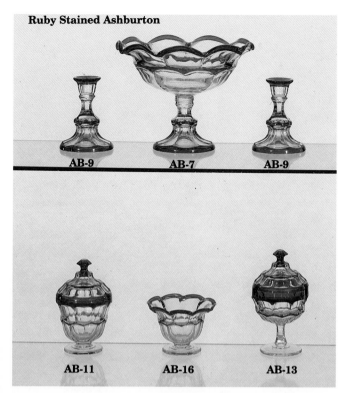

AB-9   AB-7   AB-9

AB-11   AB-16   AB-13

Ruby Stained Panel Grape

PB-1   PG-134

PG-26   PG-20   PG-65   PG-20

PG-103   PG-86   BG-33

Grossman Era Ruby

ML-4   ML-1

ML-20   440-1   ML-8   AS-1

340-2   EH-130   EH-124

1516-1   1513-1   PG-121   EH-73

Ruby & Ruby Stain

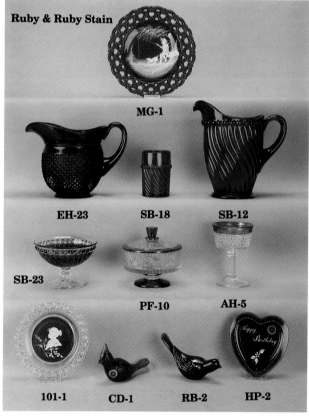

MG-1

EH-23   SB-18   SB-12

SB-23   PF-10   AH-5

101-1   CD-1   RB-2   HP-2

Ruby Ashtrays

EH-171   CO-11   1972-1   EH-102   CO-11

Ruby Stain in Crystal

PB-1　WB-3　WB-1　WB-2　1943-1

WF-37　WF-24　WF-23　WF-26

WF-32　WF-30　WF-16　WF-36

WF-33　WF-31　WF-34　WF-35　WF-12　WF-8　WF-6

Ruby Stain in Crystal

WB-3　WB-1　WB-2　WF-32

RL-3　RL-6　RL-8　WF-20

PG-20　PG-65　PG-20　PB-1　WF-31

PG-129　PG-113　BG-33　PG-103　300-2

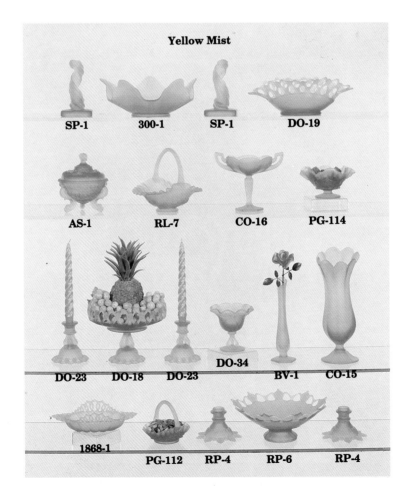

Yellow Mist

SP-1　300-1　SP-1　DO-19

AS-1　RL-7　CO-16　PG-114

DO-23　DO-18　DO-23　DO-34　BV-1　CO-15

1868-1　PG-112　RP-4　RP-6　RP-4

CODE SECTION

AB-1 Claret or juice goblet, ftd.
Colors: Crystal, amber, olive green, Bermuda Blue, brown, pink, Golden Sunset, moss green.
Availability: Crystal is more difficult to find than the later colors.
Reproductions: None known.

AB-2 Water goblet, ftd.
Colors: Crystal, amber, Bermuda Blue, brown, olive green, pink, moss green, Golden Sunset.
Availability: Most commonly found item in any color.
Reproductions: None known.

AB-3 Iced Tea Goblet, 14 oz., ftd.
Colors: Crystal, amber, Bermuda Blue, olive green, brown, pink, moss green, Golden Sunset.
Availability: All difficult to find.
Reproductions: None known.

AB-4 Iced Tea tumbler, 13 oz., flat.
Colors: Amber, Bermuda Blue, olive green, crystal, Golden Sunset, moss green.
Availability: All difficult to find.
Reproductions: None known.

AB-5 Old Fashioned or Rocks tumbler, flat.
Colors: Amber, Bermuda Blue, brown, crystal, olive green, pink, moss green, Golden Sunset.
Availability: This was the best selling piece and should be easily found in any color in certain areas.
Reproductions: None known.

AB-6 Sherbert, ftd.
Colors: Amber, brown, crystal, olive green, pink, Golden Sunset, moss green, Bermuda Blue.
Availability: All difficult to find.
Reproductions: None known.

AB-7 Compote or fruit bowl, lipped, ftd.
Colors: Crystal w/ruby stain, crystal, crystal w/platinum accent, moss green, amber, Bermuda Blue, olive green, Golden Sunset, amber.
Availability: All are difficult.
Reproductions: None known.

AB-8 Cake salver, ftd.
Colors: Crystal, Bermuda Blue, olive green, Golden Sunset.
Availability: All colors are scarce.
Reproductions: None known.

AB-9 Candleholder. Note, these were used as bases for the larger footed pieces, and are very similar to the Sawtooth candlesticks (see ST-3).
Colors: Amber, Bermuda Blue, crystal w/ruby accent, crystal, moss green, olive green, Golden Sunset.
Availability: All difficult to find.
Reproductions: None known.

AB-10 Compote or fruit bowl, flared, ftd.
Colors: Amber, Bermuda Blue, crystal, olive green, Golden Sunset.
Availability: All are very difficult.
Reproductions: None known.

AB-11 Sugar with lid. Also marketed as a candy with lid.
Colors: Amber, Bermuda Blue, crystal, olive green, crystal w/ruby stain, milk glass, milk glass w/Roses & Bows decoration, Golden Sunset, mg w/Pansy decoration.
Availability: Mg common, mg decorated versions are difficult, colors may be slightly more difficult.
Reproductions: None known.

AB-12 Creamer.
Colors: Crystal, Bermuda Blue, olive green, Golden Sunset.
Availability: Scarce due to the fact that the sugar was marketed more as a candy than as a creamer and sugar set.
Reproductions: None known.

AB-13 Compote or candy w/lid, stem ftd.
Colors: Amber, Bermuda Blue, crystal, crystal w/ruby stain, crystal mist, milk glass, milk glass w/Roses and Bows decoration, Flame, olive green, pink mist, blue mist, green mist, moss green, Golden Sunset.
Availability: Usually available, Flame and Roses & Bows may be very difficult.
Reproductions: None known.

AB-14 Pitcher, large footed.
Colors: Amber, Bermuda Blue, brown, crystal, olive green, pink, Golden Sunset.
Availability: All colors very scarce.
Reproductions: None known.

AB-15 Mint compote, footed, crimped rim.
Colors: Green marble, brown marble, purple marble, moss green, amber, Golden Sunset, Bermuda Blue, Brandywine Blue.
Availability: Marbles are scarce, other colors are difficult.
Reproductions: None known.

AB-16 Candy, footed, open, crimped rim. This is actually the sugar bottom which was turned into a candy.
Colors: Crystal w/ruby stain.
Availability: Scarce.
Reproductions: None known.

AB/CO-15 Plate, scallop rim, sherbert underliner or dinner sized.
Colors: Amber, Bermuda Blue, olive green, milk glass, Golden Sunset, moss green.
Availability: All colors are scarce, milk glass is slightly difficult.
Reproductions: None known.

AH-1 Iced tea tumbler, 11 oz, low ftd.
Colors: Milk glass, crystal.
Availability: Both are available.
Reproductions: None known.

AH-2 Water tumbler, 7-1/2 oz., low ftd.
Colors: Milk glass, crystal.
Availability: Both are available.
Reproductions: None known.

AH-3 Gingerale or juice tumbler, 5 oz., low ftd. (later called a vase by Grossman.)
Colors: Milk glass, lilac opalescent.
Availability: Scarce in milk glass, common in lilac opalescent.
Reproductions: None known.

AH-4 Water Goblet, 8 oz., hi ftd.
Colors: Milk glass, crystal, Golden Sunset, Laurel Green, Brandywine Blue, Candlelight, Brandywine Blue Opalescent.
Availability: Milk glass very common, all colors are scarce.
Reproductions: None known.

AH-5 Champagne Goblet or hi ftd. sherbert.
Colors: Milk glass, crystal, crystal w/ruby accent stain.
Availability: Mg available, crystal & crystal w/stain very difficult.
Reproductions: None known.

AH-6 Sherbert, low ftd. Rim can be straight or belled.
Colors: Milk glass, Crystal w/ruby flashing.
Availability: Scarce in both colors.
Reproductions: None known.

AH-7 Egg cup, double end.
Colors: Milk glass, crystal.
Availability: Scarce in both colors.
Reproductions: None known.

AH-8 Jug or Pitcher, 1/2 gallon applied hdl. Other companies produced a similar pitcher, but the "Hobnail" pattern is interspersed with horizontal bars. Westmoreland's Hobnail is all hobnail.
Colors: Milk glass.
Availability: Very scarce.
Reproductions: None known.

AH-9 Candlestick, 5" tall.
Colors: Milk glass, Candlelight, Lilac Opalescent, Brandywine Blue Opalescent.
Availability: Mg common, colors scarce.
Reproductions: None known.

AH-10 Salt & Pepper shakers w/chrome

lids, ftd.
Colors: Milk glass, Brandywine Blue Opalescent, Candlelight.
Availability: Mg common, colors scarce.
Reproductions: None known.

AH-11 Finger Bowl, 4-1/2", ftd.
Colors: Milk glass
Availability: scarce.
Reproductions: None known.

AH-12 Ashtray, round, 4-1/2".
Colors: Milk glass, moss green.
Availability: Mg available, moss green is difficult.
Reproductions: None known.

AH-13 Mayonnaise, ftd., 4-1/2" belled rim.
Colors: Milk glass. Also a ruffled version in Brandywine Blue Opalescent, & Candlelight called a nut dish.
Availability: Mg scarce, others very scarce.
Reproductions: None known.

AH-14 Grapefruit bowl, 6-1/2".
Colors: Milk glass.
Availability: scarce.
Reproductions: None known.

AH-15 Puff Box or Bon-Bon and cover, 5".
Colors: Milk glass, Brandywine Blue Opalescent, Candlelight.
Availability: Mg common, colors scarce.
Reproductions: None known.

AH-16 Rose Bowl, ftd., 4-1/2" (note this is the same piece as the mayo AH-13 but with a cupped rim).
Colors: Milk glass, lilac opalescent.
Availability: Both common.
Reproductions: None known.

AH-17 Cruet for oil or vinegar, 2 oz.
Colors: Milk glass, Brandywine Blue Opalescent, Candlelight.
Availability: Mg common, colors scarce.
Reproductions: None known.

AH-18 Sugar bowl, open, 3-1/2" high.

Colors: Milk glass, Brandywine Blue Opalescent, Candlelight, Lilac Opalescent.
Availability: Mg common, colors scarce.
Reproductions: None known.

AH-19 Creamer, 3-1/2" high.
Colors: Milk glass, Brandywine Blue Opalescent, Candlelight, Lilac Opalescent.
Availability: Mg common, colors scarce.
Reproductions: None known.

AH-20 Celery Dish, oval, 10" x 5-1/2".
Colors: Milk glass, Brandywine Blue Opalescent, Candlelight.
Availability: Mg available, all colors scarce.
Reproductions: None known.

AH-21 Pickle dish, oval, 8" x 4".
Colors: Milk glass, Candlelight, Brandywine Blue Opalescent.
Availability: Mg difficult, Candlelight and Brandywine Blue Opalescent are very scarce.
Reproductions: None known.

AH-22 Bowl, belled rim, 7".
Colors: Milk glass, Brandywine Blue Opalescent. Candlelight may also have been produced.
Availability: All are scarce.
Reproductions: None known.

AH-23 Bowl, belled rim, 9-1/2".
Colors: Milk glass, Brandywine Blue Opalescent, Candlelight.
Availability: Mg scarce, colors very scarce.
Reproductions: None known.

AH-24 Bowl, belled rim, 5-1/2".
Colors: Milk glass, Brandywine Blue Opalescent, Candlelight.
Availability: All are scarce.
Reproductions: None known.

AH-25 Bowl, cupped rim, 8".
Colors: Milk glass, Lilac Opalescent.
Availability: Both available.
Reproductions: None known.

AH-26 Cup, can be used with American

Hobnail or Beaded Edge.
Colors: Milk glass.
Availability: Common.
Reproductions: None known.

AH-27 Compote, footed flared, 8" dia., 4" hi.
Colors: Milk glass
Availability: Common.
Reproductions: None known

AH-28 Butter or Cheese dish with lid, 5-1/2".
Colors: Milk glass, Lilac Opalescent, for
Levay: Aquamarine and Ruby.
Availability: Mg & Lilac Opal common,
Aquamarine & Ruby very scarce.
Reproductions: None known.

AH-29 Compote, belled ftd., 6" dia., 5-3/4" hi.
Colors: Milk glass.
Availability: Common.
Reproducitons: None known.

AH-30 Compote, crimped rim, hi ftd., 6-1/2".
Colors: Brandywine Blue Opalescent,
Candlelight, Lilac Opalescent.
Availability: Brandywine Blue Opal. &
Candlelight very scarce, Lilac Opal difficult.
Reproductions: None known.

AH-31 Compote, crimped rim, hi ftd., 7".
Colors: Brandywine Blue Opalescent,
Candlelight, Lilac Opalescent.
Availability: Lilac Opal scarce, others very
scarce.
Reproductions: None known.

AH-32 Vase, ftd., pulled top, height can vary.
Colors: Brandywine Blue Opalescent,
Candlelight, Lilac Opalescent.
Availability: All are scarce.
Reproductions: None known.

AH-33 Bowl, 9" crimped & ruffled.
Colors: Lilac Opalescent.
Availability: scarce.
Reproductions: None known.

AH-34 Vase, fluted, 11". Height may vary.
Colors: Lilac Opalescent.

Availability: Very difficult.
Reproductions: None known.

AH-35 Vase, ftd., flared, ruffled rim, 8".
Colors: Lilac opalescent.
Availability: Very difficult.
Reproductions: None known.

AH-36 Vase, ftd., 8-1/2".
Colors: Lilac Opalescent.
Availability: Very difficult.
Reproductions: None known.

AH-37 Jack-in-the-pulpit vase, ftd., 10-1/2".
Colors: Lilac Opalescent.
Availability: Scarce.
Reproductions: None known.

AH-38 Bud vase, ftd., pulled top, 8". Height
may vary.
Colors: Lilac opalescent.
Availability: Scarce.
Reproductions: None known.

AH-39 Candy compote, ruffled rim, ftd.,
6-1/2"
Colors: Lilac Opalescent.
Availability: Very difficult.
Reproductions: None known.

AH-40 Vase, ftd., double crimped, 5-1/2" tall.
Colors: Lilac opalescent.
Availability: scarce.
Reproductions: None known

AH-41 Vase, ftd., double crimped, 7" tall.
Colors: Lilac opalescent.
Availability: Scarce.
Reproductions: None known.

AH-42 Donut stand, ftd. ruffled rim, 8" dia.
Colors: Lilac opalescent.
Availability: Very scarce.
Reproductions: None known.

AH-43 Serving plate, ruffled rim, 12" dia.
Colors: Lilac opalescent.
Availability: scarce.
Reproductions: None known.

AH-44 Basket, oval, ruffled rim, ftd., 6-1/2".
Colors: Lilac opalescent.
Availability: Very scarce.
Reproductions: None known.

AH-45 Basket, round, double crimped, ftd., 6".
Colors: Lilac opalescent.
Availability: Very scarce.
Reproductions: None known.

AH-46 Mint compote, ftd., double crimped, 5-1/2".
Colors: Lilac opalescent.
Availability: Scarce.
Reproductions: None known.

AH-47 Vase, ftd., ruffled, 4-1/2".
Colors: Lilac Opalescent.
Availability: Scarce.
Reproductions: None known.

AH-48 Mint compote, ftd., double crimped, 5".
Colors: Lilac Opalescent.
Availability: Difficult.
Reproductions: None known.

AH-49 Chalice, tall ftd., (shown on back cover). This Chalice is 9-1/2" tall and 3-7/8" diameter. This item is not listed in any catalog which I own.
Colors: Milk glass, other colors are possible.
Availability: Very scarce to rare.
Reproductions: None known.

AS-1 Argonaut Shell Line #1048, covered candy, 3 dolphin feet, 6". Be careful, Vallerysthal also made a version of this candy but it will be smaller in diameter. This version from France is usually found in a dark blue opaque glass.
Colors: Almond, mint green, milk glass, mg w/mop, mint green mist, almond mist, antique blue, antique blue mist, apricot mist, blue pastel, dark blue mist, Brandywine Blue, Golden Sunset, Laurel Green, green mist, lilac mist, purple marble, green marble, brown marble, amber, crystal mist, pink mist, Bermuda Blue, Lilac Opalescent, yellow mist, Honey Carnival, Ice Blue Carnival, light blue mist, ruby, pink pastel, mg mop w/hp shells. For Levay: butterscotch carnival (1980, 400 made) and pink carnival.
Availability: Mg available, colors are very difficult to scarce. Carnival colors are very scarce to rare.
Reproductions: Cobalt, black mg, alexandrite, azure blue.

AS-2 Line #1048 Argonaut Shell cone shaped vase, 3 dolphin style feet.
Colors: Mg, crystal mist, mg mop, mg mop w/hp accents on shells, Golden Sunset, Electric Blue Opalescent, Electric blue Opalescent Carnival (200 made), almond.
Availability: Mg, mg mop, cry mist, almond & Colden Sunset are difficult, hand painted versions are very difficult, Electric Blue Opal plain and carnival are scarce to rare.
Reproductions: Cobalt, Cobalt carnival.

BA-1 Line #10 Bird ashtray.
Colors: Dk blue mist, light blue mist, green mist, pink mist, green marble.
Availability: Mist colors difficult, marble is very difficult.
Reproductions: None known.

BB-1 Line #1883 Blackberry, water goblet, 8 oz., footed.
Colors: Brandywine Blue, Laurel Green, Golden Sunset, mg.
Availability: All are scarce.
Reproductions: None known.

BB-2 Line #503 Bon bon, 2 hdld w/lid.
Colors: Antique blue mist, almond, blue pastel, crystal mist w/Floral Bouquet, brown mist w/Floral Bouquet, dk blue mist w/Floral Bouquet, milk glass w/Roses & Bows, crystal mist w/Roses & Bows, crystal with ruby stain w/Ruby Floral, dk blue mist w/daisy, brown mist w/daisy, green mist w/daisy, pink mist, dark blue mist, brown mist, mg w/blue Beaded Bouquet, Bermuda Blue.
Availability: Colors are difficult, decorated

examples are scarce.
Reproductions: None known.

BD-1 Bull dog door stop, 7 lbs. This item was very difficult to make in black milk glass due to the fact that black milk glass does not anneal well. A special annealing chamber had to be built in order to make this bull dog. Tiffin also made this bull dog. Different sources claim that Westmoreland had loaned Tiffin their mold in order to fill a special order for Tiffin. Tiffin's bull dog is just as rare to find as Westmoreland's. Tiffin produced this item in a black frosted color as well as others.
Colors: Black milk glass, milk glass, black mist, brown mist, Golden Sunset, moss green.
Availability: All colors extremely rare.
Reproductions: Cobalt blue, milk glass. The cobalt reproductions seem to be of very poor quality, lots of rippling and cloudy glass.

BD-2 Line #75 bulldog, 3-1/2" high. This will most often be found with rhinestone eyes.
Colors: Milk glass, black milk glass, black frosted milk glass, Golden Sunset, moss green, ruby carnival, electric blue carnival.
Availability: All colors very scarce.
Reproductions: Black satin, milk glass, cobalt, black w/red collar, mg w/red collar, cobalt w/white collar, blue ice, blue ice carnival, blue slag, pink, custard, cranberry, cranberry ice carnival.

BE-1 Bowl, oval, crimped, 6".
Colors: Mg, dec#4 Floral, dec#64-2 Fruit, dec#70 Birds, dec#74 Poultry, dec#A-28 Red Trim, dec#37 Holly.
Availability: Mg slightly difficult, dec#64-2 Fruit difficult, others scarce to rare.
Reproductions: None known.

BE-2 Salt & pepper shakers, footed.
Colors: Mg, dec#4 Floral, dec#64-2 Fruit, dec#70 Birds, dec#74 Poultry, dec#A-28 Red trim.
Availability: Mg difficult, decorations rare.
Reproductions: None known.

BE-3 Sugar, open, footed.
Colors: Mg, dec#4 Floral, dec#64-2 Fruit, dec#70 Birds, dec#74 Poultry, dec#A-28 Red trim.
Availability: Mg & dec#64-2 Fruit available, all others very scarce to rare.
Reproductions: None known.

BE-4 Creamer, footed.
Colors Mg, dec#4 Floral, dec#64-2 Fruit, dec#70 Birds, dec#74 Poultry, dec#A-28 Red trim.
Availability: Mg & dec#64-2 Fruit available, all others very scarce to rare.
Reproductions: None known.

BE-5 Saucer.
Colors: Mg, dec#4 Floral, dec#64-2 Fruit, dec#70 Birds, dec#74 Poultry, dec#A-28 Red trim.
Availability: Mg & dec#64-2 Fruit available all others scarce.
Reproductions: None known.

BE-6 Cup, this actually belongs to Line #1800, (See PL-9 for other variations.)
Colors: Mg, dec#4 Floral, dec#64-2 Fruit, dec#70 Birds, dec#74 Poultry, dec#A-28 Red trim.
Availability: Mg available, dec#64-2 slightly difficult, others scarce.
Reproductions: None known.

BE-7 Sherbert, footed.
Colors: Mg, dec#4 Floral, dec#64-2 Fruit, dec#70 Birds, dec#74 Poultry, dec#A-28 Red trim.
Availability: Mg available, dec #64-2 slightly difficult, others scarce.
Reproductions: None known.

BE-8 Tumbler, 8 oz., footed. Later in the 1970's this piece was crimped at the rim and marketed as a vase in mist colors.
Colors: Mg, dec#4 Floral, dec#64-2 Fruit, dec#70 Birds, dec#74 Poultry, dec#A-28 Red trim.
Availability: Mg & dec#64-2 Fruit available, all others scarce to very scarce.
Reproductions: None known.

BE-9 Bowl, oval, vegetable.
Colors: Mg, dec#4 Floral, dec#64-2 Fruit, dec#70 Birds, dec#74 Poultry, dec#A-28 Red trim.
Availability: All very scarce to rare.
Reproductions: None known.

BE-10 Bowl, round 5", fruit.
Colors: Mg, dec#4 Floral, dec#64-2 Fruit, dec#70 Birds, dec#74 Poultry, dec#A-28 Red trim, mg w/teddy bears, elephants, squirrels or dogs. (The last decorations were part of a child sized set.)
Availability: Mg available, others scarce. child's decorations rare.
Reproductions: None known.

BE-11 Relish, oval, 3 part.
Colors: Mg, dec#4 Floral, dec#64-2 Fruit, dec# 70 Birds, dec#74 Poultry, dec#A-28 Red trim.
Availability: All very scarce to rare.
Reproductions: None known.

BE-12 Bowl, oval (no reference to size).
Colors: Mg, dec#4 Floral, dec#64-2 Fruit, dec#70 Birds, dec#74 Poultry, dec#A-28 Red trim.
Availability: All very scarce to rare.
Reproductions: None known.

BE-13 Torte plate, 15" round, may have entire Zodiac impressed on back of plate.
Colors: Mg, dec#4 Floral, dec#64-2 Fruit, dec#70 Birds, dec#74 Poultry, dec#A-28 Red Trim, crystal or crystal w/stain accents w/Zodiac.
Availability: Mg & dec#64-2 Fruit are difficult, all other decorations are scarce.
Reproductions: None known. Note this particular mold is rusting away in the factory and cannot be remade today unless another mold is made.

BE-14 Platter, oval, 2 handles.
Colors: Mg, dec#4 Floral, dec#64-2 Fruit, dec#70 Birds, dec#74 Poultry, dec#A-28 Red trim.
Availability: All very scarce to rare.
Reproductions: None known.

BE-15 Dinner plate, 10-1/2", depressed ctr, wide rim.
Colors: Mg, dec#4 Floral, dec#64-2 Fruit, dec#70 Birds, dec#74 Poultry, dec#A-28 Red trim.
Availability: Mg difficult, dec#64-2 Fruit very difficult, others very scarce.
Reproductions: None known.

BE-16 Lunch plate, 8-1/2", may be croup shape or regular. Also can be found in crystal with a Zodiac design on back of plate, or Bob Cratchet decoration.
Colors: Mg, cry, dec#4 Floral, dec#64-2 Fruit, dec#70 Birds, dec#74 Poultry, dec#A-28 Red trim, crystal or crystal w/stain with Zodiac.
Availability: Mg difficult, cry w/dec rare, other decorations scarce.
Reproductions: None known.

BE-17 Salad plate, 7"croup shape.
Colors: Mg, dec#4 Floral, dec#64-2 Fruit, dec#70 Birds, dec#74 Poultry, dec#A-28 Red trim, mg w/teddy bears, elephants, squirrels or dogs. (This last decoration was a part of a child sized set.)
Availability: Mg & dec#64-2 Fruit are usually available, others are scarce, the child's decoration will be rare.
Reproductions: None known.

BE-18 B&B plate, 6" regular shape.
Colors: Mg, dec#4 Floral, dec#64-2 Fruit, dec# 70 Birds, dec#74 Poultry, dec#A-28 Red trim.
Availability: Mg slightly difficult, all others scarce.
Reproductions: None known.

BF-1 Line #3 Butterfly, large.
Colors: purple marble, antique blue, almond, purple carnival (a limited edition for the Historical Glass Museum Foundation in 1977), yellow mist, pink mist, brown marble, mint green, green mist, dk blue mist, green marble, Antique Blue Mist, vaseline, brown mist.
Availability: Purple carn very scarce, others difficult to scarce.
Reproductions: None known.

BG-1 Torte plate, 15", round.
Colors: Milk glass, mg w/dec#85 Pastel Fruit.
Availability: Very scarce due to the size of the plate and its ability to crack with use.
Reproductions: None known.

BG-2 Dinner plate, 10-1/2", round. See BG-41 for square version.
Colors: Milk glass, may be found with dec#32 on milk glass.
Availability: Very scarce in milk glass, rare with any decoration.
Reproductons: Milk glass, black milk glass, Black glass may be gold handpainted in the center.

BG-3 Luncheon plate, 8-1/2", round. See BG-41 for square version.
Colors: Milk glass, mg w/dec#85 Pastel Fruit.
Availability: Mg scarce, decorated rare.
Reproductions: Milk glass.

BG-4 Salad or dessert plate, 7", round.
Colors: Milk glass.
Availability: Scarce.
Reproductions: Milk Glass.

BG-5 Bread and butter plate, 6", round.
Colors: Milk glass.
Availability: Scarce.
Reproductions: 5" milk glass version.

BG-6 Mayonnaise, 4-1/2", footed.
Colors: Milk glass.
Availability: Scarce.
Reproductions: Mg w/green leaves and gold grapes. Top rim will be lipped.

BG-7 Salt & pepper shakers, ftd., chrome lids.
Colors: Milk glass.
Availability: Slightly difficult.
Reproducitons: Milk glass, milk glass with green leaves & gold grapes.

BG-8 3 pc. Mayonnaise set. consists of 1 round fruit cocktail bowl, 1 saucer, and 1 (#1837) ladle.

Colors: Milk glass.
Availability: Set complete scarce.
Reproductions: None at this time.

BG-9 Sugar bowl, open, square.
Colors: Milk glass, mg w/dec#86 Green & Gold, Golden Sunset.
Availability: Mg available, decorated mg is scarce, Golden Sunset is scarce.
Reproductions: Milk glass, milk glass with green leaves & gold grapes.

BG-10 Creamer, square.
Colors: Milk glass, mg w/dec#86 green & gold, Golden Sunset.
Availability: Mg available, decorated mg is scarce, Golden Sunset is scarce.
Reproductions: Milk glass, milk glass with green leaves & gold grapes.

BG-11 Cup and saucer.
Colors: Milk glass.
Availability: Both pieces are scarce.
Reproductions: Milk glass, milk glass with green leaves & gold grapes.

BG-12 Water goblet, round ftd., 8 oz.
Colors: Milk glass, mg w/dec#85 Pastel Fruit. Note goblet in Golden Sunset has square foot.
Availability: All colors are scarce.
Reproductions: None at this time.

BG-13 Iced tea tumbler, flat 10 oz.
Colors: Milk Glass.
Availability: Scarce.
Reproductions: None at this time.

BG-14 Water tumbler, flat, 8 oz.
Colors: Milk Glass.
Availability: Scarce.
Reproductions: None at this time.

BG-15 Juice tumbler, flat, 5 oz.
Colors: Milk glass.
Availability: Very scarce.
Reproductions: None at this time.

BG-16 Parfait, round footed, may also be referred to as a vase.

Colors: Milk glass.
Availability: scarce.
Reproductions: Mg, mg w/green leaves and gold grapes. The rims of these are lipped and are sold as vases.

BG-17 Fruit cocktail bowl, round, 3-1/2".
Colors: Milk Glass.
Availability: Scarce.
Reproductions: None at this time.

BG-18 Sherbert, low footed, bell shape. This piece was also sold as a planter with a crimped rim.
Colors: Milk glass.
Availability: Scarce.
Reproductions: In crimped rim version milk glass w/green & gold hp.

BG-19 Bowl & cover, square, 9" tall, high footed.
Colors: Milk glass, golden sunset, and the following decorations on milk glass: dec#915 Gold, dec#32 Roses & Bows, dec#85 Pastel Fruit, dec#86 Green & Gold.
Availability: Mg & dec#32 available, all others are very difficult.
Reproductions: Black mg, amberina, milk glass, mg w/green, cobalt, pink & gold hp. Examples may be found with or without lids.

BG-20 Bowl, 7", square, flared rim, footed. Note: This & BG-21 are the same except one has a lid. They were sold both ways.
Colors: Milk glass, Golden Sunset, and the following decorations on milk glass: dec#32 Roses & Bows, dec#85 Pastel Fruit, dec#86 Green & Gold.
Availability: Mg available, all others are scarce.
Reproductions: Milk glass & milk glass w/green leaves & gold grapes, pink. May be found with or without lid.

BG-21 Bowl, 7" square, flared rim, ftd w/lid. Same as BG-20 with a lid.
Colors: Milk glass, milk glass with the following decorations: dec#915 Gold, dec#32 Roses & Bows, dec#85 Pastel fruit, dec#86

Green & gold.
Availability: Mg available, all others scarce to rare due to the addition of the lid.
Reproductions: Milk glass & milk glass w/green leaves & gold grapes, pink, cobalt, red and amber. May be found with or without lid.

BG-22 Vase, bell, crimped rim, round ftd., 9".
Colors: Milk glass, Milk glass with the following decorations: dec#85 Pastel Fruit, dec#86 Green & Gold.
Availability: Mg scarce, decorated rare.
Reproductions: Frosted blue & possibly others.

BG-23 Vase, bell, plain rim, round ftd., 9". Same as BG-22 except for rim.
Colors: Milk Glass & mg w/dec#86 Green & Gold.
Availability: Mg scarce, decorated rare.
Reproductions: Frosted blue is possible since the above vase was produced but this vase is not shown. Other variations are also possible.

BG-24 Candlestick, square, 4". Note these were used as bases on many footed pieces.
Colors: Almond, Golden Sunset, milk glass, mg w/dec#85 Pastel Fruit & dec#86 Green & Gold.
Availability: Mg common, decorated scarce, other colors scarce.
Reproductions: Black milk glass, milk glass, cobalt, red, amber, amberina, pink, & mg w/green leaves & gold grapes.

BG-25 Bowl, flared, square, footed, 9". Note this piece does not have a lid.
Colors: Almond, milk glass & mg with dec#86 Green & Gold.
Availability: Mg available, almond & decorated are scarce.
Reproductions: Milk glass, black milk.

BG-26 Bowl & cover, referred to as a square puff box at times, 4".
Colors: Brandywine Blue, Golden Sunset, Laurel Green, milk glass, and milk glass

with these decorations: dec#32 roses & bows, dec#85 Pastel Fruit, dec#86 Green & Gold, dec#915 gold.
Availability: Mg common, dec#32 & dec#915 available, all others scarce.
Reproductions: None at this time.

BG-27 Ashtray, square, 6-1/2".
Colors: Brandywine Blue, Golden Sunset, Laurel Green, milk glass, and these decorations on mg: dec#915 Gold, dec#32 Roses & Bows, dec#85 Pastel Fruit, dec#86 Green & Gold, mg w/sporting dogs (a series of 4 dogs.)
Availability: Mg & dec#32 available, other decorations are difficult, the sporting dogs, Brandywine blue, Golden Sunset and Laurel Green are the scarcest.
Reproductions: None at this time.

BG-28 Ashtray, square, 5".
Colors: Golden Sunset, milk glass and these decorations on milk glass: dec#915 Gold, dec#32 Roses & Bows, dec#85 Pastel Fruit, dec#86 Green & Gold, mg w/sporting dogs (a series of 4 dogs.)
Availability: Mg common, dec#32 & dec#915 available, all others scarce.
Reproductions: Black milk glass plain or with gold decoration, milk glass, and milk glass w/green leaves & gold grapes.

BG-29 Ashtray, square, 4".
Colors: Brandywine Blue, Golden Sunset, Laurel Green, milk glass, and these decorations on milk glass: dec#915 Gold, dec#32 Roses & Bows, dec#85 Pastel Fruit, dec#86 Green & Gold, mg w/sporting dogs (a series of 4 dogs), mg w/bird in tree scenes.
Availability: Mg & dec#32 common, dec#915 available, all others scarce.
Reproductions: None at this time.

BG-30 Cigarette box & cover, 4" x 6".
Colors: Milk glass, Golden sunset, and these decorations on milk glass: dec#32 Roses & Bows, dec#915 Gold, dec#85 Pastel Fruit, dec#86 Green & gold.
Availability: Mg common, decorated scarce, Golden Sunset very scarce.

Reproductions: Milk glass, black milk glass, mg w/green leaves & gold grapes, black glass w/gold accents, cobalt, mg w/Roses & Bows.

BG-31 Bowl, flared, footed, 5". Note this and BG-32 are the same item except for the addition of a lid. They were marketed both ways.
Colors: Milk glass, mg w/dec#86 Green & Gold.
Availability: Mg available, decorated scarce.
Reproductions: None at this time.

BG-32 Bowl, flared w/lid footed, 5". May be found with or without lid.
Colors: Brandywine blue, Golden sunset, Laurel Green, milk glass, milk glass with these decorations: dec#32 roses & Bows, dec#85 Pastel Fruit, dec#86 Green & Gold.
Availability: Mg & dec#32 available, all others scarce.
Reproductions: None at this time.

BG-33 Honey and cover, low footed, 5".
Colors: Brandywine Blue, almond, crystal w/ruby accent, crystal velvet, dk blue mist, Golden sunset, crystal mist w/dec#32-1 Roses & Bows, green mist, honey amber carnival, mint green, yellow mist, milk glass & milk glass with these decorations: dec#915 Gold, dec#32 Roses & Bows, dec#85 Pastel Fruit, dec#86 Green & Gold, almond mist, mint green mist, Ice Blue Carnival, antique Green.
Availability: Mg & mg w/dec#32 common, crystal velvet, Brandywine Blue & Golden Sunset and carnival colors are scarce, all others are available.
Reproductions: Cobalt, milk glass, black milk glass.

BG-34 Bowl and cover, square, footed, 7" tall
Colors: Golden Sunset, milk glass, and milk glass with these decorations: dec#915 Gold, dec#32 Roses & Bows, dec#85 Pastel Fruit, dec#86 Green & Gold.
Availability: Mg & dec#32 available, all others scarce.
Reproductions: None at this time.

BG-35 Vase, crimped rim, footed, 6". Note this piece is the same as the parfait with the top crimped. (BG-16)
Colors: Mg & mg w/dec#85 Pastel Fruit or dec#86 Green & Gold.
Availability: All are scarce.
Reproductions: Milk Glass, mg w/green & gold hp.

BG-36 Bowl, flared, low square, 7". Note see BG-37, these are the same pieces with and without a lid. They were marketed either way.
Colors: Golden Sunset, milk glass & milk glass w/dec#86 Green and Gold.
Availability: Mg available, decorated scarce.
Reproductions: None at this time.

BG-37 Bowl, flared, low, square, 7", with lid. Note BG-36 may be found with or without a lid.
Colors: Milk glass, mg w/dec#85 Pastel Fruit or dec#86 Green & Gold, Golden Sunset.
Availability: More difficult to find with the lid than without. Mg is available, Golden sunset & decorated mg is scarce.
Reproductions: None at this time.

BG-38 Cake salver, skirted, square, footed 11".
Colors: Milk glass.
Availability: Very scarce.
Reproductions: None at this time.

BG-39 Bowl, flared, low, square, 9".
Colors: Milk glass.
Availability: scarce.
Reproductions: None at this time.

BG-40 Canape tray, 2 tier, chrome center hdl.
Colors: Milk glass.
Availability: Very scarce.
Reproductions: None at this time.

BG-41 Luncheon Plate, square 8-1/2". Also available in a 12-1/2" size.
Colors: golden Sunset, some may be found in mg.

Availability: Golden Sunset scarce, mg if found at all would be rare.
Reproductions: None known.

BG-42 Canape Tray, center handled, 1 tier, 7-1/4" diameter.
Colors: Milk glass, possibly others.
Availability: Very difficult to scarce.
Reproductions: None known.

BK-1 Line #750 Basket small flat, 4" diameter.
Colors: Antique blue mist, apricot mist, blue pastel, dark blue mist, light blue mist, pink mist, crystal mist, green mist, brown marble, green marble, purple marble, antique blue mist w/Beaded Bouquet, antique blue w/Beaded Bouquet, mint green w/Beaded Bouquet, almond w/Beaded Bouquet, milk glass w/Beaded Bouquet, milk glass w/blue wedding bells, crystal mist with crystal handle w/wedding bell, crystal mist w/China Rose, crystal mist w/Holly, almond w/Almond Rose, milk glass w/Holly, dk blue mist w/daisy, green mist w/daisy, lilac mist w/daisy, yellow mist w/daisy, brown mist w/daisy, crystal mist w/dogwood, mint green w/dogwood, pink mist w/dogwood, dk blue mist w/Floral Bouquet, brown mist w/Floral Bouquet, crystal mist w/Floral Bouquet, almond w/Floral Spray, milk glass w/Floral Spray, ruby w/Mary Gregory style bonnet girl, dk blue mist w/Mary Gregory style, crystal with ruby stain w/Mary Gregory, milk glass w/Rose & Gold trim, milk glass w/red hearts, rose & bow, crystal w/ruby stain w/Ruby Floral, ruby w/Ruby Floral, milk glass w/strawberry, pink pastel, yellow mist, brown mist, ruby, ruby w/Snow Flower, mg w/China Rose, mg mop w/pastel flowers, almond w/Dogwood, mg w/purple Beaded Bouquet, butterscotch carnival (1980, 400 made), almond, lilac opalescent, pink mist w/Snow Flower, pink mist w/Daisy, lt blue mist w/Daisy, mg, mg w/dec#32, black mg.
Availability: All slightly difficult.
Reproductions: Cobalt, crystal, cranberry ice, cranberry ice carnival, milk glass Mother of Pearl, black amethyst, black with hp Rose,

vaseline, and amethyst mop. Any or all of these colors may be hand painted with any of the original style of hand paintings. These new versions will almost always bear the circular "Westmoreland" mark on the bottom of the basket.

BK-2 Line #750 Basket, flat, 6" x 9" tall. Please note that the actual measurements are 9" to the top of the handle, 5" to the top of the basket base. The 6" refers to the diameter.
Colors: Dark blue mist, green mist, mg w/dec#32, ruby w/Ruby Floral.
Availability: All scarce.
Reproductions: None known.

BL-1 Line #456/ME/222 Ballerina mint dish or ashtray, 8-3/4" long.
Colors: Black milk glass, black milk glass w/frosted accents, moss green, Golden Sunset.
Availability: Original examples are rare.
Reproductions: New examples are 7-1/2" long, which is much smaller than the originals. Cobalt, cobalt carnival, aquamarine/teal, vaseline.

BS-1 Line #462 breakfast stack set, includes sugar (bottom) with or without holders for salt & pepper shakers (which are absent from photo), a creamer (middle) and tray or cover on top. These pieces are circa 1920's. A mustard jar w/sq domed lid was also available.
Colors: Crystal, pink, green.
Availability: The entire set is rare in any color, the shakers are the most difficult item to find. Individual pieces can be found to make up a set.
Reproductions: None known.

BV-1 Line #229 bud vases, hex ftd, height can vary from 5" to 11".
Colors: almond, mint green, almond w/daisy decal, milk glass, Golden Sunset, antique blue mist, black milk glass, blue pastel, dk blue mist, Brown mist, flame, pink mist, crystal mist, green mist, Brandywine Blue,

Laurel Green, moss green, light blue mist, olive green, mint green mist, dk blue mist w/daisy, lilac mist w/daisy, green mist w/daisy, crystal mist w/50th anniv, mg mop w/30th anniv, mg w/blue Beaded Bouquet, almond w/Beaded Bouquet, mint green w/Beaded Bouquet, yellow mist w/daisy, brown mist w/daisy, antique blue mist w/Beaded Bouquet, crystal mist w/dogwood, mint green w/dogwood, pink mist w/dogwood, brown mist w/Floral Bouquet, crystal mist w/Floral Bouquet, dk blue mist w/Floral Bouquet, crystal mist w/Floral Spray, almond w/Floral Spray, milk glass w/Roses & Bows, crystal mist w/Roses & Bows, milk glass mop w/Roses & Bows, milk glass w/strawberry, Bermuda Blue, lilac opalescent, pink pastel, crystal mist w/25 anniv, almond w/dogwood, almond mist, mg w/purple Beaded Bouquet, yellow mist, ruby, ruby w/Snow flower, pink mist w/Snow flower, mg mop.
Availability: All are available, decorated versions may be difficult.
Reproductions: None known.

BV-2 Line #1902 Bud vase, round ftd, pulled top. Height can vary.
Colors: amber, Bermuda Blue, apricot mist, dk blue mist, lilac, Brandywine Blue, brown marble, purple marble, green marble, lilac mist w/daisy, green mist w/daisy, dk blue mist w/daisy, yellow mist w/daisy, Golden sunset, mg, pink mist, crystal mist, lt blue mist, green mist, mg w/Roses & Bows, lt blue mist w/Daisy, pink mist w/Daisy, black mg.
Availability: All colors are difficult.
Reproductions: None known.

CD-1 Line #11 Cardinal, solid glass.
Colors: Crystal, ruby, purple marble, dk blue mist, green mist, lt blue mist, apricot mist, ruby carnival.
Availability: All slightly difficult.
Reproductions: Ruby, purple carnival, orange slag, cobalt.

CD-2 Carolina Dogwood bowl, 8" crimped & ruffled. This was a very old pattern that was

revived in later years and produced in very limited editions for Levay. An 8" basket & 10" plate are also produced in this pattern.
Colors: Ruby carnival, Amethyst opalescent, Amethyst Opalescent Carnival (only 33 made).
Availability: Bowl, basket and plate are all rare.
Reproductions: None known.

CG-2 Line #108 Cherry & Grape 5"creamer and sugar. Both creamer and sugar were sold with lids.
Colors: Milk glass, milk glass w/hand painted cherries and grapes, turquoise carnival (limited edition).
Availability: Mg difficult, mg hp scarce, turquoise carn rare.
Reproductions: None known.

CH-1 Bowl, cupped, footed, 8-1/2" dia., 8-1/2" tall.
Colors: Milk glass.
Availability: Very scarce.
Reproductions: None at this time.

CH-2 Bowl, bell, footed, 10-1/2" dia., 8-1/2" tall.
Colors: Milk glass.
Availability: Very scarce.
Reproductions: None at this time.

CH-3 Bowl, straight sided, footed, 9" dia., 8-1/2" tall.
Colors: Milk glass.
Availability: Very Scarce.
Reproductions: None at this time.

CH-4 Bowl, cupped, low, 8-1/2" dia, 4-1/2" tall.
Colors: Milk glass.
Availability: Very Scarce.
Reproductions: None at this time.

CH-5 Bowl, bell, low, 10-1/2" dia, 4-1/2" tall.
Colors: Milk glass.
Availability: Very scarce.
Reproductions: None at this time.

CH-6 Creamer, 3-3/4" high.
Colors: Milk glass & decorated mg (dec#64), turquoise carnival (in 1980 as a limited edition).
Availability: mg available, decorated scarce, carnival very scarce.
Reproductions: Milk glass, mg w/decorated cherries, mg w/22kt gold accents, and cobalt.

CH-7 Sugar, open, 3-1/4" tall.
Colors: Milk glass & decorated mg (dec#64), turquoise carnival (in 1980 as a limited edition.)
Availability: Mg available, decorated scarce, carnival very scarce.
Reproductions: Milk glass, mg w/decorated cherries, mg w/22kt gold accents, and cobalt.

CH-8 Bowl, straight sided, low, 9" dia., 4-1/4" tall.
Colors: Milk glass.
Availability: Very scarce.
Reproductions: None at this time.

CH-9 Cookie jar and cover, 7-1/2" tall, 7" dia., sometimes referred to as the Plantation Cookie Jar.
Colors: Milk glass, lilac pastel, mint green, decorated milk glass (dec#64), and almond. For Levay: chocolate glass in 1982, cobalt carnival in 1978 limited edition of 300, ice blue carnival in 1977 limited edition of 250, lilac opalescent in 1982 limited edition of 500, lime green carnival limited edition of 125, purple slag in 1978, purple slag carnival in 1977-78 limited edition of 200, ruby or cerese in 1979, ruby carnival in 1978 limited edition of 2000, ruby slag in 1982, purple carnival (200 made), turquoise carnival in 1980.
Availability: Mg difficult to find, lilac opalescent very scarce and decorated mg is very scarce, mint green & almond rare. All Levay carnival colors very rare.
Reproductions: Milk glass, black milk glass, milk glass w/decorated cherries, cobalt, ruby, black mg w/gold decorated cherries, milk glass w/gold cherries.

CH-10 Cookie jar and cover, footed, 7" dia., 12" tall.
Colors: Milk glass.
Availability: Very rare.
Reproductions: Milk glass, mg w/gold painted cherries, and cobalt.

CH-11 Candlestick, 4".
Colors: Milk glass.
Availability: Very scarce.
Reproductions: Milk glass, cobalt blue, mg w/22 kt gold hp cherries, and cobalt.

CH-12 Honey and cover, footed, 5-1/2". May have either a thumbprint lid or a cherry lid. The thumbprint lid is more difficult to find.
Colors: Milk glass, decorated mg (dec#64), milk glass w/Holly, milk glass w/Roses & Bows, amber, green marble, purple marble, Golden Sunset. For Levay: Cobalt carnival in 1978 limited edition of 500.
Availability: Mg available, decorated & colors scarce. Levay color rare.
Reproductions: None at this time.

CK-5 Line #602 Chick Egg Cup. (On Back Cover.)
Colors: Milk glass, mg w/red trim hp.
Availability: Both usually available.
Reproductions: None known.

CL-1 Line #1972 Mini Lite candle light. This candle lamp consists of a glass base and a separate glass shade. A crystal candle cup was originally part of this lamp. The candle cups are usually missing from today's examples on the market, although this does not seem to bother collectors or effect pricing.

Two different styles of shades were produced. One shade is very plain and is the one most often found with decorations or decals. The other was designed to simulate a stained glass window. This will have squares all around the shade in rows. A stained glass version was produced and was simply called "multi colored." Other colors are available in the "windowed" version, and some will be decorated, usually with Beaded Bouquet. A

child's night light version was also produced with different types of animal decals.

Because so many different combinations can be collected, the base colors and shade colors and decorations will be listed separately. See the lamp section for the correct combinations. In 1983 Grossman showed the same mini lite shade on a wood base, which was 8" tall. The name of this version is the same.

These mini lamps were produced from 1972, hence the line number. They were produced until the company closed.
Base Colors: Wood, pink mist, crystal, crystal mist, milk glass, ruby, almond, mint green, green mist, dk blue mist, purple marble, green marble, black milk glass, lt blue mist.
Shade Colors: Pink mist snow flower, cry mist w/strawberry, pheasants, blue jay, owl, bunnies, cardinal, peacocks, blue butterfly, robin w/peach blossoms, china rose, mallard, raccoon, squirrels, Andrea West Rooster, Andrea West Country floral, multi-color butterfly, floral spray, antique fruit, dogwood, blue wedding bells, delicate rose, grapes, 25th anniv., 50th anniv., yellow rose, fruit (called Della Robbia, a decal), roses & bows, eagle & flag, holly, ruby w/snow flower, several different Mary Gregory style, ruby floral, 40th anniv., multi-colored (like stained glass—note this was a hand painted stain coloration on crystal), brown mist w/daisy, floral bouquet, green mist w/dogwood (sometimes referred to as "Floral" in catalogs), floral bouquet, daisy, plain green mist, almond w/beaded bouquet, mint green w/beaded bouquet, mint green w/strawberry, dk blue mist w/daisies, several different Mary Gregory style, floral bouquet, dogwood, Brandywine blue plain, crystal mist plain, blue mist plain, yellow mist w/daisies, crystal with ruby stain w/Ruby Floral, crystal mist w/red hearts, roses & bows, cry mist w/cardinal & holly, cry mist w/Oriental, yellow mist w/Floral Spray, cry mist w/white & pink Bells, cry mist w/Holly, cry mist w/Christmas tree, mint green w/Christmas Bouquet, cry mist w/Nursery rhyme, crys mist w/Monkey & Banana, cry mist w/Bunny

Playmates, cry mist w/Clown, cry mist w/Teddy Bear, cry mist w/Circus, cry mist w/Dog playmates.

Availability: Later combinations such as the various animals and birds will be slightly difficult to find because the present owners have not tired of them as yet. The hardest mini lites will be the beaded bouquet hand painted items in mint green and almond, as well as any Mary Gregory style and child's examples. Anniversary examples will be difficult to find mostly because they did not sell well at gift shops. All others seem to be in sufficient supply to keep collectors happy.

Reproductions: None known.

CM-1 Line #1 Camel covered dish. Sometimes referred to as Humphrey or a laying dromedary.

Colors: Green mist, milk glass, yellow mist, Antique blue, lilac mist, and Cobalt, Turquoise carnival and Emerald Green Carnival in limited editions for Levay.

Availability: All originals are very difficult to find, any carnival examples would be considered rare.

Reproductions: Milk glass, cobalt, vaseline, mg mop.

CO-1 Water goblet, footed.

Colors: Bermuda Blue, crystal, brown, moss green, Golden Sunset, Laurel Green, olive green.

Availability: Crystal available, colors are more difficult to find.

Reproductions: None known.

CO-2 Claret or juice goblet, footed.

Colors: Bermuda Blue, brown, crystal, moss green, Golden sunset, olive green.

Availability: Crystal difficult, colors scarce.

Reproductions: None known.

CO-3 Sherbert, low footed.

Colors: Bermuda Blue, brown, crystal, moss green, Golden Sunset, olive green.

Availability: All are difficult to find.

Reproductions: None known.

CO-4 Iced tea tumbler, flat, 16 oz.

Colors: Crystal, brown, moss green, Bermuda Blue, olive green, Golden Sunset.

Availability: All difficult to find.

Reproductions: None known.

CO-5 Iced tea tumbler, flat, 13 oz.

Colors: crystal, Golden Sunset, moss green, olive green, Bermuda Blue.

Availability: All are very difficult to find.

Reproductions: None known.

CO-6 Pitcher or jug, flat, 8" at tallest point.

Colors: crystal, Bermuda Blue, Golden Sunset, olive green, and for Levay: Blue carnival in 1976 limited edition of 100 sets, purple carnival (50 sets made), ice blue carnival (130 sets made).

Availability: Colors scarce, any carnival is rare.

Reproductions: None known.

CO-7 Old Fashioned or rocks tumbler, flat, 4" tall.

Colors: Crystal, and for Levay Blue Carnival in limited edition sets of 100 in 1976, purple carnival (50 sets made), ice blue carnival (130 sets made).

Availability: Crystal difficult to find. Any carnival is rare.

Reproductions: None known.

CO-8 Juice tumbler, flat.

Colors: Crystal

Availability: Scarce.

Reproductions: None known.

CO-9 Candlestick, tall. Note these are very similar to a Northwood Candlestick.

Colors: Crystal, Bermuda Blue, olive green, Golden Sunset, pink mist, pink pastel, blue pastel, lt blue mist, Laurel green, Brandywine Blue.

Availability: All colors are scarce.

Reproductions: Cobalt w/flower decal, possibly others.

CO-10 Compote or fruit bowl, lipped, footed.

Colors: Crystal, Bermuda Blue, olive green, Golden Sunset, pink pastel, pink mist, blue

pastel, lt blue mist.
Availability: All colors are scarce.
Reproductions: None known.

CO-11 Ashtray, round, available in 5" or 7".
Colors: Bermuda Blue, crystal, pink, blue pastel or Golden sunset with a Wedding saying in the center of the ashtray, crystal, flame, green marble, mint green, purple marble, black milk glass, olive green, almond, ruby, brown marble.
Availability: Available in most colors, Wedding saying may be slightly more difficult.
Reproductions: None known.

CO-12 Cigarette lighter.
Colors: Crystal, moss green, black milk glass, Bermuda Blue, Golden Sunset, olive green, black milk glass mist.
Availability: all are difficult to find.
Reproductions: None known.

CO-13 Iced tea goblet, low footed, 14 oz.
Colors: Crystal, moss green, Golden Sunset, olive green.
Availability: All are difficult to find.
Reproductions: None known.

CO-14 Heart shaped bon-bon, 1 handled. This item bears no markings at all but does have a ground bottom. Ground bottoms added to the cost of the items. This practice was discontinued when the difficult times arrived.
Colors: Laurel Green, crystal and possible others.
Availability: All are scarce.
Reproductions: None known.

CO-15 Vase, ftd., swung, height can vary.
Colors: Golden Sunset, Laurel Green, Brandywine Blue, apricot mist, green mist, lt blue mist, black milk glass, brown mist, flame, crystal mist, pink mist, green marble, purple marble, brown marble, milk glass w/purple Beaded Bouquet, lilac mist w/daisy, yellow mist w/daisy, green mist w/daisy, dk blue mist w/daisy, milk glass w/Roses &

Bows, Bermuda Blue, olive green, amber, yellow mist, brown mist w/Daisy, dk blue mist, mg.
Availability: Golden Sunset, Laurel Green & Brandywine Blue scarce. Marble colors scarce. All decorated examples very scarce. Others are slightly difficult.
Reproductions: None known.

CO-16 Sweetmeat, 2 handled, hi ftd., 6" tall.
Colors: Green marble, purple marble, apricot mist, milk glass, mg w/dec #32, green mist, dk blue mist, brown mist, crystal mist, pink mist brown marble, apricot mist, moss green, milk glass w/purple Beaded Bouquet, Golden Sunset, olive green, lt blue mist, Bermuda Blue, yellow mist.
Availability: Colors scarce, mg & mg w/hp very difficult.
Reproductions: None known.

CO-17 Jack-in-the-pulpit vase, hex ftd., 6-3/8" tall. Height may vary.
Colors: Antique blue, antique blue mist, antique blue mist w/dec#32, crystal w/ruby stain, flame, ruby w/Ruby Floral, Golden Sunset, ruby, green mist, lt blue mist, ruby w/Snow Flower, dk blue mist.
Availability: Colors difficult, decorated items very scarce.
Reproductions: None known.

CO-18 Sugar, flat, open. This item as well as the creamer may bear the Keystone "W" mark. These were produced in the 1960's in Laurel Green and the old Keystone marking was retained to prove to the public that it was an original reproduction of an older piece.
Colors: Crystal, Laurel Green, Golden Sunset, Brandywine Blue, olive green, moss green.
Availability: All Scarce.
Reproductions: None known.

CO-19 Creamer, flat. See above description.
Colors: Crystal, Laurel Green, Golden Sunset, Brandywine Blue, olive green, moss green.
Availability: All scarce
Reproductions: None known.

CO-20 Sugar, large, flat w/lid, 2 hdld. (On Back Cover.)
Colors: Crystal, Golden Sunset, Laurel Green, Brandywine Blue, olive green, moss green.
Availability: All scarce.
Reproductions: None known.

CP-1 Line #502 Stippled Heart cup plate, 3-3/8" diameter.
Colors: Crystal, Brandywine Blue, Laurel Green, Golden Sunset, moss green, Bermuda Blue, olive green.
Availability: cry common, colors slightly difficult.
Reproductions: Red, honey amber, crystal.

CP-2 Line #503 Henry Clay cup plate, 3-3/8" diameter.
Colors: Crystal, Brandywine Blue, Laurel Green, Golden Sunset, moss green, olive green, Bermuda Blue.
Availability: Cry common, colors slightly difficult.
Reproductions: None known.

CP-3 Line #506 Wedding Day cup plate, 3-3/8" diameter. This is a humorous cup plate. It shows a couple smiling on their wedding day. Turned a different way it shows the same couple three weeks later frowning!
Colors: Crystal, Brandywine Blue, Laurel Green, Golden Sunset, moss green, olive green, Bermuda Blue.
Availability: Cry common, colors slightly difficult.
Reproductions: None known.

CP-4 Line #507 "Sandwich 1831 Eagle" cup plate, 3-3/8" diameter. As with all of the other cup plates they were copied from older molds.
Colors: Crystal, Brandywine Blue, Laurel Green, Golden Sunset, moss green, Bermuda Blue, olive green.
Availability: Cry common, colors slightly difficult.
Reproductions: None known.

CP-5 Line #508 "Valentine" cup plate, 3-3/8" diameter. This cup plate has harps on the rim with a heart with an arrow bisecting it in the center.
Colors: Crystal, Brandywine Blue, Laurel Green, Golden Sunset, moss green, olive green, Bermuda Blue.
Availability: Cry common, colors slightly difficult.
Reproductions: Crystal, azure blue.

CT-1 Line #1 Cat on lacy oblong base. The base is line #1870. Base measures 5" x 8" long and 6-1/2" tall. These cats usually have glass eyes. Westmoreland sometimes paired different colored tops and bottoms together on these.
Colors: Caramel marble, milk glass, purple marble, green marble, cobalt carnival (limited edition of 1000), white carnival and pink carnival (both very limited), purple slag carnival (500 made), antique blue.
Availability: Mg is slightly difficult, any color is scarce with carnival colors being very scarce.
Reproductions: None known.
(See Book 2)

CT-2 Line #18 Cat on oval vertical rib base, 5-1/2" long.
Colors: Purple marble, milk glass, ruby carnival (1000 made), ruby marble (1982, 500 made), black carnival (experimental color), cobalt carnival (1000 made), purple marble carnival (500 made).
Availability: All carnival colors are rare, black carnival is extremely rare, other colors are scarce.
Reproductions: Blue mg, milk glass, cobalt, mg mop, topaz, mg mop w/hp, topaz hp. According to the "Towne Crier Newsletter" all of these repros have the circular "Westmoreland" mark.

DH-1 Line #51 double hands mint dish or card holder. This piece is sometimes referred to as Queen Victoria hands by collectors.
Colors: Milk glass, mg w/gold dec, mg w/roses & bows, mint green, almond, antique blue, antique green.

Availability: Mg available, mg w/dec #32 available, colors scarce.
Reproductions: Cobalt.

DK-2 Duck on oval vertical rib 5" base. This duck was produced for Levay, although it was originally in the regular line.
Colors: Milk glass, ruby carnival (1000 made), black carnival (experimental), Aurora Cobalt Blue Carnival.
Availability: All are scarce to rare.
Reproductions: Cobalt carnival, cobalt.

DO-1 Water goblet, footed, 9 oz. This piece was later flared and crimped at the rim and called a sweetmeat (DO-34). A vase which has a pulled effect was also made from this piece (DO-35).
Colors: Crystal for goblet only.
Availability: Scarce.
Reproductions: None known

DO-2 Water tumbler, footed, 8 oz.
Colors: Crystal.
Availability: scarce.
Reproductions: None known.

DO-3 Iced tea tumbler, flat, 12 oz.
Colors: Crystal.
Availability: Scarce.
Reproductions: None known.

DO-4 Wine goblet, footed.
Colors: Crystal.
Availability: Scarce.
Reproductions: None known.

DO-5 Cocktail goblet, footed.
Colors: Crystal.
Availability: Scarce.
Reproductions: None known.

DO-6 Sherbert, footed.
Colors: Crystal.
Availability: Scarce.
Reproductions: None known.

DO-7 Bowl or nappy, round, 7".
Colors: Crystal.

Availability: Scarce.
Reproductions: None known.

DO-8 Bowl, cupped lacy edge, 9", low.
Colors: Crystal.
Availability: Scarce.
Reproductions: None known.

DO-9 Plate, lacy edge, 11", also in 12".
Colors: Crystal, milk glass, ruby.
Availability: Crystal scarce, mg available, ruby difficult.
Reproductions: 12" in milk glass, milk glass w/red small flowers decal, blue frosted, black milk glass plain or with floral handpaintings in white and gold colors.

DO-10 Six-pointed rose bowl, flat.
Colors: Crystal.
Availability: Scarce.
Reproductions: None known.

DO-11 Plate, salad, 7", lacy edge, star center.
Colors: Crystal.
Availability: Scarce.
Reproductions: None known.

DO-12 Plate, 9", no lace, star center.
Colors: Crystal.
Availability: Scarce.
Reproductions: None known.

DO-13 Bowl, belled lacy edge, 14" also 12" flat.
Colors: Crystal, milk glass and ruby.
Availability: Crystal scarce, mg available, ruby slightly difficult.
Reproductions: Frosted blue, black milk glass w/o floral handpainting in gold and white colors, milk glass plain or with red floral decoration.

DO-14 Bowl, belled, no lace, flat, star center, 12", also 13" with turned edge.
Colors: Crystal.
Availability: 12" scarce, 13" very scarce.
Reproductions: None known.

DO-15 Plate, lacy edge, plain center, 14".

Colors: Crystal, milk glass.
Availability: Crystal scarce, milk glass available.
Reproductions: None known.

DO-16 Epergne set, 2 piece.
Colors: Crystal.
Availability: Extremely rare.
Reproductions: None known.

DO-17 Plate, 14" star center, no lace.
Colors: Crystal.
Availability: Scarce.
Reproductions: None known.

DO-18 Bowl, cupped, footed, 10". Grossman also produced an 8-3/4" version of this bowl.
Colors: 10": Antique blue mist, apricot mist, Brandywine Blue, brown mist, almond, almond mist, dark blue mist, crystal mist, Golden Sunset, green mist, Laurel Green, milk glass, Mint Green, Mint Green mist, moss green, pink mist, lilac, lilac mist, yellow mist, Bermuda Blue, Olive green, amber, lt. blue mist. 8-3/4": Lilac opalescent, pink pastel, blue pastel, mg.
Availability: Most colors are available in both sizes. Lilac and apricot mist may be more difficult.
Reproductions: Milk glass.

DO-19 Bowl, oval crimped, 12" flat. Also in 10-1/2" size. The 12" may also be found in a candlestick footed version.
Colors: 10-1/2" in mg only. 12" in apricot mist, black milk glass, Brandywine Blue, brown marble, brown mist, almond, flame, Golden Sunset, green marble, green mist, Laurel Green, Mint Green, moss green, lilac, purple marble, ruby, dark blue mist, green marble, amber, pink mist, crystal mist, lt blue mist, Bermuda Blue, olive green and yellow mist.
Availability: 10-1/2" size scarce. 12" in flame, lilac, marble colors are scarce, all others available.
Reproductions: None known.

DO-20 Plate, lacy edge, 11" also in 12-1/2" and 14".

Colors: 11" milk glass, 14" crystal and milk glass, 12-1/2" ruby.
Availability: 11" available, 14" crystal scarce, milk glass available, ruby slightly difficult.
Reproductions: None known.

DO-21 Compote & cover, 10" high, footed.
Colors: Milk glass, moss green, Golden Sunset.
Availability: All are very scarce.
Reproductions: None known.

DO-22 Cake salver, footed, 11".
Colors: Apricot mist, dk blue mist, green mist, milk glass, mint green, pink mist.
Availability: Mg available, all others difficult.
Reproductions: None known.

DO-23 Candlestick, 4-1/2". These were also used as bases on all footed items.
Colors: Black milk glass, dark blue mist, Brandywine Blue, almond, almond mist, Flame, Golden Sunset, green mist, Laurel Green, lilac, Blue Pastel, milk glass, mint green, mint green mist, moss green, pink mist, pink pastel, yellow mist, apricot mist, amber, crystal mist, Bermuda Blue, ruby, lilac opalescent, lt blue mist.
Availability: Mg, mint green, almond, green mist are common, flame, black milk glass & lilac are scarce. All others are available to slightly difficult.
Reproductions: Milk glass, black mg, cobalt.

DO-24 Bowl, belled, 9", low footed. Also made in a 12" flat version.
Colors: Milk glass.
Availability: Difficult.
Reproductions: Black milk glass with rim crimped may have a floral design in white and gold colors.

DO-25 Banana bowl, footed, 11".
Colors: Milk glass.
Availability: Available.
Reproductions: None known.

DO-26 Rose bowl, low ftd, 6", cupped rim.

Colors: Crystal, milk glass.
Availability: Mg available, crystal scarce.
Reproductions: Milk glass, black mg.

DO-27 Bowl, turned edge, 9-1/2", flat.
Colors: Milk glass, ruby.
Availability: Both difficult.
Reproductions: A 12" version was produced in milk glasss by Plum Glass.

DO-28 Bowl, round, 8".
Colors: Milk glass.
Availability: Available.
Reproductions: None known.

DO-29 Bowl, belled footed, 12". Also in 9".
Colors: 12" Brandywine Blue, Golden Sunset, Laurel Green, milk glass, lilac, lilac mist. 9" Crystal & mg.
Availability: 12" mg common, all other colors difficult. 9" crystal scarce, milk glass available.
Reproductions: None known.

DO-30 Bowl, belled, footed, 9" dia., 7-1/2" high.
Colors: Milk glass.
Availability: Scarce.
Reproducitons: None known.

DO-31 Bowl, rose, footed, 6" dia., 8" high.
Colors: Milk glass.
Availability: Very scarce.
Reproductions: None known.

DO-32 Bowl, crimped, footed, 10-1/2" diameter.
Colors: Crystal, milk glass.
Availability: Both very scarce.
Reproductions: A flat version of this bowl was reproduced in milk glass and black mg.

DO-33 Rose bowl, flared rim, 6-1/2" dia, 3-1/2" high.
Colors: Milk glass.
Availability: Rare. These did not sell well so very few were produced.
Reproductions: None known.

DO-34 Sweetmeat, footed, ruffled rim. This was made from the water goblet.
Colors: Almond, mint green, milk glass, mg w/roses & bows, mg w/blue beaded bouquet, amber, yellow mist, pink mist, almond mist, mint green mist, Bermuda Blue, almond w/beaded bouquet, antique blue, antique blue mist, Brandywine Blue, Laurel Green, dk blue mist, brown mist, green mist, lilac mist, purple marble, green marble, brown marble, mint green w/Beaded Bouquet, antique blue w/Beaded Bouquet, antique blue mist w/Beaded Bouquet, crystal mist w/Roses & Bows, almond w/Almond Rose, ruby w/Ruby Floral, apricot mist.
Availability: Mg available, hp items scarce, colors very difficult.
Reproductions: None known.

DO-35 Vase, footed, swung. Height may vary. This item was produced from the water goblet mold.
Colors: Green mist, dark blue mist.
Availability: Both scarce.
Reproductions: None known.

DP-1 Line #1049 Dolphin candlestick, hex base, 4" tall.
Colors: Milk glass, almond, almond mist, crystal mist, black milk glass, antique blue mg, antique blue mist.
Availability: Mg common, other colors scarce to rare.
Reproductions: Cobalt, ruby, black mg, alexandrite, azure blue.

DP-2 Line #1049 Dolphin shell bowl, footed, 8".
Colors: Milk glass, black milk glass, crystal mist, antique blue, antique blue mist, almond, almond mist, mg mop.
Availability: Mg common, other colors scarce to rare.
Reproductions: Black mg, cobalt, alexandrite.

DP-3 Line #1049 Dolphin center handled serving tray. The edge of this tray may be scalloped or octagonal.

Colors: Almond, almond mist, crystal mist, antique blue, antique blue mist.
Availability: All colors very difficult to scarce.
Reproductions: Black mg, alexandrite.

DP-4 Line #1049 Dolphin candlestick, hex base, 9" tall. Several companies throughout the years have made these types of candlesticks.
Colors: Milk glass, black milk glass, almond, crystal mist, antique blue mist, antique blue, pink pastel, pink mist, blue pastel, lt blue mist, Brandywine Blue Opalescent (made for A.A. Importing, according to Bob Rupp).
Availability: Mg available, others colors are scarce.
Reproductions: Cobalt, black mg, alexandrite, azure blue.

DP-6 Line #1049 Dolphin shell bowl, footed, 12".
Colors: Antique blue mist, almond, milk glass, crystal mist.
Availability: This large version is more scarce than that of the small version. All colors very scarce to rare.
Reproductions: None known.

DP-8 Line #1049/1 Dolphin lamp. This lamp was originally a product of the Boston & Sandwich Glass Company. These types of lamps were oil lamps. Westmoreland used the design and turned it into an electric lamp. Another type of Dolphin lamp was made from the large dolphin candlestick (DP-4). Both of these lamps were produced during the 1920's.
Colors: Pink, crystal, green, amber and blue.
Availability: All colors are very scarce.
Reproductions: None known, at this time. Although since the tall candlestick (DP-4) is being reproduced, it may be only a matter of time before lamp parts are added to the candlestick.

DR-1 Plate, luncheon, 9".
Colors: Crystal, crystal w/dk stain, crystal w/pastel stain, cry w/yl mist stain.

Availability: Difficult to find.
Reproductions: None known.

DR-2 Plate, salad, 7-1/2".
Colors: Crystal, crystal w/dk stain, crystal w/pastel stain.
Availability: Difficult to find.
Reproductions: None known.

DR-3 Water goblet, 8 oz. 6", footed.
Colors: Crystal, crystal w/dk stain, crystal w/pastel stain, milk glass, Antique blue milk, mg w/gold dec.
Availability: Crystal and milk glass are common, all stain pieces difficult, Antique Blue and gold dec. are scarce.
Reproductions: None known.

DR-4 Iced tea tumbler, footed, 11 oz.
Colors: Crystal, crystal w/dk stain, crystal w/pastel stain, milk glass.
Availability: Crystal and mg are available, stained tumblers are difficult.
Reproductions: None known.

DR-5 Water tumbler, footed, 8 oz.
Colors: Crystal, crystal w/dk stain, crystal w/pastel stain, milk glass.
Availability: Crystal, mg and dk stain are available, pastel stain is difficult.
Reproductions: None known.

DR-6 Cocktail or claret goblet, 3-1/4 oz.
Colors: Crystal, crystal w/dk stain, crystal w/pastel stain, milk glass.
Availability: All colors are difficult.
Reproductions: None known.

DR-7 Sherbert, low footed.
Colors: Crystal, crystal w/dk stain, crystal w/pastel stain, milk glass.
Availability: Mg available, all others are difficult.
Reproductions: None known.

DR-8 Creamer, individual, footed.
Colors: Crystal, crystal w/dk stain, crystal w/pastel stain, milk glass.
Availability: Dark stain and mg common,

crystal available, pastel difficult.
Reproductions: None known.

DR-9 Sugar, individual, footed.
Colors: Crystal, crystal w/dk stain, crystal w/pastel stain, milk glass.
Availability: Dk stain and milk glass are common, crystal available, pastel stain is difficult.
Reproductions: None known.

DR-10 Shakers, salt & pepper, footed.
Colors: Crystal, crystal w/dk stain, crystal w/pastel stain, milk glass.
Availability: All are difficult.
Reproductions: None known.

DR-11 Cup and saucer.
Colors: Crystal, crystal w/dk stain, crystal w/pastel stain.
Availability: Crystal available, all others are difficult.
Reproductions: None known.

DR-12 Water tumbler, flat, 8 oz. 3-3/4" tall.
Colors: Crystal, crystal w/dk stain, crystal w/pastel stain, milk glass. For Levay: Cobalt carnival in 1978 limited to 150 sets, turquoise carnival in 1980 limited to 400 sets.
Availability: Mg available, all others difficult. Levay colors very rare.
Reproductions: None known.

DR-13 Bowl or nappy, cupped, 1 handle, 6-1/2". Also available in flared 10" and heart shaped versions.
Colors: Crystal, crystal w/dk stain.
Availability: Scarce.
Reproductions: None known.

DR-14 Mint compote, footed, 6-1/2".
Colors: Crystal, crystal w/dk stain.
Availability: Difficult.
Reproductions: None known.

DR-15 Candlestick, 4".
Colors: Crystal, crystal w/stain.

Availability: Available in both.
Reproductions: None known.

DR-16 Bowl, bell, 12".
Colors: Crystal, crystal w/dk stain.
Availability: Crystal available, stain is scarce.
Reproductions: None known.

DR-17 Domed candy jar & cover, 1/2 lb. footed, 7" tall.
Colors: Almond, Golden Sunset, crystal, crystal mist w/dec#32-1, crystal w/dk stain, mg w/mother of pearl finish and pastel painted fruit, milk glass, mg mother of pearl plain, mint green, milk glass w/dec#32, moss green, amber, pink carnival (500 made), mg mop w/Roses & Bows, mint green mist, almond mist.
Availability: Mg, mg w/dec#32 available, all others are difficult to scarce.
Reproductions: None known.

DR-18 Bowl, round, 4-1/2". Other sizes which were manufactured: 6", 7-1/2" and 9".
Colors: Crystal, crystal w/dk stain.
Availability: All difficult to find.
Reproductions: None known.

DR-19 Torte plate, 14". This is also found with a turned up edge or plain edge.
Colors: Turned edge only appear in crystal, plain edge appear in crystal or crystal w/dk stain.
Availability: Turned edge are scarce, plain edge are very difficult.
Reproductions: None known.

DR-20 Bowl, heart shaped, 1 handled, 8".
Colors: Crystal, crystal w/dk stain.
Availability: Both are difficult.
Reproductions: None known.

DR-21 Champagne goblet, hi footed, 4-3/4" high.
Colors: Crystal, crystal w/dk stain, crystal w/pastel stain, milk glass.
Availability: Mg and crystal available, both stain colors are difficult.
Reproductions: None known.

DR-22 Gingerale or juice tumbler, flat, 5 oz.
Colors: Crystal, crystal w/dk stain.
Availability: Both are very difficult.
Reproductions: None known.

DR-24 Iced tea tumbler, flat, 12 oz., this will be found in a straight or bell version.
Colors: Crystal, crystal w/dk stain.
Availability: Both very difficult.
Reproductions: None known.

DR-25 Finger bowl w/underplate, bowl 5", plate is 6".
Colors: Crystal, crystal w/dk stain.
Availability: Very difficult.
Reproductions: None known.

DR-26 Candelabra, 2-lite.
Colors: Crystal w/dk stain.
Availability: Very scarce.
Reproductions: None known.

DR-27 Pitcher or jug, 32 oz., 7", flat.
Colors: Crystal, crystal w/dk stain. For Levay: Cobalt carnival in 1978 limited to 150 sets, turquoise carnival in 1980 limited to 400 sets.
Availability: Crystal scarce, stain is very scarce. Levay colors very rare.
Reproductions: None known.

DR-28 Basket, 1 handle, round, 9", also available in 12", 12-1/2" and 8-1/2".
Colors: Crystal, crystal w/dk stain.
Availability: All are very scarce.
Reproductions: None known.

DR-29 Basket, 1 handle, oval, 12", also in 16".
Colors: Crystal, crystal w/dk stain.
Availability: All are very scarce.
Reproductions: None known.

DR-30 Rose Bowl Compote or mint, ruffled rim, stem footed. This piece was produced from a water goblet. All production was for Levay.
Colors: Ruby, ruby carnival (2000 made).

Availability: Ruby scarce, ruby carnival is very scarce to rare.
Reproductions: None known.

EGG-1 Line #1, Egg shaped trinket box, 2 pieces. Most often found with some type of hand painting or decal. Productions started on the egg for the 1973 catalog and continued until 1983. REPRODUCTIONS ABOUND!!!
Colors: Dark blue mist w/daisy, dark blue mist w/floral bouquet, green mist w/daisy, yellow mist w/daisy, crystal mist w/floral bouquet, strawberry, china rose, dogwood, floral spray, 25th anniv., 50th anniv., Andrea West Rooster, Andrea West Country Floral, bunnies, pheasants, mallards, cardinal, owl, antique fruit, Antique Blue w/Beaded Bouquet, Almond w/Beaded Bouquet, Floral Spray, pink mist w/dogwood, ruby w/40th anniv., several Mary Gregory style including Bonnet girl on picket fence, mg mop w/30th anniv., dk blue mist w/white cameo, ruby w/white cameo, mint green w/Beaded Bouquet, antique blue mist w/Beaded Bouquet, lilac mist w/daisy, brown mist w/daisy, mint green w/dogwood, brown mist w/Floral Bouquet, mg mop w/red hearts, rose & bow, plain dark blue mist.
Availability: None of the above combinations are easily found. The scarce examples include any Beaded Bouquet or Mary Gregory style items. All other examples are very difficult to find.
Reproductions: Cobalt, red and green. Most of the reproductions will be hand painted with a Mary Gregory scene, Shirley Temple decal or a Rose. Note that most of the originals are artist signed and dated. The decal originals will bear no signature or date. The hand painted reproductions may be signed by L. Plues. If the reproductions are dated the date will be post 1985, which assures the buyer that it is new. Not many examples of these "New" examples are dated.

EH-1 Iced tea tumbler, round footed, 12-1/2 oz.

Colors: Crystal, milk glass.
Availability: Both available.
Reproducitons: None known.

EH-2 Water tumbler, round footed, 9 oz.
Colors: Crystal
Availability: Available.
Reproducitons: None known.

EH-3 Tumbler, round footed, 7 oz.
Colors: Crystal.
Availability: Available.
Reproductions: None known.

EH-4 Parfait, round footed.
Colors: Crystal.
Availability: Scarce.
Reproductions: None known.

EH-5 Sherbert/Champagne, high round footed.
Colors: Crystal.
Availability: Slightly difficult.
Reproductions: None known.

EH-6 Sherbert, low round footed.
Colors: Crystal.
Availability: Available.
Reproducitons: None known.

EH-7 Cocktail goblet, 3 oz., round ftd.
Colors: Crystal.
Availability: Scarce.
Reproductions: None known.

EH-8 Water goblet, 8 oz., round ftd.
Colors: Crystal, milk glass, pink pastel.
Availability: All are common.
Reproductions: None known.

EH-9 Claret goblet, 5 oz., round ftd.
Colors: Crystal.
Availability: Available.
Reproductions: None known.

EH-10 Wine goblet, 2 oz., round footed.
Colors: Crystal.
Availability: Difficult.
Reproductions: None known.

EH-11 Cordial, round ftd.
Colors: Crystal.
Availability: Difficult.
Reproductions: None known.

EH-12 Old Fashioned Cocktail tumbler, flat.
Colors: Crystal.
Availability: Scarce.
Reproductions: None known.

EH-13 Whiskey or shot glass, flat, 1-1/2 oz., also available in 3 oz. size.
Colors: Crystal. For Levay ruby in 1982-83.
Availability: Both scarce when originals.
Reproductions: Ruby - which is more amberina than true ruby. Possibly others.

EH-14 Gingerale Tumbler, flat, 5 oz.
Colors: Crystal.
Availability: Available.
Reproductions: Crystal by Plum Glass. A bud vase in a light turquoise was also made from this piece.

EH-15 Water tumbler, flat, 8 oz.
Colors: Crystal. For Levay: ruby, and ruby carnival in 1981 limited to 200 sets.
Availability: Crystal difficult. Levay colors very rare.
Reproductions: None known.

EH-16 Iced tea tumbler, flat, 10 oz.
Colors: Crystal, milk glass.
Availability: Both difficult.
Reproductions: None known.

EH-17 Iced tea tumbler, flat, 12 oz.
Colors: Crystal.
Availability: Scarce.
Reproductions: None known.

EH-18 Cruet, 2 oz. with stopper, 5" tall.
Colors: Crystal, milk glass. For Levay and regular line in pink pastel in 1983.
Availability: Mg common, crystal available, pink scarce.
Reproductions: None known.

EH-19 Cruet, 6 oz. with stopper, 6-1/4" tall.

Colors: Crystal, milk glass. For Levay in ruby.
Availability: Mg common, crystal available, ruby scarce.
Reproductions: None known.

EH-20 Cruet, 6 oz. no handles, with stopper.
Colors: Crystal.
Availability: Scarce.
Reproductions: None known.

EH-21 Decanter with stopper, 20 oz.
Colors: Crystal.
Availability: Very scarce.
Reproductions: None known.

EH-22 Pitcher or jug, flat, 1 qt. also in 1/2 gallon size.
Colors: Crystal. For Levay: Ruby carnival in 1981 limited to 200 sets.
Availability: Crystal very scarce. Ruby carnival very rare.
Reproductions: None known.

EH-23 Pitcher, or jug, bulbous, 38 oz., also in 23 oz. and 60 oz. sizes.
Colors: Crystal. For Levay: Ruby and ruby carnival in 1982 limited to 75.
Availability: Crystal very scarce, ruby and ruby carnival rare.
Reproductions: None known.

EH-24 Creamer, hexagonal 4-1/4", ftd.
Colors: Crystal, milk glass, pink pastel, Golden Sunset, ruby.
Availability: Crystal and mg common, pink available, ruby and Golden Sunset are scarce.
Reproductions: None known.

EH-25 Sugar, hexagonal 4-1/4", ftd.
Colors: Crystal, milk glass, pink pastel, Golden Sunset, ruby.
Availability: Crystal and mg common, pink available, ruby and Golden Sunset are scarce.
Reproductions: None known.

EH-26 Creamer, flat, hexagonal shape.
Colors: Crystal, amber, ruby.

Availability: Crystal common, others slightly difficult.
Reproductions: None known.

EH-27 Sugar, flat, hexagonal shape.
Colors: Crystal, amber, and ruby.
Availability: Crystal common, others slightly difficult.
Reproductions: None known.

EH-28 Shakers, salt & pepper, round, ftd. With either plain or rayed ft.
Colors: Crystal, milk glass, pink pastel, ruby.
Availability: Crystal and mg available, pink and ruby slightly difficult.
Reproductions: None known.

EH-29 Compote, bell, footed, 5-1/2".
Colors: Crystal, milk glass.
Availability: Both common.
Reproductions: None known.

EH-30 Plate, dinner, 10" pointed edges.
Colors: Crystal.
Availability: Scarce.
Reproductions: None known.

EH-31 Plate, luncheon, 8" pointed edges. Plates also available in 6-1/2" salad & 5-1/2" bread & butter.
Colors: Crystal.
Availability: 8" common, all others scarce.
Reproductions: None known.

EH-32 Plate, pie, narrow rim, 7".
Colors: Crystal.
Availability: Scarce.
Reproductions: None known.

EH-33 Plate, luncheon, plain edge, 8-1/2"
Colors: Crystal.
Availability: Scarce.
Reproductions: None known.

EH-34 Plate, depressed center, 6-1/2".
Colors: Crystal.
Availability: Scarce.
Reproductions: None known.

EH-35 Cream soup, 2 hdld. w/cream soup plate, 6-1/2" dia., plain edge.
Colors: Crystal, milk glass.
Availability: Very scarce.
Reproductions: None known.

EH-36 Cup & saucer, saucer is round.
Colors: Crystal and milk glass.
Availability: Cups are more plentiful than the saucers, but both are available.
Reproductions: None known.

EH-37 Finger bowl, 4-1/2", finger bowl plate, 6-1/2" pointed edges.
Colors: Crystal, milk glass.
Availability: Both very scarce.
Reproductions: None known.

EH-38 Plate, 3-part grill. 10-1/2".
Colors: Crystal.
Availability: Scarce.
Reproductions: None known.

EH-39 Relish, 3-part, rimmed, 8".
Colors: Crystal, milk glass.
Availability: Slightly difficult.
Reproductions: None known.

EH-40 Mayonnaise, belled flat, 6" dia. x 2-1/2" tall.
Colors: Crystal, milk glass. Grossman produced a 5" version in pink pastel.
Availability: All slightly difficult.
Reproductions: None known.

EH-41 Bowl or nappy, squared, 6".
Colors: Crystal.
Availability: Scarce.
Reproductions: None known.

EH-42 Bowl or nappy, round, 8".
Colors: Crystal, pink pastel.
Availability: Both slightly difficult.
Reproductions: None known.

EH-43 Bowl or nappy, round, 6".
Colors: Crystal.
Availability: Difficult.
Reproductions: None known.

EH-44 Bowl or nappy, round, 5".
Colors: Crystal, milk glass.
Availability: Difficult.
Reproductions: None known.

EH-45 Bowl or nappy, round, 4-1/2".
Colors: Crystal, milk glass - mg may have fruit decoration in center.
Availability: Crystal available, mg slightly difficult, fruit scarce.
Reproductions: None known.

EH-46 Bowl or nappy, belled 5-1/2".
Colors: Crystal, milk glass, and mg w/hp fruit.
Availability: Crystal and mg difficult, mg w/hp fruit is scarce.
Reproductions: None known.

EH-47 Bowl or nappy, belled & rimed, 7-1/2".
Colors: Crystal.
Availability: Scarce.
Reproductions: None known.

EH-48 Bowl, belled, 11". A 12" version was produced for Levay in 1980.
Colors: 11" crystal, 12" ruby.
Availability: Both scarce.
Reproductions: None known.

EH-49 Bowl, flared, 12".
Colors: Crystal, ruby.
Availability: Very scarce.
Reproductions: None known.

EH-50 Compote, round, footed, 5". Also produced in a 5-1/2" version.
Colors: Crystal, milk glass, pink pastel.
Availability: Crystal & mg common, pink available.
Reproductions: None known.

EH-51 Compote, honey, footed, 6" dia. x 4-1/2" tall.
Colors: Crystal, milk glass, pink pastel.
Availability: All available.
Reproductions: None known.

EH-52 Bowl, oval, crimped, 12", also in 10".

Colors: Crystal, milk glass, ruby.
Availability: Crystal and mg available, ruby scarce.
Reproductions: None known.

EH-53 Candy jar & cover, cone shape, 1/2 lb., footed, 7-1/2" tall.
Colors: Crystal, milk glass, Golden Sunset, crystal w/ruby flashing.
Availability: Crystal & mg common, Golden Sunset difficult, flashed scarce.
Reproductions: None known.

EH-54 Cigarette box & cover, 4-1/2" x 2-1/2".
Colors: Crystal, milk glass.
Availability: Mg common, crystal difficult.
Reproductions: None known.

EH-55 Hat, high, used for a cigarette jar.
Colors: Crystal, milk glass, purple marble, Golden Sunset.
Availability: Crystal & mg common, others are scarce.
Reproductions: Cobalt, cobalt carnival, ruby, ruby carnival, purple marble.

EH-56 Hat ashtray, low.
Colors: Crystal, milk glass, Golden Sunset.
Availability: All very difficult.
Reproductions: None known.

EH-57 Ashtray, round, 4-1/2".
Colors: Crystal.
Availability: Very difficult.
Reproductions: None known.

EH-58 Nut dish or salt dip, individual, footed, very small, 3".
Colors: Crystal, milk glass, Brandywine Blue, ruby, moss green.
Availability: Crystal & mg common, others slightly difficult.
Reproductions: Cobalt, red carnival, ruby, sky blue, milk glass, vaseline and many other colors. This piece has been reissued so much it is almost uncollectible.

EH-59 Ashtray, 3".

Colors: Crystal.
Availability: Slightly difficult.
Reproductions: None known.

EH-60 Coaster, round, 3".
Colors: Crystal.
Availability: Scarce.
Reproductions: None known.

EH-61 Bowl, grapefruit, 6-1/2" rimed.
Colors: Crystal, cry w/black trim.
Availability: Both are scarce.
Reproductions: None known.

EH-62 Bon Bon, 1 handled, hexagonal, 5" x 7".
Colors: Crystal, milk glass, amber.
Availability: Mg and crystal available, amber is difficult.
Reproductions: None known.

EH-63 Pickle dish, oval, 8".
Colors: Crystal, milk glass.
Availability: Both difficult.
Reproductions: None known.

EH-64 Bowl, crimped, flat, 6".
Colors: Crystal.
Availability: Available.
Reproductions: Frosted Blue as a bowl Frosted blue & black milk glass made into a basket. Also in milk glass made into a 7" oval basket. This may have red flower decals. Also made into a heart shaped 1 handled bon bon in milk glass.

EH-65 rose bowl, 6", flat, cupped rim, 4-1/2" tall.
Colors: Crystal, milk glass.
Availability: Both available.
Reproductions: Turquoise blue, cobalt blue and possibly others.

EH-66 Rose Bowl, 4" dia. x 3" tall, flat, cupped rim.
Colors: Crystal, milk glass, pink pastel.
Availability: All available.
Reproductions: Turquoise blue, cobalt and possibly others.

EH-67 Rose bowl, 6-pointed, 8" also in 7" dia x 4-1/2" tall.
Colors: Crystal, milk glass, pink pastel, ruby, almond.
Availability: Crystal and mg common, pink slightly difficult, almond scarce, ruby rare.
Reproductions: None known.

EH-68 Candelabra, 2 lite.
Colors: Crystal, milk glass.
Availability: Both scarce.
Reproductions: None known.

EH-69 Candy w/lid, round 3 footed, 6". Also marketed without a lid.
Colors: Crystal, Golden Sunset, milk glass, pink pastel, ruby.
Availability: Crystal & mg very difficult, others scarce.
Reproductions: None known.

EH-70 Marmalade w/cover and spoon, 5-1/4". The lid is notched to accept the spoon. This may also be found with a chrome lid.
Colors: Crystal, milk glass.
Availability: Both available, usually spoon is missing though!
Reproductions: None known.

EH-71 Candlestick, 3-1/2".
Colors: Crystal, milk glass, Golden Sunset, pink pastel.
Availability: Crystal & mg common, others difficult.
Reproductions: None known.

EH-72 Bowl, round, crimped, 9-1/2".
Colors: Crystal, milk glass, pink pastel.
Availability: All available.
Reproductions: None known.

EH-73 Basket, 9" tall, handled, flat.
Colors: Light blue mist, crystal, Golden Sunset, lilac opalescent, milk glass, pink pastel, pink mist, ruby, blue pastel and ruby slag (for Levay), turquoise carnival (for Levay in 1980).
Availability: Mg common, Golden Sunset,

Lilac Pastel scarce, all others are slightly difficult.
Reproductions: Milk glass, cobalt, ice blue, dark amber, black milk glass, cranberry ice, cranberry ice carnival, blue ice, Rhode Island Red (an amberina color), Bermuda Blue, blue ice carnival, pink, cobalt carnival.

EH-74 Celery dish, oval, 12" also in 9".
Colors: 12" crystal, milk glass, 9" crystal only.
Availability: All slightly difficult.
Reproductions: None known.

EH-75 Torte plate, 14" pointed edge, also in 20-1/2".
Colors: Crystal, ruby.
Availability: Both very scarce.
Reproductions: None known.

EH-76 Punch bowl, base, ladle & cups.
Colors: Crystal, turquoise (1940's).
Availability: Both are rare especially complete.
Reproductions: None known.

EH-77 Iced tea tumbler, sq. ftd. 11oz.
Colors: Crystal.
Availability: Slightly difficult.
Reproductions: None known.

EH-78 Water tumbler, sq. ftd., 9 oz.
Colors: Crystal.
Availability: Available.
Reproductions: None known.

EH-79 Water tumbler, sq. ftd., 7 oz.
Colors: Crystal.
Availability: Difficult.
Reproductions: None known.

EH-80 Gingerale tumbler, sq. ftd., 5 oz.
Colors: Crystal.
Availability: Difficult.
Reproductions: None known.

EH-81 Water goblet, sq. ftd., 8 oz.
Colors: Crystal, cry w/black foot, mg, cobalt (depressions era, old).
Availability: Crystal and mg available, black

foot scarce, cobalt is rare.
Reproductions: None known.

EH-82 Cocktail goblet, sq ftd. 3 oz.
Colors: Crystal.
Availability: Scarce.
Reproductions: None known.

EH-83 Sherbert, low, sq. ftd.
Colors: Crystal.
Availability: Available.
Reproductions: None known.

EH-84 Sherbert/Champagne, high, sq. ftd.
Colors: Crystal.
Availability: Available.
Reproductions: None known.

EH-85 Wine goblet, sq. ftd., 2 oz.
Colors: Crystal.
Availability: Slightly difficult.
Reproductions: None known.

EH-86 Cordial, sq. ftd.
Colors: Crystal.
Availability: Difficult.
Reproductions: None known.

EH-87 Oyster coctail, sq. ftd. Same as EH-88 without lid or spoon.
Colors: Crystal, milk glass. Milk glass was only marketed as a mustard.
Availability: Both available.
Reproductions: None known.

EH-88 Mustard, sq. ftd., w/lid & spoon. Lid is notched to accept the spoon.
Colors: Crystal, milk glass.
Availability: Both complete, slightly difficult.
Reproductions: None known.

EH-89 Shakers, salt & pepper, sq. ft.
Colors: Crystal, ruby, pink pastel.
Availability: All slightly difficult.
Reproductions: None known.

EH-90 Creamer, sq. ftd.
Colors: Crystal.

Availability: available.
Reproductions: None known.

EH-91 Sugar, sq. ftd.
Colors: Crystal.
Availability: Available.
Reproductions: None known.

EH-92 Compote, round bowl, sq ftd, 5".
Colors: Crystal.
Availability: Available.
Reproductions: None known.

EH-93 Compote, belled bowl, sq. ftd, 5-1/2".
Colors: Crystal.
Availability: Available.
Reproductions: None known.

EH-94 Honey compote, sq ftd., 6".
Colors: Crystal.
Availability: Available.
Reproductions: None known.

EH-95 Candlestick, sq. base, 5-1/2".
Colors: Crystal.
Availability: Very scarce.
Reproductions: None known.

EH-96 Bowl or nappy, square, 4-1/2".
Colors: Crystal.
Availability: Scarce.
Reproductions: None known.

EH-97 Fingerbowl, sq. ftd.
Colors: Crystal.
Availability: Scarce.
Reproductions: None known.

EH-98 Dinner plate, square, 10".
Colors: Crystal.
Availability: Very scarce.
Reproductions: None known.

EH-99 Cup & square saucer.
Colors: cups; crystal and milk glass. Saucers; crystal, black milk glass.
Availability: Crystal and milk glass available, black saucers scarce.
Reproductions: None known.

EH-100 Fingerbowl, flat round, with 6" square plate.
Colors: Crystal.
Availability: Both pieces scarce.
Reproductions: None known.

EH-101 Cheese dish & dover, 6" also in 8-3/4".
Colors: Crystal, aquamarine (for Levay), ruby (for Levay).
Availability: Crystal scarce, Levay colors are rare.
Reproductions: None known.

EH-102 Ashtray, square, 4-1/2". Also produced in an 8" square size (see EH-171).
Colors: Black milk glass, crystal, Golden Sunset, milk glass, mint green, almond.
Availability: Crystal and mg common, all others difficult.
Reproductions: Black milk glass.

EH-103 Luncheon plate, square, 8-3/4".
Colors: Crystal, crystal w/black stripe.
Availability: Crystal available, black stripe scarce.
Reproductions: None known.

EH-104 Plate, 6" square. Fingerbowl liner.
Colors: Crystal.
Availability: Difficult.
Reproductions: None known.

EH-105 Flower holder, sq. ftd., 6-1/2".
Colors: Crystal, milk glass.
Availability: Both available.
Reproductions: None known.

EH-106 Ivy ball, crimp top, sq. ftd., 6-1/2".
Colors: Crystal, milk glass.
Availability: Crystal difficult, milk glass is very common.
Reproductions: None known.

EH-107 Iced tea tumbler, barrel shape, ftd.
Colors: Crystal.
Availability: Scarce.
Reproductions: Milk glass made into a carafe by pulling the rim and adding an applied handle.

EH-108 Water goblet, barrel shaped, ftd. 8 oz.
Colors: Crystal, antique blue, milk glass.
Availability: Crystal scarce, antique blue very scarce to rare, mg available.
Reproductions: Crystal, pink mist with a ruffled rim called a mint dish, and turquoise blue swung vase made from this goblet.

EH-109 Water tumbler, barrel shape, ftd. 9 oz.
Colors: Crystal.
Availability: Scarce.
Reproductions: None known.

EH-110 Gingerale tumbler, barrel shape, ftd.
Colors: Crystal.
Availability: Scarce.
Reproductions: None known.

EH-111 Champagne goblet, barrel shape, ftd.
Colors: Crystal, milk glass.
Availability: Both scarce.
Reproductions: None known.

EH-112 Sherbert, high footed, barrel shape.
Colors: Crystal, milk glass.
Availability: Both scarce.
Reproductions: None known.

EH-113 Wine goblet, 2-1/4 oz., barrel shape, ftd.
Colors: Crystal.
Availability: Very scarce.
Reproductions: Crystal and milk glass as a wine, pink made into a small mint by ruffling the rim.

EH-114 Cordial, barrel shape, ftd., 1 oz.
Colors: Crystal.
Availability: Very scarce.
Reproductions: Blue mist made into a bud vase by pulling the top rim.

EH-115 Urn & cover, 11" barrel shape, sq. ftd. Also marketed as a 8" vase-no lid.
Colors: Crystal, mg, crystal w/ruby stain.
Availability: All colors are scarce.
Reproductions: None known.

EH-116 Cocktail goblet, barrel shape, 3-1/2 oz., ftd.
Colors: Crystal.
Availability: Scarce.
Reproductions: None known.

EH-117 Sherbert, low ftd., barrel shape.
Colors: Crystal.
Availability: Scarce.
Reproductions: None known.

EH-118 Canister w/lid, round, 32 oz., 7" tall.
Colors: Milk glass.
Availability: Extremely rare.
Reproductions: None known.

EH-119 Planter or jardiniere, 4" high, same as bottom of EH-118.
Colors: Milk glass, crystal.
Availability: Both extremely rare.
Reproductions: None known.

EH-120 Canister w/lid, round, 42 oz., 8" tall.
Colors: Milk glass.
Availability: Extremely rare.
Reproductions: None known.

EH-121 Planter or jardiniere, 5-1/2" high, same as bottom of EH-120.
Colors: Milk glass.
Availability: Extremely rare.
Reproductions: None known.

EH-122 Canister w/lid, round, 55 oz., 10" tall.
Colors: Milk glass.
Availability: Extremely rare.
Reproductions: None known.

EH-123 Planter or jardiniere, 7-1/2" high, same as bottom of EH-122.
Colors: Milk glass.
Availability: Extremely rare.
Reproductions: None known.

EH-124 Bowl, round, 2 handled, footed, 6" high, 8" dia. Sometimes referred to as Loving Cup.
Colors: Milk glass, Golden Sunset, blue pastel, pink pastel, lilac opalescent, ruby, pink mist, lt blue mist, crystal.
Availability: Mg available, others very difficult to scarce.
Reproductions: None known

EH-125 Vase, swung, flat, 12" tall, height will vary.
Colors: Milk glass.
Availability: Scarce.
Reproductions: None known.

EH-126 Vase, swung, flat, 14" tall, height will vary. Also in 10" size.
Colors: Milk glass, Brandywine Blue, Golden Sunset, Laurel Green.
Availability: Both 10" and 14" scarce in mg, colors very scarce to rare.
Reproductions: None known.

EH-127 Bowl, round bowl, sq. ft., 6-1/2" crimped rim.
Colors: Milk glass.
Availability: Difficult.
Reproductions: None known.

EH-128 Compote, crimped, 5", stemmed, round ft.
Colors: Brandywine Blue, Golden Sunset, Laurel Green, milk glass, pink opalescent, pink pastel.
Availability: Mg available, others difficult.
Reproductions: None known.

EH-129 Vase or compote, crimped edge, 4-1/2", round ftd.
Colors: Golden Sunset, milk glass.
Availability: Mg available, Golden Sunset difficult.
Reproductions: None known.

EH-130 Candlestick, 9".
Colors: Light blue mist, blue pastel, crystal, lilac opalescent, milk glass, pink pastel, pink mist, ruby. May also be found in the depression era colors of pink, green and turquoise.
Availability: Mg and crystal available, all others difficult, depression era examples are scarce.
Reproductions: None known.

EH-131 Bowl, oval, diamond foot, 9" x 5-1/2" high.
Colors: Milk glass, Golden Sunset, crystal.
Availability: Mg available, Golden Sunset scarce.
Reproductions: None known.

EH-132 Ashtray, 3-1/2" oblong.
Colors: Milk glass.
Availability: Available.
Reproductions: None known.

EH-133 Cigarette jar & cover, round, flat.
Colors: Milk glass.
Availability: Difficult.
Reproductions: None known.

EH-134 Fan vase or napkin holder, ftd., 5" high.
Colors: Milk glass, Golden Sunset.
Availability: Mg available, Golden Sunset scarce.
Reproductions: None known.

EH-135 Bowl, oval, crimped, 10" also in 12".
Colors: Crystal, milk glass.
Availability: Both available.
Reproductions: None known.

EH-136 Bowl, round, turned edge, shallow, 10".
Colors: Milk glass.
Availability: Scarce.
Reproductions: None known.

EH-138 Basket, round, 1 handle, 5" x 3-1/2" tall.
Colors: Crystal, milk glass.
Availability: Both common.
Reproductions: None known.

EH-139 Line #300 Individual condiment set consisting of a tray 4-1/2" x 3-1/4", an open salt dish, 1 cruet w/stopper, and 1 pepper shaker 3-3/4" tall.
Colors: Crystal, milk glass.
Availability: Trays and salts are usually available but cruets and peppers are the scarce items to find.

Reproductions: Salt dips only in black milk glass, cobalt, milk glass, amberina, green slag, rubina, morning glory, apple green, ice blue, cobalt, ruby, vaseline and sky blue. The other pieces in this set have been reproduced in cobalt, crystal, pink and milk glass. These have been produced in Taiwan.

EH-140 Ashtray, 3 footed, round, deep.
Colors: Milk glass.
Availability: Available.
Reproductions: None known.

EH-141 Butter dish & cover, oblong, 1/4 lb.
Colors: Crystal, milk glass, Golden Sunset. For Levay, ruby limited to 200.
Availability: Crystal and mg difficult, ruby and Golden sunset very scarce to rare.
Reproductions: Cobalt, ruby, black milk glass.

EH-142 Salt shaker & pepper mill, metal tops and bottoms.
Colors: Milk glass.
Availability: Difficult.
Reproductions: None known

EH-143 Cigarette lighter, oval.
Colors: Milk glass.
Availability: Very difficult.
Reproductions: None known

EH-144 Ashtray, square w/Moon landing logo.
Colors: Milk glass.
Availability: Scarce.
Reproductions: None known.

EH-145 Trivet, round, 3 footed.
Colors: Crystal.
Availability: Scarce.
Reproductions: None known.

EH-146 Nut dish, 3-1/4" tall x 4-3/8 " long, oval, diamond shape ft.
Colors: Crystal, milk glass.
Availability: Scarce.
Reproductions: None known.

EH-147 Snack server, canter handled, 2 tier.

Colors: Brandywine Blue, Golden Sunset, Laurel Green.
Availability: All colors are very scarce.
Reproductions: None known.

EH-148 Boric Acid bottle w/stopper. These were also marketed as perfume bottles. These were mainly made in the 1930's and 1940's. The writing on the bottle will add to it's value. Perfumes will not have any writing. Mouthwash and lotion bottles were also produced, but these will have a wider stopper and bottle opening than the perfume bottle.
Colors: Turquoise, milk glass, green, pink, amber, cobalt, antique blue, crystal.
Availability: Perfumes: Mg common, colors very difficult. Bottles with writing scarce in any color.
Reproductions: None known.

EH-149 Bowl, rolled edge, belled, 10-3/4".
Colors: Green, turquoise, amber, pink, crystal.
Availability: All scarce.
Reproductions: None known.

EH-150 Bowl, bell, 9-1/2".
Colors: Amber, green, turquoise, pink.
Availability: All very difficult.
Reproductions: None known.

EH-151 Line #300 candy jar and cover, square ftd., 1/2 lb., 9" tall. This piece is often referred to as English Hobnail but was always marketed as "Waterford". See #300-2 for companion piece.
Colors: Crystal, milk glass, crystal w/ruby stain.
Availability: All available.
Reproductions: None known.

EH-152 Torte or serving plate, 13".
Colors: Pink pastel.
Availability: Slightly difficult.
Reproductions: None known.

EH-153 Vase, swung, flat, 10-1/2".
Colors: Pink pastel.

Availability: Difficult.
Reproductions: None known.

EH-154 Vase, bud, ftd., pulled rim, 11".
Colors: Pink pastel.
Availability: Difficult.
Reproductions: Turquoise blue.

EH-155 Mint compote, shallow double crimped, stemmed ftd., 5".
Colors: Pink pastel.
Availability: Difficult.
Reproductions: None known.

EH-156 Serving plate, rolled edge, 12".
Colors: Pink pastel.
Availability: Difficult.
Reproductions: None known.

EH-157 Basket, oval, flat 7".
Colors: Pink pastel.
Availability: Difficult.
Reproductions: None known.

EH-158 Banana bowl, flat, oval 8".
Colors: Pink pastel.
Availability: Very difficult.
Reproductions: Cobalt.

EH-159 Bowl, flared, double crimped, 12".
Colors: Pink pastel.
Availability: Difficult.
Reproductions: None known.

EH-160 Candle ball, ftd., 6" tall.
Colors: Pink pastel.
Availability: Difficult.
Reproductions: None known.

EH-161 Donut stand, stem ftd., 6".
Colors: Pink pastel.
Availability: Very difficult.
Reproductions: None known.

EH-162 Basket, ruffled, flat, 6-1/2".
Colors: Pink pastel.
Availability: Very difficult.
Reproductions: Crystal mist, black mg, cobalt, Bermuda Blue.

EH-163 Bud vase, mini, 5" tall.
Colors: Pink pastel.
Availability: Difficult.
Reproductions: Blue frost.

EH-164 Bud vase, mini, 3" tall.
Colors: Pink pastel.
Availability: Difficult.
Reproductions: None known.

EH-165 Basket, square, flat, 7-1/2".
Colors: Pink pastel.
Availability: Very difficult.
Reproductions: None known.

EH-166 Mint compote, shallow double crimped, 5" stemmed ftd.
Colors: Pink pastel.
Availability: Difficult.
Reproductions: None known.

EH-167 Mint compote, shallow ruffled, 5" stemmed ftd.
Colors: Pink pastel.
Availability: Difficult.
Reproductions: None known.

EH-168 Bowl, mint, double crimped, flat, 6".
Colors: Pink pastel.
Availability: Difficult.
Reproductions: Blue frost.

EH-169 Ivy or rose vase, 6 pointed, 3" flat.
Colors: Pink pastel.
Availability: Very difficult.
Reproductions: None known.

EH-170 Bowl or bon-bon, square, flat, 6-1/2".
Colors: Pink pastel.
Availability: Difficult.
Reproductions: None known.

EH-171 Ashtray, 7-3/4" to 8" square.
Colors: Mint green, almond, ruby, mg, Golden Sunset.
Availability: All scarce.
Reproductions: None known.

EH-172 Vase, footed, crimped, rim, 6-1/4"

tall. This vase was produced during the Grossman years and was made from the barrel shaped water goblet.
Colors: Pink pastel.
Availability: Slightly difficult.
Reproductions: Pink frost.

EH-180 Puff box with cover, 5" diameter. See back cover for the photo of this item.
Colors: Crystal, milk glass & depression era pink, green, turquoise, cobalt blue.
Availability: Crystal & mg slightly difficult, colors are scarce with turquoise and cobalt being the hardest to find.
Reproductions: None known.

EM-1 Elf Mug or Stein. This stein has 3 different scenes with German writing describing each scene. This stein originally had a cone shaped lid which was sealed to the bottom with wax and sold as a condiment item. These originals were in milk glass. The later carnival versions were produced for Levay in 1983 and 1984 and did not have lids. A "Lovers" stein was also produced in the same manner and the same colors as below.
Colors: Milk glass (very early), ruby carnival (1000 or less made, usually signed and dated but not always), black carnival (an experimental color in 1984).
Availability: Mg very rare (the lid is the rarest part), ruby carnival very scarce, black carnival rare.
Reproductions: None as yet but be aware that Greentown Glass also made a very similar mug in a green or blue milk glass.

EV-1 Elite vase, flat 7-1/4" tall x 3" dia. This vase was a mold which was revived by David Grossman for a Levay limited edition of 1000.
Colors: Ruby carnival (1983), other carnival colors such as black carnival may exist but were not shown in any Levay catalogs.
Availability: Any carnival color is rare.
Reproductions: None known.

FF-1 Fan & File Line #303 child's punch set,

or salesman's sample. 4-1/2" tall punch bowl w/attached foot, 1" cups. This was made as early as the 1920's but the most commonly found examples are from the Grossman era. Grossman planned on issuing a set once per year from 1982 through 1989 to celebrate the company's 100 years of productions. Only 3 years worth were produced. This set was also sold to Levay in very limited quantities and special colors.

Colors: For Levay: pink carnival, pink, ruby carnival (2000 made), turquoise carnival, aurora blue carnival, electric blue carnival (500 made), cobalt carnival, crystal carnival (500 made), marigold carnival (400 made), vaseline carnival, ice blue carnival, honey amber carnival, ruby or cerese in 1979, emerald green opalescent in 1975. For Grossman: Blue pastel-1982, ruby in 1983, crystal in 1984. Other 1920's colors may exist but would be considered very rare today.

Availability: Levay colors very scarce to rare, Grossman colors scarce.

Reproductions: Blue ice, blue ice carnival, blue milk glass, cobalt, vaseline, amethyst, cranberry ice, cranberry ice carnival, Bermuda Blue, milk glass, and alexandrite. These repros may or may not be marked with a "Keystone R", according to the "Towne Crier Newsletter."

FF-2 Fan & File line #299 child's butter dish w/domed lid. This appeared as early as the 1920's. The next reissue occurred in the 1950 catalog in milk glass. Grossman also produced these for retail sales as well as for Levay. This piece was also called a jelly. Dimensions are 3-1/2" dia. x 2-1/2" tall.

Colors: For Levay: Ruby, cobalt carnival, pink carnival, red carnival, marigold carnival (500 made), purple carnival (1000 made), Brandywine Blue, electric blue carnival (500 made), green, ice blue carnival (1000 made), pink, vaseline carnival, Aurora cobalt carnival, crystal, crystal carnival (500 made). For the regular line: milk glass, ruby, crystal, Golden Sunset.

Availability: Mg available, all other colors scarce. Levay colors are very scarce to rare.

Reproductions: None known.

FF-3 Fan & File Line #299 sugar, open or spooner 2-1/2". This piece has the same history as the item above.

Colors: For Levay: Ruby, cobalt carnival, pink carnival, red carnival, marigold carnival (500 made), purple carnival (1000 made), Brandywine Blue, electric blue carnival (500 made), crystal, crystal carnival (500 made), green, ice blue carnival (1000 made), pink, vaseline carnival. For the regular line: Milk glass, ruby, crystal, Golden Sunset.

Availability: Mg available, all other colors scarce, Levay colors are very scarce to rare.

Reproductions: None known.

FF-4 Fan & File Line #299 child's creamer, 2-1/2" tall. See FF-2 for descriptions and dates.

Colors: For Levay: Ruby, Aurora cobalt carnival, pink carnival, red carnival, marigold carnival (500 made), purple carnival (1000 made), Brandywine blue, electric blue carnival (500 made), crystal, crystal carnival (500 made), green, ice blue carnival (1000 made), pink, vaseline carnival. For the regular line: Milk glass, ruby, crystal, Golden Sunset.

Availability: Mg available, all other colors scarce, Levay colors are very scarce.

Reproductions: None known.

FF-5 Fan & File #299 child's sugar w/lid, 3-1/4" tall. See FF-2 for descriptions and dates.

Colors: Grossman: Crystal, milk glass, ruby. For Levay: Marigold carnival (500 made), purple carnival (1000 made), Brandywine blue, electric blue carnival (500 made), cobalt carnival, green, ice blue carnival (1000 made), pink, pink carnival, ruby carnival, vaseline carnival, crystal carnival (500 made).

Availability: the covered sugar is much more difficult to find than the open sugar/spooner.

Reproductions: None known.

FF-6 Fan & File #299 child's banana stand, ftd., 6-1/2". See FF-2 for descriptions and dates.
Colors: Grossman: Crystal, ruby.
Availability: All colors very scarce.
Reproductions: Alexandrite, vaseline, cobalt, amethyst.

FF-7 Fan & File #299 child's cake plate, ftd., 7". See FF-2 for descriptions and dates.
Colors: Grossman: Crystal, ruby.
Availability: All colors very scarce.
Reproductions: Alexandrite, vaseline, cobalt, amethyst.

FL-1 Line #1700 "Flute" or "Arch" pitcher, 8-1/4" tall. This line as a complete set was shown in the 1912 catalog. The pitcher and tumbler, which is 4" tall was reissued for Levay in very limited amounts.
Colors: Crystal carnival w/cardinal decal (300 sets made), crystal carnival plain (300 sets made).
Availability: Cardinal decal very scarce to rare, plain crystal carnival scarce.
Reproductions: None known.

FMN-1 Line #2 Forget-me-not border, 2 tier tid bit tray, center handled. Top plate is 7" dia., bottom plate is 11", and the tray complete is 5-1/2" tall.
Colors: Milk glass, moss green, Golden Sunset.
Availability: Mg available, moss green and golden sunset are difficult.
Reproductions: None known.

FR-1 Line #81, Fruits punch set. Consists of 5 quart punch bowl cupped, belled or straight rim, punch base, punch cups, and #1800 ladle.
Colors: Milk glass, cobalt carnival (100 sets made), lilac opalescent (500 sets), ice blue carnival, honey amber carnival, turquoise carnival (100 sets), purple carnival (100 sets), almond.
Availability: Mg slightly difficult, other colors very scarce to rare. Note mg set has mg ladle, color sets will have a crystal ladle, almond sets will have almond ladle.
Reproductions: None known.

144

GS-1 Line #1900 Grandma's Slipper.
Colors: Black mg, almond, cobalt carnival, crystal mist, yellow mist (sometimes called chartreuse), dark blue mist, brown mist, Antique Blue mist, Antique Blue, mint green, ice blue carnival, honey amber carnival, green mist, milk glass mop. any of these colors may have a hand painted touch of flowers.
Availability: Carnival colors are scarce, but all others colors are only slightly difficult.
Reproductions: Ruby, cobalt.

HB-1 Line #1857 Heart shaped chocolate box w/heart and arrow finial on lid.
Colors: Dark blue mist, green mist, almond w/Almond Rose, milk glass w/Roses & Bows, crystal mist w/25th anniv., crystal mist w/50th anniv.
Availability: All scarce.
Reproductions: Cobalt, ruby, aquamarine/teal.

HB-2 Line #1902 Heart shaped small trinket box w/lid.
Colors: Dark blue mist w/daisy, green mist w/daisy dec., mg w/dec#32, mg mop w/Roses & Bows, ruby w/Ruby Floral, antique blue w/Beaded Bouquet, brown mist w/Floral Bouquet, mint green w/Beaded Bouquet, almond w/Beaded Bouquet, almond w/Almond Rose, lilac mist w/daisy, brown mist w/daisy, crystal mist w/Floral Bouquet, yellow mist w/daisy, dark blue mist w/Floral Bouquet, crystal w/ruby stain w/Ruby Floral, ruby w/Snowflower.
Availability: Colors difficult, decorated examples are very difficult.
Reproductions: Cobalt, ruby, blue satin with or without hand paintings. Decorations include any Mary Gregory style, rose or Shirley Temple, Tom Mix or Hopalong Cassidy decals. The latter usually appears on cobalt only.

HH-1 Line #550 High Hob sweetmeat, 6-1/2" oval, ftd. also called a candy at times.
Colors: Crystal, purple carnival, pink carnival, emerald green opalescent (150

made), purple slag carnival, Brandywine Blue Opalescent, Butterscotch, vaseline opalescent, aurora cobalt blue carnival (1000 made), royal blue, green marble.

Availability: Crystal very difficult, all carnival colors were limited editions for Levay and are considered very scarce to rare.

Reproductions: None known.

HH-2 Line #550 High Hob water tumbler, 4" tall, flat.

Colors: Pink carnival (200 sets made), emerald green opalescent (150 sets made), purple slag carnival (76 sets made), aurora cobalt blue carnival (800 sets made), royal blue, electric blue opalescent carnival (150 sets made), electric blue opalescent (200 sets made), purple carnival (300 sets made), butterscotch (55 sets made), purple (300 sets made).

Availability: All listed above were produced for Levay in limited amounts and are considered very scarce to rare. Crystal may also be found and would date to the early part of this century. Crystal is also very scarce.

Reproductions: None known.

HH-3 Line #550 High Hob water pitcher.

Colors: Aurora cobalt blue carnival (800 sets made), pink carnival (200 sets made), electric blue opalescent carnival (150 sets made), electric blue opalescent (200 sets made), purple carnival (300 sets made), emerald green opalescent (150 sets made), butterscotch (55 sets made), purple slag carnival (76 sets made), purple (300 sets made), royal blue.

Availability: All colors listed above were produced in limited quantities for Levay and are considered very scarce to rare. Crystal may also be found but would date back to the early part of the century. Crystal is considered very scarce.

Reproductions: None known.

HN-1 Line #1 Hen on basketweave base, 7-1/2" long x 5-3/4" wide. This may also be found on a #1870 lacy rim base.

Colors: Brandywine Blue, Laurel Green,

Golden Sunset, mg, mg w/hp accents, green marble, lilac mist, yellow opaque, almond w/hp accents, ruby, purple marble, antique blue mg w/mg head, all antique blue, crystal, ruby slag, chocolate glass, electric blue carnival (500 made), crystal carnival (1500 made), pink carnival, turquoise carnival in 1980.

Availability: Mg and mg hp common, all other colors very scarce.

Reproductions: Blue milk glass, purple slag and light pink. These repros are from AA Importing and are of poor quality so they should pose no problems. They do not have any type of markings at all.

HN-2 Line #2 Hen on basketweave base, 5-1/2" x 4" wide. Dimensions may vary on this hen. The hens made for Levay will be 5" long.

Colors: Brandywine Blue, Laurel Green, Golden Sunset, mg, mg w/hp accents, dk blue mist, black milk glass w/hp accents, green mist, antique blue, olive green, Bermuda Blue. For Levay: Ruby slag carnival (500 made), purple slag carnival (500 made), ruby carnival (1000 made), black carnival (experimental color), cobalt carnival (1000 made), purple marble, vaseline.

Availability: Mg & mg hp available, all other colors very scarce. Levay colors very scarce to rare.

Reproductions: 5-1/2" (will have circular "Westmoreland" mark according to the "Towne Crier Newsletter") mg w/hp, mg mop w/hp, mg, mg mop, blue milk glass, vaseline, vaseline carnival, Bermuda Blue, mg w/amethyst accents, blue ice, aquamarine /teal, topaz, purple slag, light pink, cobalt, cobalt carnival, black milk glass. 5" (will have no marking, these are made for A.A. Importing) repros include: Cobalt, pink, crystal, aqua, light blue, blue milk glass, blue, green, black w/mg head, grey w/mg head, lavendar opaque, blue and white slag, amethyst carnival and ruby. These 5" repros may have a wide rim base.

HP-2 Line #1820 Heart shaped coaster. Part

of a set which includes spade, club & diamond. (See CL-2, DI-1, & SP-2 for other examples).
Colors: Black mg, apricot mist, almond, crystal w/ruby stain, ruby w/Happy Birthday hp, mg w/red heart, rose & bow, ruby w/Ruby Floral, dk blue mist w/daisy, crystal with ruby stain w/Cameo, ruby w/Mary Gregory style Bonnet girl, brown mist w/Cameo, mg mop w/Cameo, almond w/Cameo, ruby w/white Cameo, crystal with ruby stain w/Ruby Floral, pink mist w/Snow flower, Ruby w/Snow Flower.
Availability: All difficult, especially the hand painted varieties.
Reproductions: None known.

IR-1 Line #60 Ivy ring, 12" diameter. These is also a 7" version of this ivy ring. These were first made in the 1950's. These were very difficult to make because they had to be hand blown. All ivy rings were very limited in production. The last catalog showing the ivy rings was the 1970 catalog.
Colors: Crystal, black milk glass (which is so thin that it appears to be more amethyst than black), Golden Sunset, cry w/pk flashing.
Availability: All colors rare.
Reproductions: None known. I don't believe any of the glass companies have any employees with the skills to manufacture this any longer. This type of glass is a lost art.

LB-1 Line #20 Love Birds covered dish, oval. Dimensions are 6-1/2" long x 5-1/4" tall.
Colors: Milk glass, apricot mist, dark blue mist, pink mist, crystal mist, green mist, moss green, green marble, purple marble, brown marble, lt blue mist, Bermuda blue, Golden Sunset, olive green, yellow mist, Antique Blue Mist, mint green, mg mop, almond, caramel marble, Antique Blue, black mg, Brandywine Blue. For Levay: Pink carnival (500 made), butterscotch carnival (400 made), vaseline (400 made), Black carnival (experimental color in 1985).
Availability: Levay colors, especially pink carnival are rare, all other colors very

difficult to scarce. Milk glass available.
Reproductions: Ruby, alexandrite, azure blue, blue milk glass.

LE-1 Plate, 11"
Colors: Milk glass, black milk glass, dark blue mist. Mostly decorated. Decorations include 8 different game birds, floral, or Mary Gregory style designs.
Availability: All scarce.
Reproductions: None known.

LE-2 Cake salver, 11" dia., ftd., 5" high.
Colors: Milk glass.
Availability: Scarce.
Reproductions: None known.

LE-3 Bowl, flared, 10-1/4", footed.
Colors: Milk glass.
Availability: Scarce.
Reproductions: None known.

LE-4 Banana bowl, 12", ftd., 8-1/2" high.
Colors: Milk glass.
Availability: Scarce.
Reproductions: None known.

LE-5 Candlesticks, 4".
Colors: Milk glass.
Availability: Available.
Reproductions: None known.

LE-6 Bowl, round, 8-1/2", flat.
Colors: Milk glass, mg w/flower bouquet hp.
Availability: Very scarce.
Reproductions: None known.

LE-7 Bowl, flared, 11-1/2", flat.
Colors: Milk glass.
Availability: Very scarce.
Reproductions: None known.

LE-8 Bowl, cupped, 10" ftd., also in 11" belled version.
Colors: Milk glass.
Availability: Scarce.
Reproductions: None known.

LF-1 Line #1923 Leaf salad plate or bon bon,

9". Also available in a 12" size which was marketed as a tray for salad, sandwiches or cake. First available in the 1950 catalog.
Colors: Both 9" and 12" in milk glass only.
Availability: 9" available, 12" scarce.
Reproductions: 9" and 12" pink and pink frost.

LF-2 Line #1923 Leaf dessert plate or bon bon 6". This line was shown as early as 1950 in milk glass. Basically sold as a salad or dessert set. The small 6" size sold the best out of all of the sizes and was then marketed as a bon bon.
Colors: Brandywine Blue, Laurel Green, Golden Sunset, milk glass, green marble, purple marble, milk glass w/roses & bows dec., pink mist, dark blue mist, brown mist, antique blue mist.
Availability: Mg available, mg w/roses and bows difficult, all other colors scarce to very scarce.
Reproductions: Pink and pink frost.

LJ-1 Line #304 "Lil Jo" or Flute mini pitcher or creamer, 4" tall. This child's set or salesman's sample was produced during the depression era, although most examples found today are those made for Levay.
Colors: Ruby carnival, ruby, crystal carnival, crystal, cobalt, cobalt carnival, cobalt w/white flowers, crystal w/black & white flowers, emerald green, emerald green carnival, emerald green w/white flowers, purple carnival (1977, 500 made).
Availability: All very scarce.
Reproductions: Cobalt plain or with Shirley Temple, Tom Mix or Hopalong Cassidy decals and cobalt carnival, or vaseline.

LJ-2 Line #304 Lil Jo or Flute tumbler, 2" tall, flat. this item was sold with LJ-1 as a child's water set.
Colors: Ruby carnival, ruby, electric blue, electric blue carnival, amberina, amberina carnival, crystal carnival, crystal, cobalt, cobalt carnival, cobalt w/white flowers, crystal w/black & white flowers, emerald green, emerald green carnival, emerald

green w/white flowers, purple carnival (1977, 500 sets made).
Availability: All very scarce.
Reproductions: Cobalt, vaseline, and cobalt carnival.

LO-1 Torte plate, 13".
Colors: Crystal w/ruby stain, pink opalescent.
Availability: Crystal w/stain scarce, pink opalescent difficult.
Reproductions: None known.

LO-2 Candlestick, 3-1/2". If turned upside down this item becomes a mint dish.
Colors: Amber, apricot mist, lt blue mist, crystal w/ruby stain, crystal mist, flame, green mist, lilac pastel, moss green, pink mist, pink opalescent, milk glass, mg w/mother of pearl, black milk glass, dark blue mist, Golden Sunset.
Availability: Mg, lilac pastel, pink opalescent are available. Flame, crystal w/ruby stain are scarce. All others are slightly difficult.
Reproductions: None known.

LO-3 Bowl, cupped, 9". Also in a flared 12", see LO-31.
Colors: Amber, apricot mist, lt blue mist, black milk glass, crystal w/ruby stain, flame, green mist, moss green, pink mist, pink opalescent, milk glass, mg w/mother of pearl, dark blue mist, crystal mist, Golden Sunset, olive green, Bermuda Blue.
Availability: Mg & green mist are available: flame, black mg, crystal w/ruby stain are scarce. All others are slightly difficult.
Reproductions: Cobalt, vaseline.

LO-4 Bowl, oval, 11-1/2" ftd. May be lipped.
Colors: Crystal w/ruby stain, milk glass, black milk glass.
Availability: Mg available, others difficult.
Reproductions: None known.

LO-5 Bowl, 4", mayonnaise, may be cupped.
Colors: Crystal w/ruby stain, milk glass, mg w/rose decoration, crystal mist, mg mop, other colors date earlier.

Availability: Mg available, others are difficult to scarce.
Reproductions: Cobalt, vaseline.

LO-6 Plate, 7", mayonnaise liner.
Colors: Crystal w/ruby stain, milk glass, mg w/rose decoration, crystal mist, mg mop, other colors date earlier.
Availability: Mg available, others are difficult to scarce.
Reproductions: None known.

LO-7 Line #1933 vase, oval, square ftd., 10".
Colors: Milk glass, mg w/gold decoration.
Availability: Very scarce to rare.
Reproductions: None known.

LO-8 Line #1933 vase, oval, ftd., 2 handled, 10-1/2".
Colors: Milk glass.
Availability: Very scarce to rare.
Reproductions: None known.

LO-9 Line #1933 cornucopia vase, 7" footed.
Colors: Milk glass, crystal.
Availability: Both colors are difficult.
Reproductions: None known.

LO-10 Candlestick, ruffled, ftd., 3".
Colors: Flame, pink opalescent, Golden Sunset, Bermuda Blue, olive green, lt blue mist, green mist, apricot mist.
Availability: Flame & Golden Sunset scarce, others slightly difficult.
Reproductions: None known.

LO-11 Vase, pulled 10" footed.
Colors: Light blue mist, black milk glass, crystal mist, flame, green mist, pink mist, pink opalescent, milk glass, apricot mist, dark blue mist, mg w/pansy dec#34, Bermuda Blue, olive green, Golden Sunset, and flame mist.
Availability: Decorated mg, flame, flame mist, black mg are scarce. All others slightly difficult.
Reproductions: None known.

LO-12 Bowl, flared, lipped, 11".

Colors: Pink opalescent.
Availability: Available.
Reproductions: None known.

LO-13 Vase, lily, footed, 6".
Colors: Pink opalescent.
Availability: Available.
Reproductions: None known.

LO-14 Vase, 6" footed, pinched scalloped top.
Colors: Pink opalescent.
Availability: Available.
Reproductions: None known.

LO-15 Compote, mint, round ftd., 6", pointed rim.
Colors: Light blue mist, black milk glass, milk glass, crystal mist, flame, green mist, pink mist, pink opalescent, Bermuda Blue, moss green, olive green, Golden Sunset.
Availability: Mg, pink opal, moss green are available. Flame, black milk glass, Bermuda Blue, Golden Sunset are scarce. All others are slightly difficult.
Reproductions: None known.

LO-16 Basket, star shape, footed, 8".
Colors: Pink opalescent.
Availability: Difficult.
Reproductions: None known.

LO-17 Basket, oval, footed, 8".
Colors: Pink opalescent.
Availability: Difficult.
Reproductions: None known.

LO-18 Glow ball or candleholder, footed, 4-1/2".
Colors: Pink opalescent.
Availability: Difficult.
Reproductions: None known.

LO-19 Compote, mint, star footed, lipped edge, 5-1/2".
Colors: Apricot mist, light blue mist, crystal mist, flame, green mist, pink mist, pink opalescent, green marble, purple marble,

dark blue mist, amber, milk glass, Bermuda Blue, olive green Golden Sunset, Brandy-wine Blue, black mg.
Availability: Mg, crystal mist available. Flame scarce. All others difficult.
Reproductions: None known.

LO-20 Bell, 4", hook handle. Looks like an umbrella.
Colors: Pink opalescent.
Availability: Difficult.
Reproductions: None known.

LO-21 Vase, mini, ruffled, footed, 5".
Colors: Pink opalescent.
Availability: Difficult.
Reproductions: None known.

LO-22 Vase, mini jack-in-the-pulpit, 6", footed.
Colors: Pink opalescent.
Availability: Difficult.
Reproductions: Black mg, cobalt, amethyst, blue ice.

LO-23 Vase, mini lily, 4-1/2", footed.
Colors: Pink opalescent.
Availability: Difficult.
Reproductions: None known.

LO-24 Vase, mini crimped, 5", footed.
Colors: Pink opalescent.
Availability: Difficult.
Reproductions: None known.

LO-25 Vase, mini bud, 6-1/2", footed.
Colors: Pink opalescent.
Availability: Difficult.
Reproductions: None known.

LO-26 Candelabra, triple branch, 5-1/4" tall, 8" long.
Colors: Light blue mist, crystal mist, green mist, milk glass, pink mist.
Availability: All difficult.
Reproductions: None known.

LO-27 Compote, 8-1/4" dia., 6" tall. Several sizes of this type of compote were produced during the depression era. Several colors may exist.
Colors: Green mist, green, pink and possibly others.
Availability: All scarce.
Reproductions: None known.

LO-28 Perfume bottle, tall and very slender, w/ball shaped stopper. This item is essentially made from a bud vase and a special tool is used to form the top rim of the perfume. All production of this item was very limited. These have been reproduced in several colors. The dark amber bottle is the only definite original Westmoreland bottle in the picture.
Colors: Dark amber, pink, pink mist, green, black mg.
Availability: Very few originals exist. These were made in very limited production, thus all colors are rare.
Reproductions: Cranberry ice w/satin accents, cranberry ice, cobalt, pink, pink mist, pink clear w/mist accents, blue ice, blue ice satin, blue ice clear w/mist accents.

LO-29 Shaker, footed. This item was produced during the depression era. It may be found in other colors.
Colors: Crystal, possibly others.
Availability: Very scarce.
Reproductions: None known.

LO-30 Puff box, round with lid. Produced during the depression era. May be found in other colors. This piece has not been reproduced like the perfume bottles, as yet.
Colors: Pink, pink mist, possibly others.
Availability: Very scarce.
Reproductions: None known.

LO-31 Bowl, flared, 12".
Colors: Black milk glass, flame, pink mist, crystal mist, green mist, light blue mist, Bermuda Blue, olive green, Golden Sunset, milk glass.
Availability: All colors are scarce to very scarce.
Reproductions: None known.

LOV-1 Line #241 Lily of the Valley Vase, 7" tall. May have a slight flare to the rim, or may have a cupped rim. The cupped rims usually are found on the carnival versions.
Colors: Milk glass, mint green, electric blue opalescent carnival (500 made), antique green, crystal carnival (400 made), electric blue opalescent, ruby.
Availability: Mg available, mint green and antique green are scarce, all carnival colors are rare.
Reproductions: Milk glass, cobalt.

MC-1 Line #1013 mini candelabra, triple branch, 4-1/2" footed. Child's or salesman's sample.
Colors: Crystal, dark blue mist, apricot mist, green mist, light blue mist, ruby, blue pastel, lavendar, pink pastel.
Availability: All colors are very difficult. Crystal may be only slightly difficult.
Reproductions: Crystal, vaseline, mg mop.

MC-2 Mini chamberstick w/finger hole, 1". This appears to have been produced only for the 1984 Grossman catalog.
Colors: Crystal
Availability: Scarce.
Reproductions: Cobalt.

MG-1 Line #2 Forget-me-not border plate, 8". This plate can be found plain in either white or black milk glass. But most often these plates will be found with some sort of hand painted decoration in the center. The most commonly found is that of the Mary Gregory style. These plates may also be found in 7" and 11" sizes in milk glass only. These were most often used in the 2 tier tidbit server (see FMN-1).
Colors: Black milk glass, dark blue mist, ruby, milk glass, all with or without decorations, crystal mist w/China Rose, black milk glass w/Oriental Poppy, crystal mist w/wedding bells, mg w/China rose, brown mist w/Mary Gregory style, antique blue milk glass.
Availability: Ruby and dark blue mist is

more difficult than that of milk or black, with decorations in all colors are very difficult.
Reproductions: Cobalt with or without hp decorations.

MJ-9 Holland or Dutch scene mustard jar w/lid. This hexagonal mustard has a lid which sits more flush to the rim than that of MJ-8. The same type of scenes are protrayed. The lid for this mustard and that of the MJ-8 mustard are interchangeable. Remnants of hand painting are also found on this mustard jar. *(See Book 2 for MJ-8)*
Colors: Mg, mg w/various hand paintings.
Availability: Either is very scarce.
Reproductions: None known.

ML-1 Candlestick, 4-3/4" tall. Grossman later crimped the tops on these which made them 5-1/2" tall.
Colors: 4-3/4" milk glass, mint green. 5-1/2" Blue pastel, lilac opalescent, pink pastel, ruby.
Availability: 4-3/4" difficult. 5-1/2" very difficult.
Reproductions: Crystal, crystal mist, black milk glass, and cobalt. These repros will have the circular "Westmoreland" mark according to the "Towne Crier Newsletter."

ML-2 Bowl, bell, 10" dia., 4-1/2" high, ftd.
Colors: Milk glass.
Availability: Very difficult.
Reproductions: Turquoise blue with top rim cupped, black milk glass, and cobalt. These repros are marked with the "WG" mark according to the "Towne Crier Newsletter."

ML-3 Bowl, rose, ftd., 4-1/2" dia., 4-1/2" high.
Colors: Milk glass, for Levay purple carnival limited to 200.
Availability: Mg slightly difficult.
Reproductions: Frosted pink, marketed as a mini punch bowl.

ML-4 Bowl, crimped, footed, 10" dia., 5-1/2" high.
Colors: Blue pastel, lilac opalescent, milk

glass, pink pastel, ruby, mint green, for Levay purple carnival limited to 200.
Availability: All colors difficult. Levay colors rare.
Reproductions: Black milk glass in 9". Black milk glass and pink in 12" size as a basket w/applied handle.

ML-5 Compote & cover, footed, 4-1/2" dia., 6" high with lid. Note lid will not fit on ML-6. A plain rim is needed.
Colors: Milk glass, ruby.
Availability: Slightly difficult.
Reproductions: None known.

ML-6 Compote, open, footed, 4-1/2" x 4-1/2". Note that this compote requires no lid, since it has a rippled type edge. ML-5 has a plain rim which enables the lid to fit.
Colors: Milk glass.
Availability: Available.
Reproductions: Some items were made into baskets, ruffled, or made exactly as the original. Crystal, crystal mist, milk glass, black milk glass.

ML-7 Bowl, square, crimped, ftd., 4-1/2" dia., 4-1/2" tall.
Colors: Milk glass.
Availability: Scarce.
Reproductions: See ML-6.

ML-8 Chocolate box and cover, round, flat, 6-1/2" dia., 3-3/4" high.
Colors: Dark blue mist, blue pastel, green mist, lilac mist, lilac opalescent, milk glass, moss green, pink pastel, ruby, light blue mist.
Availability: All colors very difficult.
Reproductions: Cobalt, crystal, crystal frost.

ML-9 Sugar, twig like handles.
Colors: Mint green, milk glass, ruby.
Availability: Mint green and ruby very scarce, milk glass common.
Reproductions: Black milk glass, crystal, black mg w/22kt gold hp. These repros will have the circular "Westmoreland" mark according to the "Towne Crier Newsletter."

Although I have found some will bear a Keystone PG mark for Plum Glass.

ML-10 Creamer, twig like handles.
Colors: Mint green, milk glass, ruby.
Availability: Mint green and ruby very scarce, milk glass common.
Reproductions: Black milk glass, crystal, black mg w/22kt gold hp. These repros will have the circular "Westmoreland" mark according to the "Towne Crier Newsletter." Although I have found some will bear a Keystone PG mark for Plum Glass.

ML-11 Bowl, round, crimped, ftd., 4-1/2" dia., 4-1/2" tall. This item was later reproduced as a basket.
Colors: Milk glass.
Availability: Difficult.
Reproductions: Black mg as a basket, see ML-6.

ML-12 Bowl or nappy, cupped, 6" dia., 2" high.
Colors: Milk glass.
Availability: Difficult.
Reproductions: None known.

ML-13 Bowl or nappy, round, 7" dia., 1-3/4" high.
Colors: Milk glass.
Availability: Difficult.
Reproductions: None known.

ML-14 Bowl or nappy, turned edge, 8" dia., 1-3/16" high.
Colors: Milk glass.
Availability: Difficult.
Reproductions: None known.

ML-15 Cookie jar & cover, 8" dia., 7-1/4" high.
Colors: Milk glass. For Levay: Purple carnival limited to 200.
Availability: Mg scarce, Levay colors rare.
Reproductions: None known.

ML-16 Bowl, cupped, ftd., 8" dia., 7-1/4" high (Cookie jar bottom).

Colors: Milk glass. (Note this may be found in purple carnival, but in order to be correct it must have a lid as in ML-15.)
Availability: Mg scarce.
Reproductions: None known.

ML-17 Rose bowl, 6 pointed, 8" dia., x 6" tall, low ftd.
Colors: Milk glass.
Availability: Available.
Reproductions: None known.

ML-18 Bowl, rippled edge, footed, 7-1/2" dia., 4" high.
Colors: Milk glass.
Availability: Scarce.
Reproductions: None known.

ML-19 Bowl or compote, ruffled & crimped, ftd., 7-1/2".
Colors: Blue pastel, lilac mist, green mist, dark blue mist, antique green, ruby, pink pastel, lilac opalescent, purple carnival (200 made).
Availability: All colors are scarce.
Reproductions: None known.

ML-20 Basket, oval, ftd., 14", 1 handle. This is a Grossman design. An 11" basket was produced for Levay from this mold in purple carnival (only 200 were made).
Colors: 14" lilac opalescent, ruby, blue pastel, pink pastel, milk glass. 11" purple carnival (200 made).
Availability: All colors scarce, carnival is rare.
Reproductions: Black milk glass, mg.

NH-1 Line #1707 fan vase or napkin holder, ftd., 5" tall. these will be found with several different decals. This item was introduced in 1981.
Colors: Crystal mist w/china rose, black mg w/Oriental poppy, black mg plain, crystal mist w/Andrea West Country Floral, crystal mist w/Andrea West Rooster, crystal mist w/strawberry, crystal mist w/hp grape decoration, crystal mist w/Antique Fruit. All except grape design are decals.
Availability: All decals & grapes are slightly

difficult to find.
Reproductions: None known.

OD-1 Line #10 Oval duck on rimed base. The oval base measures 8" long x 6" wide. The Duck top measures 8-3/8" long beak to tail and 4-1/4" wide. Several reproductions exist. Originals are marked with a "W" with a "G" mark, most reproductions have the circular Westmoreland mark. Unmarked examples may be a product of Tiffin Glass. Tiffin produced the exact same covered duck in brown, cornsilk yellow, amber, pink, citron green, beige opal, green opal, white opal and crystal, according to Fred Bickenheuser's "Tiffin Glassmaster's Book III". Bickenheuser also states that the dimensions for this duck are 8" long, 5" high and 6" wide.
Colors: Crystal carnival (1500 made), Aurora Cobalt Blue Carnival (150 made), milk glass mist, purple marble, antique blue mist, milk glass, light blue mist, crystal mist, almond mop, milk glass w/gold rubbed feathers, antique blue, almond, dark blue mist, mint green, caramel marble, mg mop, purple marble carnival and black carnival (experimental).
Availability: Original carnival colors made for Levay are scarce, mint green, almond and antique blue are also scarce. Purple marble is very scarce. All others are very difficult.
Reproductions: Cobalt, cobalt carnival aquamarine/teal, milk glass, mg mop, cobalt & mg slag, purple slag and blue milk glass. The blue milk glass is an import via A.A. Importing Company. This is not a consistent blue color and appears very chalky. The cobalt example is usually very slimy or oily. Bubbles and other debris will be found in the glass. The cobalt carnival may not be slimy because of the carnival treatment. The underside of the duck top is usually void of a carnival treatment. This is where it will be slimy or oily. Also look for the circular "Westmoreland" marking. This mark is usually on these reproductions.

OOB-1 Line #10 Owl on 2 books. This owl is 3-1/2" tall and is usually marked with the

"W" with superimposed "G". Be aware that Degenhart also makes a similar owl, but theirs is usually marked on the bottom with a "D". All reproductions of the Westmoreland owl usually have the "WG" mark also.
Colors: Almond, antique blue, mint green, green mist, dark blue mist, yellow mist, yellow opaque, pink opaque, blue opaque, cobalt carnival, Brandywine Blue, Electric Blue Carnival (1500 made), purple marble (500 made), ruby, light blue mist, black mg mist, milk glass, apricot mist, ruby carnival (3000 made).
Availability: All are slightly difficult.
Reproductions: Black mg, cobalt, cobalt carnival, vaseline, vaseline carnival, ruby, ruby carnival, pink milk glass, pink frost, blue ice, blue ice carnival, mg mop, caprice blue, lime green, blue frost, blue, amber, milk glass, pink.

OQ-1 Juice tumbler, flat, 5 oz.
Colors: Milk glass. For Levay electric blue opalescent carnival in 1976 limited to 6,000, electric blue opalescent in 1974-1976, ruby carnival (1000 sets made).
Availability: Milk glass very difficult. Levay colors very rare.
Reproductions: None known

OQ-2 Pitcher or jug, 1 pint, 7-1/2" tall. Note the 6" plate is used under this pitcher in the batter set.
Colors: Milk glass. For Levay: Electric blue opalescent in 1976, electric blue opalescent carnival in 1974-76 limited edition of 1000, ruby carnival (1000 sets made).
Availability: Mg available, Levay colors rare.
Reproductions: None known.

OQ-3 Water goblet, footed, 8 oz.
Colors: Milk glass, Brandywine Blue, Golden Sunset, Laurel Green, crystal, crystal w/ruby stain in 1978.
Availability: Mg common, others scarce.
Reproductions: None known.

OQ-4 Sherbert, low footed.
Colors: Milk glass.

Availability: Scarce.
Reproductions: None known.

OQ-5 Wine goblet, footed, 2 oz.
Colors: Milk glass.
Availability: Scarce.
Reproductions: None known.

OQ-6 Iced tea tumbler, flat, 11 oz.
Colors: Milk glass, crystal, crystal w/ruby stain in 1978, purple marble in 1978.
Availability: Mg and crystal scarce, other colors very scarce to rare.
Reproductions: None known.

OQ-7 Cruet w/stopper, 6 oz. Older versions will have a different taller stopper.
Colors: Milk glass. For Levay: Ruby carnival in 1979-83 limited edition of 3000, crystal, crystal w/ruby stain in 1978, ruby or cerise in 1979.
Availability: Mg and crystal available, any others very scarce. Levay colors are rare.
Reproductions: None known.

OQ-8 Candlestick, 4".
Colors: Milk glass.
Availability: Available.
Reproductions: None known.

OQ-9 Water tumbler, flat, 9 oz.
Colors: Milk glass, antique blue, moss green, honey carnival. For Levay: Ice blue carnival in 1975, cobalt in 1978, cobalt carnival in 1978 limited to 150 sets, dark lime green in 1974-76 limited to 125 sets, lime green carnival limited to 125 sets, mg mop, purple slag in 1978, purple slag carnival in 1978 limited to 150 sets, ruby carnival in 1983 limited to 1000 sets, white carnival in 1979 limited to 1500 sets, electric blue opalescent carnival (6000 made), purple carnival, black carnival (experimental).
Availability: Mg available, all others scarce, Levay colors are rare.
Reproductions: Cobalt and cobalt carnival.

OQ-10 Pitcher or jug, 3 pint, 8-1/2" tall.

Colors: Milk glass, antique blue mg, honey carnival, moss green. For Levay: Ice blue carnival in 1975, purple marble in 1978, white carnival in 1979 limited to 1500 sets, cobalt carnival in 1978 limited to 150 sets, cobalt in 1978, crystal w/ruby stain in 1978, crystal, dark lime green in 1974-7 limited to 100 sets, lime green carnivel limited to 125 sets, purple slag carnival in 1978 limited to 150 sets, black carnival, ruby carnival, purple carnival.
Availability: Mg available, others scarce, Levay colors are rare.
Reproductions: Cobalt, cobalt carnival.

OQ-11 Cheese dish, w/dome lid, 4-1/2" tall.
Colors: Milk glass. For Levay: Ruby carnival in 1983 limited to 500, aquamarine, cobalt in 1978, crystal in 1978, crystal w/ruby stain in 1978, ice blue carnival in 1975, purple slag in 1978, purple slag carnival in 1978 limited to 500, ruby.
Availability: Mg available, Levay colors very scarce to rare.
Reproductions: Cobalt, cobalt carnival.

OQ-12 Relish dish, 3 part, 9", round.
Colors: Crystal, milk glass.
Availability: Both scarce.
Reproductions: None known.

OQ-13 Butter dish & cover, 1/4 lb.
Colors: Milk glass.
Availability: Slightly difficult.
Reproductions: Cobalt, cobalt carnival.

OQ-14 Mayonnaise, bell, footed, 5".
Colors: Milk glass.
Availability: Scarce.
Reproductions: Cobalt.

OQ-15 Mayonnaise, round, footed, 4-1/2".
Colors: Milk glass.
Availability: Scarce.
Reproductions: Cobalt.

OQ-16 Shakers, salt & pepper, flat.

Colors: Milk glass. Mg w/hp Forget-Me-Nots. For Levay: Ice blue carnival in 1975 and ruby carnival in 1983.
Availability: Mg common, Levay colors very scarce to rare, any hand painted examples scarce.
Reproductions: None known.

OQ-17 Oval tray, used for condiment or perfume set, 13" x 6".
Colors: Milk glass. Note even on decorated perfume sets the tray is plain.
Availability: Very scarce.
Reproductions: None known.

OQ-18 Pickle dish, oval, 10" flat.
Colors: Milk glass.
Availability: Scarce.
Reproductions: None known.

OQ-19 Sugar, open, flat, individual, 3-1/2".
Colors: Milk glass.
Availability: Slightly difficult.
Reproductions: None known.

OQ-20 Creamer, flat, individual, 3-1/2".
Colors: Milk glass.
Availability: Slightly difficult.
Reproductions: None known.

OQ-21 Syrup pitcher, flat, 3 oz., 3-1/4" tall. Note a saucer is used under this pitcher in the batter set.
Colors: Milk glass.
Availability: Rare.
Reproductions: None known.

OQ-22 Fruit cocktail bowl, footed, 3-1/2".
Colors: Milk glass.
Availability: Rare.
Reproductions: None known.

OQ-23 Bread & butter plate, 6".
Colors: Milk glass.
Availability: Very scarce.
Reproductions: None known.

OQ-24 Salad plate, 8-1/2".
Colors: Milk glass.

Availability: Very scarce.
Reproductions: None known.

OQ-25 Dinner plate, 10-1/2".
Colors: Milk glass.
Availability: Extremely rare.
Reproductions: None known.

OQ-26 Bowl or nappy, bell, footed, 5-1/2".
Colors: Milk glass.
Availability: Very scarce.
Reproductions: None known.

OQ-27 Bowl or nappy, round, footed, 4-1/2".
Colors: Milk glass.
Availability: Very scarce.
Reproductions: None known.

OQ-28 Bowl or nappy, flat, round, 8".
Colors: Milk glass.
Availability: Very scarce.
Reproductions: None known.

OQ-29 Cup, coffee or tea, flared rim, footed.
Colors: Milk glass. For Levay: Purple carnival limited to 400.
Availability: Mg very scarce, Levay colors very rare.
Reproductions: None known.

OQ-30 Bowl or nappy, round, flat, 4".
Colors: Milk glass.
Availability: Rare.
Reproductions: None known.

OQ-31 Creamer, large, 4" tall.
Colors: Milk glass, mg w/forget-me-not hand painting. For Levay: Ice Blue Carnival in 1975, ruby carnival in 1983 limited to 500, crystal w/ruby stain in 1978.
Availability: Mg common, hand painted scarce, Levay colors very scarce to rare.
Reproductions: Cobalt, cobalt carnival.

OQ-32 Sugar, open, 4" tall.
Colors: Milk glass. For Levay: Ice blue carnival in 1975, ruby carnival in 1983 limited to 500, crystal, crystal w/ruby stain in 1978.

Availability: Mg scarce, Levay colors very scarce to rare.
Reproductions: None known.

OQ-33 Bowl, round, footed, 10-1/2" dia., 4-1/2" tall.
Colors: Milk glass.
Availability: Rare.
Reproductions: None known.

OQ-34 Sugar & cover, 6-1/2" tall. Also marketed as a candy dish.
Colors: Milk glass, almond, crystal mist w/dec#32-1, mg w/dec#32, mg w/forget-me-not hand painting, mint green, pink mist, antique blue mg, dark blue mist, antique blue mist, brown mist, mg mop, antique green. For Levay: Ice blue carnival in 1975, ruby carnival in 1983 limited to 500, crystal in 1978, crystal w/ruby stain in 1978, pink.
Availability: Mg slightly difficult, hp examples scarce, Levay colors are very scarce to rare, other colors very difficult.
Reproductions: Cobalt, cobalt carnival.

OQ-35 Compote & cover, low ftd., 5" square. This item was also referred to as a covered honey.
Colors: Antique blue mist, milk glass, ruby, antique blue mg, crystal, crystal w/ruby stain in 1978, mg w/hp Forget-Me-Not.
Availability: Mg available, others are scarce.
Reproductions: Cobalt.

OQ-36 Sweetmeat & cover, high footed, 6-1/2" high.
Colors: Milk glass, Brandywine Blue, Golden Sunset, Laurel Green, crystal, crystal w/ruby stain, ruby, mg w/forget-me-not hp.
Availability: Mg available, other colors are scarce, hp is also scarce.
Reproductions: None known.

OQ-37 Perfume bottle w/stopper, flat, 5 oz. Note these were very difficult to make. A special tool was needed to press the lip of the bottle. Very few of these were produced.
Colors: Milk glass, mg w/forget-me-not.

Availability: Very scarce to rare.
Reproductions: None known.

OQ-38 Puff box & cover, footed, 4-1/2".
Colors: Crystal, milk glass, purple carnival for Levay, ruby carnival also for Levay, mg w/forget-me-not.
Availability: All very scarce to rare.
Reproductions: None known.

OQ-39 Saucer or syrup pitcher underplate.
Colors: Milk glass, purple carnival for Levay limited to 400.
Availability: Mg slightly difficult, Levay colors very rare.
Reproductions: None known.

OQ-40 Bowl, cupped, octagon ftd., 6".
Colors: Milk glass.
Availability: Slightly difficult.
Reproductions: Blue frost.

OQ-41 Box & cover, square, 3-1/2" x 5-1/2" high.
Colors: Milk glass, possibly some carnival colors, mg w/Roses & Bows, crystal.
Availability: Mg plain & dec scarce, carnival rare, crystal scarce.
Reproductions: Cobalt.

OQ-42 Punch set, consisting of 8 quart 14" dia. bell shape punch bowl, skirted pedestal, punch cups (which are not belled like the regular cups), #1800 glass ladle, red plastic punch cup hooks.
Colors: Milk glass.
Availability: Extremely rare.
Reproductions: None known.

OQ-43 Bowl, crimped, skirted ft., 9".
Colors: Milk glass.
Availability: Very scarce.
Reproductions: None known.

OQ-44 Cake salver, skirted ft, 11". Also in 12" version w/a bell foot (see OQ-49).
Colors: Milk glass, crystal.
Availability: Both versions very scarce.
Reproductions: None known.

OQ-45 Bowl, bell, skirted ft., 9".
Colors: Milk glass.
Availability: Very scarce.
Reproductions: None known.

OQ-46 Bowl, cupped, skirted ft., 7".
Colors: Milk glass.
Availability: Very scarce.
Reproductions: None known.

OQ-47 Banana bowl, skirted ft., 11".
Colors: Milk glass.
Availability: Very scarce.
Reproductions: Pink.

OQ-48 Ashtray, square, 6-1/2".
Colors: Milk glass.
Availability: Slightly difficult.
Reproductions: None known.

OQ-49 Cake salver, skirted rim, bell ft., 12".
Colors: Milk glass.
Availability: Very scarce.
Reproductions: None known.

OQ-50 Cigarette box & cover, 5" x 4".
Colors: Milk glass, mg w/forget-me-not, mg w/gold line decoration.
Availability: Mg difficult, others scarce to very scarce.
Reproductions: None known.

OQ-51 Bowl, shallow, round, skirted ft., 9".
Colors: Milk glass.
Availability: Scarce.
Reproductions: None known.

OQ-52 Ashtray, square, 4".
Colors: Milk glass, olive green, mg w/forget-me-not hp flower.
Availability: All difficult, hp versions are scarce.
Reproductions: None known.

OQ-53 Bowl, shallow, round, flat, 9", 2-1/4" high.
Colors: Milk glass.
Availability: Very scarce to rare.
Reproductions: None known.

OQ-54 Bowl, lipped, footed, 12" x 4" high.
Colors: Milk glass.
Availability: Very scarce to rare.
Reproductions: None known.

OQ-55 Bowl, flared, footed, 13".
Colors: Milk glass.
Availability: Very scarce to rare.
Reproductions: None known.

OQ-56 Vase, flat, bell top, 9" tall.
Colors: Milk glass.
Availability: Very scarce.
Reproductions: None known.

OQ-57 Bowl, round, octagon ft., 7-1/2".
Colors: Milk glass, mg w/forget-me-not, crystal.
Availability: Mg common, dec. scarce, crystal difficult.
Reproductions: Turquoise blue.

OQ-58 Fan vase, octagon ft., 9".
Colors: Milk glass, mg w/dec #32.
Availability: Mg common, dec. scarce.
Reproductions: None known.

OQ-59 Celery vase, pinched top, round ft., 6-1/2" tall.
Colors: Crystal, honey carnival, ice blue carnival for Levay in 1975, milk glass, mg w/dec#32, ruby carnival for Levay.
Availability: Mg common, all others scarce.
Reproductions: None known.

OQ-60 Vase, bell, footed, 9".
Colors: Milk glass.
Availability: Very scarce.
Reproductions: None known.

OQ-61 Jardiniere, straight sided, ftd., 6-1/2".
Colors: Milk glass.
Availability: Very scarce.
Reproductions: None known.

OQ-62 Jardiniere, cupped rim, ftd., 6-1/2".
Colors: Milk glass.

Availability: Very scarce.
Reproductions: None known.

OQ-63 Vase, swung, flat, 14" approximately.
Colors: Milk glass.
Availability: Very scarce.
Reproductions: None known.

OQ-64 Torte cake salver, bell footed, 10-5/8" diameter, 5" tall.
Colors: Milk glass.
Availability: Rare.
Reproductions: None known.

PB-1 Line #757 Pansy basket w/split handle, 4-1/2" dia., This basket was easily made and usually produced when workers worked overtime on Saturdays.
Colors: Crystal w/ruby stain, almond, mint green, milk glass, antique blue, crystal, Golden Sunset, Brandywine Blue, Laurel Green, flame, green marble, purple marble, mint green mist mg w/Roses & Bows, mg mop w/Roses & bows, mg w/pansy dec#34, almond mist, Bermuda Blue, olive green, crystal w/purple, ruby and yellow stain, mg mop plain, antique green.
Availability: Mg common, colors and decorations are very difficult to scarce.
Reproductions: None known.

PF-1 Vase, hand blown, flat, 14".
Colors: Crystal, Golden Sunset.
Availability: Both scarce.
Reproductions: None known.

PF-2 Bowl, bell, footed, 9-1/2". (Note #3 Doric candlestick bases are used.)
Colors: Crystal, Golden Sunset.
Availability: Both scarce.
Reproductions: None known.

PF-3 Banana bowl, footed, 10". (Note #3 Doric candlestick bases are used).
Colors: Crystal, Golden Sunset.
Availability: Both scarce.
Reproductions: None known.

PF-4 Bowl, crimped, footed, 10". (Note #3

Doric candlestick bases are used).
Colors: Crystal, Golden Sunset.
Availability: Both scarce.
Reproductions: None known.

PF-5 Hurricane shade, hand blown, 12".
Colors: Crystal, Golden Sunset.
Availability: Both scarce.
Reproductions: None known.

PF-6 Bowl, flat, round, 12".
Colors: Crystal, Golden Sunset.
Availability: Both scarce.
Reproductions: None known.

PF-7 Candlestick, 3". (Note a double branch version is also available.)
Colors: Crystal, Golden Sunset.
Availability: Both scarce.
Reproductions: None known.

PF-8 Bowl, grapefruit, 6-1/2" w/rim.
Colors: Crystal, Golden Sunset.
Availability: Both scarce.
Reproductions: None known.

PF-9 Bow, oval, 2 handles, 8" x 11".
Colors: Crystal, Golden Sunset.
Availability: Both very scarce.
Reproductions: None known.

PF-10 Jelly & cover, ftd. Also called a candy. Note milk glass version has pattern on inside of lid only.
Colors: crystal, milk glass, crystal w/ruby stain accents, Golden Sunset.
Availability: Golden sunset scarce, all others difficult.
Reproductions: None known.

PF-11 Snack server, 2 tier, center handled. 7-1/2" bonbon is on top & dinner plate is used for the bottom.
Colors: Crystal, Golden Sunset.
Availability: Both very scarce.
Reproductions: None known.

PF-12 Cake salver, 10", ftd. (Note #3 doric candlestick base is used).

Colors: Crystal, Golden sunset.
Availability: Both very scarce.
Reproductions: None known.

PF-13 Bon bon or bowl, crimped edge, 7-1/2".
Colors: Crystal, Golden Sunset.
Availability: Both scarce.
Reproductions: None known.

PF-14 Relish dish, 2 handled, 5 part, oval.
Colors: Crystal, Golden Sunset.
Availability: Both scarce.
Reproductions: None known.

PF-15 Bowl or nappy, round, flat, 6-1/2".
Colors: Crystal, Golden sunset.
Availability: Both very scarce.
Reproductions: None known.

PF-16 Tray, oval, 2 handled, 5" x 8-1/2". This tray is used for creamer & sugar.
Colors: Crystal, Golden sunset.
Availability: Both very scarce.
Reproductions: None known.

PF-17 Sugar, open, footed.
Colors: Crystal, Golden Sunset.
Availability: Both very difficult.
Reproductions: None known.

PF-18 Creamer, footed.
Colors: Crystal, Golden Sunset.
Availability: Both very difficult.
Reproductions: None known.

PF-19 Goblet, water, footed, 8 oz.
Colors: Crystal, Golden Sunset, Brandywine Blue, Laurel Green.
Availability: Crystal and Golden Sunset slightly difficult, others scarce.
Reproductions: None known.

PF-20 Tumbler, iced tea, flat, 12 oz.
Colors: Crystal, Golden Sunset.
Availability: Both scarce.
Reproductions: None known.

PF-21 tumbler, water, flat, 10 oz., 4-3/4" tall.
Colors: Crystal, Golden sunset. For Levay:

Purple carnival in 1980 limited to 165 sets.
Availability: All scarce to rare.
Reproductions: None known.

PF-22 Tumbler, juice, flat, 6 oz.
Colors: Crystal, Golden Sunset.
Availability: Both very scarce.
Reproductions: None known.

PF-23 Sherbert, low footed.
Colors: Crystal, Golden Sunset.
Availability: Both slightly difficult.
Reproductions: None known.

PF-24 Cup & saucer.
Colors: Crystal, Golden Sunset.
Availability: Both scarce.
Reproductions: None known.

PF-25 Salt & pepper shakers, footed.
Colors: Crystal, Golden sunset.
Availability: Both scarce.
Reproductions: None known.

PF-26 Plate, 7", dessert.
Colors: Crystal, Golden Sunset.
Availability: Both scarce.
Reproductions: None known.

PF-27 Plate, 8", salad or luncheon.
Colors: Crystal, Golden Sunset.
Availability: Both very scarce.
Reproductions: None known.

PF-28 Plate, 10-1/2", dinner.
Colors: Crystal, Golden Sunset.
Availability: Both very scarce to rare.
Reproductions: None known.

PF-29 Plate, 13", torte.
Colors: Crystal, Golden Sunset.
Availability: Both rare.
Reproductions: None known.

PF-30 Punch set, consists of belled punch bowl, punch base, 12 cups, and 1-1800 ladle.
Colors: Crystal. For Levay: Purple carnival in 1980 limited to 100 sets.
Availability: All colors very rare.
Reproductions: None known.

PF-31 Pitcher, flat, 54 oz., w/ice lip.
Colors: Crystal. For Levay: Purple carnival in 1980 limited to 165 sets.
Availability: All colors rare.
Reproductions: None known.

PF-32 Goblet, iced tea, low footed, 12 oz.
Colors: Crystal, Golden Sunset.
Availability: Scarce.
Reproductions: None known.

PF-33 Cordial, 2 oz. footed. (Shown on back cover).
Colors: Crystal, possibly others.
Availability: Very difficult to scarce.
Reproductions: None known.

PG-1 Epergne, 3 pieces, consisting of: 14" flared epergne bowl, 5" base (which is interchangeable with the punch bowl set), and 8-1/2" epergne vase, belled. Also available in 2 piece without a base.
Colors: Almond, mint green, milk glass.
Availability: Mg rare, colors extremely rare.
Reproductions: None known.

PG-2 Jardiniere, cupped rim, ftd., 5".
Colors: Milk glass, mg w/22kt gold.
Availability: Mg scarce, gold rare.
Reproductions: None known.

PG-3 Epergne, w piece, consisting of: 9" lipped bowl and 8-1/2" epergne vase.
Colors: Milk glass.
Availability: Rare.
Reproductions: None known.

PG-4 Jardiniere, cupped rim, ftd., 6-1/2".
Colors: Milk glass, mg w/22kt gold.
Availability: Mg scarce, gold rare.
Reproductions: None known.

PG-5 Canape set, consisting of: 12-1/2" canape tray, round; 3-1/2" fruit cocktail, round; Line #1837 ladle.

Colors: Milk glass.
Availability: Scarce.
Reproductions: None known.

PG-6 Epergne set, consisting of: 12" lipped bowl, 5" base (which is interchangeable with punch set), 8-1/2" epergne vase. Also available in a 2 piece version without base.
Colors: Milk glass.
Availability: Rare.
Reproductions: None known.

PG-7 Jardiniere, cupped rim, ftd, 4", also listed in catalogs as a rose bowl.
Colors: Milk glass, antique green.
Availability: Both scarce.
Reproductions: None known.

PG-8 Sauce boat with oval underliner. Underliner has an indent for the boat.
Colors: Milk glass.
Availability: Slightly difficult.
Reproductions: None known.

PG-9 Vase, bell rim, ftd., 11-1/2" tall. Also available in a straight version.
Colors: Milk glass.
Availability: Rare.
Reproductions: None known.

PG-10 Vase, bell rim, ftd., 9".
Colors: Brandywine Blue, crystal, crystal velvet, dark blue mist, Golden Sunset, Laurel Green, milk glass, mint green, almond, green mist, crystal w/ruby stain, yellow mist, mg w/Roses & Bows, black mg (experimental color for 1984), mint green mist, almond mist.
Availability: Mg very common, all other colors very difficult to scarce.
Reproductions: Black milk glass, and cobalt, usually has circular Westmoreland marking, but so does the original 1984 version.

PG-11 Vase, straight sided, ftd., 9-1/2".
Colors: Milk glass, mg w/22kt gold.
Availability: Both very scarce.
Reproductions: None known.

PG-12 Iced tea tumbler, flat, 12 oz.
Colors: Brandywine Blue, Golden Sunset, Laurel Green, milk glass, crystal, moss green, olive green.
Availability: Mg and crystal available, others scarce to very scarce.
Reproductions: Milk glass by Plum. Bottoms are not ground.

PG-13 Pitcher or jug, footed, 1 qt.
Colors: Brandywine Blue, crystal, milk glass, Golden Sunset, Laurel Green, moss green, olive green, crystal w/ruby stain. For Levay: Cobalt carnival in 1978-80 limited to 500 sets, electric blue opalescent carnival limited to 200 sets, blue opalescent in 1974-76 limited to 200 sets, lilac opalescent in 1982 limited to 500 sets, lilac opalescent carnival in 1982, lime green carnival in 1978 (250 sets made), ruby carnival in 1979-80 limited to 400 sets, Aurora Cobalt Blue Carnival (50 sets made in 1981), purple slag carnival (150 sets made), and ruby or cerese.
Availability: Mg available, crystal slightly difficult, others scarce. Levay colors very scarce to rare.
Reproductions: None known.

PG-14 Water goblet, ftd., 8 oz.
Colors: Crystal, milk glass, Laurel Green, Brandywine Blue, Golden Sunset, moss green, olive green, crystal w/ruby stain.
Availability: Mg common, crystal available, others scarce.
Reproductions: None known.

PG-15 Sherbert, low footed.
Colors: Milk glass, Brandywine Blue, Golden Sunset, Laurel Green, crystal, moss green, olive green.
Availability: Mg scarce, others very scarce to rare.
Reproductions: None known.

PG-16 Cocktail goblet, ftd., 3 oz.
Colors: Milk glass.
Availability: Very scarce.
Reproductions: None known.

PG-17 Wine goblet, ftd., 2 oz. Also made into a cigarette lighter.
Colors: Crystal, milk glass, Golden Sunset. For Levay: Lime green carnival in 1977-78 limited to 100 sets. Lighters in mg only.
Availability: Lighters very scarce. Mg and crystal wines available, other scarce. Levay colors very rare.
Reproductions: Milk glass by Plum.

PG-18 Parfait, scallop ftd. This was the first item Westmoreland produced in paneled grape.
Colors: Crystal, milk glass.
Availability: Several of these were made in mg but are still difficult to find as are the crystal versions.
Reproductions: None known.

PG-19 Old Fashioned tumbler, flat, 6 oz.
Colors: Crystal, milk glass, Golden sunset, moss green, olive green.
Availability: Crystal available, mg very difficult, Golden Sunset scarce.
Reproductions: None known.

PG-20 Candlestick, skirted bottom, 4".
Colors: Mg, Brandywine Blue, almond, cry w/ruby stain, cry velvet, Golden Sunset, Laurel Green, mg w/dec#32, mg mop w/pastel painted fruit, mg w/22kt gold, mint gr, mg mop.
Availability: Mg very common, other colors scarce to very scarce, decorated very scarce.
Reproductions: None known.

PG-21 Bowl or nappy, bell rim, ftd., 5".
Colors: Milk glass.
Availability: Scarce.
Reproductions: Blue with opalescent edges, possibly others.

PG-22 Bowl or nappy, round, 4-1/2".
Colors: Milk glass, mint green, black mg.
Availability: Mg scarce, mint green and black mg are rare.
Reproductions: Possibly black mg, since this is made out of the same mold as the puff box. Also blue with opalescent edges.

PG-23 Bowl or nappy, round, 1 handle, 5".
Colors: Milk glass.
Availability: Slightly difficult.
Reproductions: None known.

PG-24 Sugar, open, footed, 4-1/4" tall.
Colors: Milk glass.
Availability: Available.
Reproductions: None known.

PG-25 Creamer, footed, 6-1/2 oz.
Colors: Milk glass.
Availability: Slightly difficult.
Reproductions: Mg w/green & gold hp.

PG-26 Candy jar & cover, low ftd., 6-1/2" tall. Also used as a covered sugar.
Colors: Mg, cry w/ruby stain, bl mist w/daisy, br mist w/daisy, gr mist w/daisy, mg w/dec#32, mg w/22kt gold, yl mist w/daisy, mg mop w/pastel hp fruit, mg w/bl wedding bells.
Availability: Mg difficult, daisy decal slightly difficult, dec#32 scarce, crystal w/ruby accent, and 22kt gold scarce.
Reproductions: None known.

PG-27 Compote & cover, footed, 7".
Colors: Brandywine Blue, Golden Sunset, Laurel green, mg, mg mop, mg w/pansy dec. mg w/22 kt gold, mg w/roses and bows.
Availability: Mg difficult, other colors scarce to rare, decorated extremely scarce.
Reproductions: None known.

PG-28 Shaker, salt & pepper, ftd., 4-1/4" tall.
Colors: Milk glass, crystal, Brandywine Blue, Laurel Green, Golden Sunset, black milk glass, crystal velvet.
Availability: Mg common, crystal available, other colors very scarce to rare.
Reproductions: Black milk glass.

PG-29 Cruet, flat w/stopper, 2 oz.
Colors: Lt amber, cry, mg, Bermuda Blue, electric bl opalescent carnival (in 1978, 1000 made), electric bl opalescent, Brandywine Blue.
Availability: Mg available, crystal difficult, others scarce.
Reproductions: None known.

PG-30 Juice tumbler, flat, 5 oz.

Colors: Crystal, milk glass, purple carnival (500 sets made), black carnival (experimental), purple (300 sets made).
Availability: Mg and crystal scarce, carnival colors are very scarce to rare.
Reproductions: None known.

PG-31 Pitcher or jug, ftd., juice, 1 pt.
Colors: Milk glass, crystal. For Levay: Purple carnival limited to 500 sets, black carnival (experimental), purple (300 sets made).
Availability: Mg and crystal available, Levay colors very scarce to rare.
Reproductions: None known.

PG-32 Appetizer set, consisting of: 9" 3 part relish dish, round fruit cocktail, and Line#1837 ladle. Also marketed with the relish alone.
Colors: Crystal and milk glass.
Availability: Mg slightly difficult in a complete set, crystal difficult.
Reproductions: None known.

PG-33 Bowl or nappy, shallow, round, 9" dia., 2" high.
Colors: Milk glass.
Availability: Scarce to extremely scarce.
Reproductions: None known.

PG-34 Jelly & cover, also known as puff box, 4-1/2".
Colors: Crystal velvet, milk glass, mg w/dec#32, crystal mist w/dec#32-1, green marble, purple marble, mg w/Christmas holly decoration, black milk glass, mg w/22kt gold, mint green, almond.
Availability: Mg common, other colors difficult, dec#32 available, other decorations scarce.
Reproductions: Black milk glass.

PG-35 Chocolate box & cover, round, 6-1/2".
Colors: Milk glass.
Availability: Scarce.
Reproductions: None known.

PG-36 Cheese dish & cover, 7", round.
Colors: Milk glass, crystal velvet. For Levay:

Aquamarine, cobalt in 1978, purple slag in 1978, purple slag carnival in 1978 limited to 500, ruby, vaseline.
Availability: Mg slightly difficult, crystal velvet scarce. Levay colors very scarce to rare.
Reproductions: Cobalt, cobalt carnival.

PG-37 Vase, bell rim, scallop ftd., 6". Note this is made from the same mold as the parfait.
Colors: Milk glass, brown marble, mg w/dec#32, dec#32 w/Mother of Pearl, plain Mother of Pearl, purple marble, mg w/pastel painted fruit, green marble, almond mist, mint green mist, crystal velvet, almond, mint green.
Availability: Mg common, other colors difficult, mg w/dec#32 available, other decorations scarce.
Reproductions: None known.

PG-38 Sherbert, high footed.
Colors: Milk glass.
Availability: Scarce.
Reproductions: None known

PG-39 Fruit cocktail, bell rim, ftd., 4-1/2".
Colors: Milk glass.
Availability: Scarce.
Reproductions: None known.

PG-40 Fruit Cocktail, round, ftd., 3-1/2". This item is used in the appetizer set as well as the 3 piece mayo set.
Colors: Milk glass, crystal.
Availability: Mg available, crystal difficult.
Reproductions: None known.

PG-41 Mayonnaise set, consisting of: fruit cocktail, round, 3-1/2", saucer, Line #1837 ladle.
Colors: Milk glass and crystal as a set.
Availability: Slightly difficult in a set.
Reproductions: None known.

PG-42 Jardiniere, footed, straight sides, 5". Note several companies made poor copies of this piece, only colors below are Westmoreland.

Colors: Milk glass, mint green, yellow mist w/daisy, dark blue mist w/daisy, green mist w/daisy.
Availability: Mg available, mint green and decorated examples are scarce.
Reproductions: Several flashed on colors on crystal are found.

PG-43 Jardiniere, footed, straight sided, 6-1/2".
Colors: Milk glass, mg w/22kt gold.
Availability: Mg available, gold rare.
Reproductions: None known.

PG-44 Candleholder, colonial, 1 handle, 5".
Colors: Milk glass.
Availability: Slightly difficult.
Reproductions: None known.

PG-45 Sugar or spooner, lacy edge, footed with lid. Also marketed as a toothbrush caddy in mist colors with a daisy decal.
Colors: Milk glass, mg w/22kt gold, moss green.
Availability: Mg difficult, 22kt. gold and moss green scarce.
Reproductions: Mg w/green and gold hp.

PG-46 Bowl, lipped, bell ftd., 9".
Colors: Milk glass, Brandywine Blue, Laurel Green, Golden Sunset.
Availability: Mg difficult, colors very scarce.
Reproductions: None known.

PG-47 Banana bowl, bell ftd., 12".
Colors: Milk glass. For Levay: Electric blue carnival in 1978 limited to 300.
Availability: Milk glass is scarce to rare. Electric blue carnival very rare.
Reproductions: None known.

PG-48 Bowl, bell rim, bell ftd., 9-1/2".
Colors: Milk glass.
Availability: Scarce.
Reproductions: None known.

PG-49 Bowl or nut dish, oval, 6" to 6-1/2".
Colors: Crystal, crystal velvet, milk glass.
Availability: Mg available, others scarce.

Reproductions: None known.

PG-50 Mayonnaise, bell rim, stem footed, 4".
Colors: Milk glass, mg w/pastel painted fruit.
Availability: Both scarce.
Reproductions: None known.

PG-51 Vase, bud, swung, flat, 18" approx.
Colors: Milk glass.
Availability: Scarce.
Reproductions: None known.

PG-52 Vase, bud, swung, flat, 16" approx.
Colors: Milk glass.
Availability: Scarce.
Reproductions: None known.

PG-53 Vase, bud, swung, flat, 14" approx.
Colors: Milk glass, mg w/dec#32.
Availability: Mg common, dec#32 difficult.
Reproductions: None known.

PG-54 Planter, square, 4-1/2".
Colors: Milk glass, mg w/22kt gold.
Availability: Mg scarce, gold rare.
Reproductions: None known.

PG-55 Planter, oblong, 5" x 9".
Colors: Milk glass, mg w/22kt gold, mg w/Roses & Bows, yellow mist, dark blue mist, green mist.
Availability: Mg available, gold rare, mist colors very difficult.
Reproductions: None known.

PG-56 Planter, window, oblong, 3" x 8-1/2".
Colors: Milk glass, green mist, mint green, yellow mist, mg w/22kt gold, dark blue mist, antique green.
Availability: Mg available, other colors difficult, gold rare.
Reproductions: None known.

PG-57 Bowl, shallow, skirted ft., 9" 6" high. .
Colors: Milk glass.
Availability: Scarce.
Reproductions: None known.

PG-58 Bowl, oblong, 12" x 6-1/2", 3-1/8" high.

This bowl was originally marketed as a herb planter, but this did not help its sales, and it was not produced in any large quantity.
Colors: Milk glass.
Availability: Extremely rare.
Reproductions: None known.

PG-59 Cake salver, skirted rim, bell ftd., 11", 4-3/4" high. Also may be found with a skirted foot.
Colors: Milk glass.
Availability: Common. this was a very popular piece and many were made.
Reproductions: None known.

PG-60 Bowl or nappy, round, shallow, 7".
Colors: Milk glass.
Availability: Scarce.
Reproductions: None known.

PG-61 Bowl, bell rim, ftd., 9-1/2".
Colors: Milk glass.
Availability: Extremely scarce.
Reproductions: None known.

PG-62 Bowl, round, footed, 8-1/2".
Colors: Milk glass.
Availability: Extremely scarce.
Reproductions: None known.

PG-63 Cake salver, pattern around top rim of plate, skirted foot, 10", 4-1/2" high. Another version is 10-1/2" with a low vertical ribbed base. The pattern on this version is on the top also.
Colors: Milk glass.
Availability: Extremely scarce.
Reproductions: None known.

PG-64 Bowl, cupped rim, footed, 8".
Colors: Milk glass, mg w/22kt gold, mg mop, mg mop w/pastel hp fruit, black mg.
Availability: Mg available, all others scarce.
Reproductions: None known.

PG-65 Bowl, lipped rim, footed, 9".
Colors: Milk glass, Brandywine Blue, Laurel Green, Golden Sunset, crystal velvet, mg mop, crystal w/ruby stain.

Availability: Mg available, colors very scarce.
Reproductions: None known.

PG-66 Salad plate, depressed center, 7".
Colors: Milk glass.
Availability: Extremely rare.
Reproductions: None known.

PG-67 Bowl or nappy, bell rim, flat, 10".
Colors: Milk glass.
Availability: Extremely rare.
Reproductions: None known.

PG-68 Vase, bud, swung, flat, 10" approx.
Colors: Milk glass, mg w/dec#32, mint green, antique green.
Availability: Mg & dec#32 available, other colors slightly difficult.
Reproductions: None known.

PG-69 Note this is showing that the punch base or epergne base may be used on just about any type of large bowl. Most bowls had a collar on the bottom which will fit the base. See epergne sets for color and availability.

PG-70 Bowl, shallow, round, flat, 14".
Colors: Milk glass.
Availability: Extremely rare.
Reproductions: None known.

PG-71 Plate, torte, 14-1/2".
Colors: Milk glass, crystal, mg w/Christmas bouquet & holly, mg w/Bicentennial decorations.
Availability: Mg rare, crystal very scarce, decorated examples are rare.
Reproducitons: None known.

PG-72 Vase, hand blown, once referred to as a pickle jar vase, flat, 12".
Colors: Milk glass, crystal.
Availability: Both are rare.
Reproductions: None known.

PG-73 Bowl & cover, footed, 9".

Colors: Milk glass.
Availability: Scarce.
Reproductions: None known.

PG-74 Compote, lipped or ruffled rim, footed, 9". This may also be found in a crimped & ruffled version see PG-133.
Colors: Milk glass.
Availability: Scarce.
Reproductions: None known.

PG-75 Perfume or toilet bottle w/stopper, flat, 5 oz.
Colors: Milk glass, mg w/dec#32, mg w/pastel painted fruit, mg w/22kt gold.
Availability: Mg scarce, decorated rare.
Reproducitons: None known.

PG-76 Tray for dresser set, oval, 13-1/2".
Colors: Milk glass, mg w/dec#32, mg w/22 kt gold.
Availability: Mg extremely scarce, mg w/dec#32 or 22 kt gold is rare.
Reproductions: None known.

PG-77 Tray or platter, oval, 9". Also used for condiment tray.
Colors: Milk glass.
Availability: Rare.
Reproductions: None known.

PG-78 Celery vase, footed, 6". Rim may be belled or straight or crimped.
Colors: Milk glass.
Availability: Slightly difficult.
Reproductions: Scalloped rim in turquoise blue, and cobalt blue.

PG-79 Plate, bread & butter, 6".
Colors: Milk glass.
Availability: Scarce.
Reproductions: None known.

PG-80 Plate, salad or luncheon, 8-1/2".
Colors: Milk glass, Brandywine Blue, Laurel Green, Golden Sunset, mint green, crystal, milk glass w/4 different hp flowers, birds or fruits.
Availability: Mg slightly difficult, mint green

rare, others extremely scarce.
Reproductions: None known.

PG-81 Plate, dinner, 10-1/2".
Colors: Milk glass, some may have bicentennial decorations as well as other decorations, mint green.
Availability: Mg extremely scarce, any decorated plates rare, colors are also rare.
Reproductions: Have found poor quality plates with an off white color without ground bottoms but none of the companies currently reproducing items have this plate listed.

PG-82 Bowl, bell, footed, 12-1/2".
Colors: Milk glass.
Availability: Extremely scarce.
Reproductions: None known.

PG-83 Bowl, round, footed, 10-1/2".
Colors: Milk glass, mg w/22 kt gold.
Availability: Both very scarce.
Reproductions: None known.

PG-84 Bowl or nappy, belled, flat, 8".
Colors: Milk glass.
Availability: Rare.
Reproductions: None known.

PG-85 Punch set, consists of: 13" belled 8 qt. punch bowl, skirted pedestal, punch cup (regular cup is belled punch cup is not)), line #1800 ladle. Also in 11" round bowl version.
Colors: Milk glass, mg w/22kt gold dec., crystal.
Availability: Mg rare, gold extremely rare, crystal rare. Note watch for cracked punch bowls. Westmoreland had great difficulty in making these. They tended to crack and even shatter when ice cold punch was placed in them.
Reproductions: Stiegel blue opalescent by Fenton. This new punch set has a lipped and flared bowl.

PG-86 Basket, oval, split handle, 6-1/2".
Colors: Amber, brown marble, crystal velvet,

mg w/dec#32, dark blue mist, green mist, milk glass, purple marble, Bermuda Blue, yellow mist, mg w/22kt gold, mg mop w/pastel hp fruit, crystal w/ruby stain, mg mop, green marble, crystal mist w/Roses & Bows, black mg, Brandywine Blue.
Availability: Mg common, dec#32 available, others slightly difficult to scarce.
Reproductions: None known.

PG-87 Cup, flared for tea or coffee, ftd.
Colors: Milk glass, Brandywine Blue, Golden Sunset, Laurel Green.
Availability: Mg available, others rare.
Reproductions: None known.

PG-88 Saucer, also used for mayonnaise liner, and fruit cocktail liner.
Colors: Milk glass, Brandywine Blue, Golden Sunset, Laurel Green, crystal.
Availability: Mg available, others rare.
Reproductions: None known.

PG-89 Butter dish & cover, 1/4 lb.
Colors: Milk glass, Golden Sunset, crystal mist w/China Rose, crystal mist w/Antique Fruit, crystal mist w/Floral Spray, crystal mist w/strawberry, crystal mist w/Andrea West Rooster, crystal mist w/Andrea West Country Floral, crystal velvet, and vaseline for Levay in 1979-1980 limited to 500.
Availability: Mg available, Golden Sunset and vaseline rare, decal examples very difficult.
Reproductions: None known.

PG-90 Candelabra, triple branch, skirted.
Colors: Milk glass.
Availability: Rare.
Reproductions: None known.

PG-91 Creamer, individual, ftd.
Colors: Milk glass, Brandywine Blue, Golden Sunset, Laurel Green, crystal, crystal w/ruby stain, mg w/Roses & Bows.
Availability: Mg common, others rare.
Reproductions: None known.

PG-92 Sugar, individual, ftd., Marketed with or without a lid.
Colors: Milk glass, Brandywine Blue, Golden Sunset, Laurel Green, crystal, crystal w/ruby stain, mg w/Roses & Bows.
Availability: Mg common-with lid slightly difficult, others rare.
Reproductions: None known.

PG-93 Soap tray, oblong, 2 handled, 6-3/4" x 5" wide.
Colors: Milk glass, mg w/dec#32.
Availability: Both extremely scarce.
Reproductions: None known.

PG-95 Candleholder, arc shaped, 2 lite. Need 4 of these to make a circle.
Colors: Milk glass.
Availability: Extremely scarce.
Reproductions: None known.

PG-96A Canister, footed w/lid, 11-1/2" tall x 6-3/4" diameter. This is the largest of the canisters and is sometimes referred to as the cookie or cracker jar.
Colors: Milk glass, green marble, purple marble. For Levay the large sized canister was marketed as a cracker jar and produced in vaseline carnival in 1979.
Availability: All colors extremely rare. These did not sell well perhaps because they did not seal out moisture. They were not made in any large quantity or for any extended length of time.
Reproductions: None known.

PG-96B Canister w/lid, 10" tall x 5-3/4" diameter. This is the middle sized canister.
Colors: Milk glass, green marble, purple marble.
Availability: All colors extremely rare. See notes on PG-96A.
Reproductions: None known.

PG-96C Canister w/lid, 7-1/2" tall x 4-1/2" diameter. This is the smallest canister and was usually referred to as a covered jar.
Colors: Milk glass, green marble, purple marble.

Availability: All colors extremely rare. See notes on PG-96A.
Reproductions: None known.

PG-97 Bowl, crimped rim, footed, 6".
Colors: Milk glass, Brandywine Blue, Laurel Green, Golden Sunset.
Availability: Mg slightly difficult, colors very scarce.
Reproductions: None known.

PG-98 Ivy ball vase, ftd., cupped rim. Note this and PG-97 are made from the same mold with different treatments after molding.
Colors: Milk glass.
Availability: Difficult.
Reproductions: None known.

PG-99 Compote, ruffled rim, footed, 6" tall x 4-1/2" diameter.
Colors: Milk glass, Brandywine Blue, Golden Sunset, Laurel Green, mg w/pansy dec#34.
Availability: Mg difficult, others rare.
Reproductions: None known.

PG-100 This is an unfinished version of PG-99. The foot and the bowl were obviously pressed separately and the stemmed foot would be applied at a later time. This item is more of a novelty than an item which could be easily collected. Other examples may be found but would be rare.

PG-101 Shaker, flat. These shakers appear to have been blown from the cruet mold without the handle or spout. These are 4-1/2" tall.
Colors: Milk glass, mg w/holly decoration.
Availability: Mg scarce, any decoration would be considered rare.
Reproductions: None known.

PG-102 Shot glass, toothpick or child's tumbler, flat, 2-1/4" tall. This item was used with PG-135 and marketed as a child's pitcher set for Levay in very limited edition colors.
Colors: Milk glass. For Levay: Lime green carnival in 1977-78 limited to 500 sets, red

carnival in 1982, turquoise carnival (300 sets made), purple carnival, emerald green carnival.
Availability: Mg slightly difficult. Levay colors very scarce to rare.
Reproductions: None known.

PG-103 Candy dish & cover, 3 ftd.
Colors: Milk glass, crystal w/ruby stain, almond, mg w/dec#32, mg w/pansy dec#34, mg w/22kt gold, crystal velvet, ruby.
Availability: Mg available, crystal w/ruby difficult, almond scarce, others with decorations scarce.
Reproductions: None known.

PG-104 Candy dish open, ruffled rim, 3 ftd. Note this is made from the same mold as the bottom of PG-103. May also be found in a crimped and ruffled rim.
Colors: Mg, antique blue mg.
Availability: Mg available, colors may be difficult.
Reproductions: None known.

PG-105 Deviled Egg tray, center handled, 12", also a 10" version available.
Colors: Milk glass, crystal.
Availability: Mg scarce, crystal scarce.
Reproductions: None known.

PG-106 Pickle dish, oval.
Colors: Milk glass.
Availability: Slightly difficult.
Reproductions: None known.

PG-107 Bowl, round, crimped rim, 4". This bowl is available in a larger size also (see PG-129).
Colors: Milk glass.
Availability: Scarce.
Reproductions: None known.

PG-109 Bowl, oval, lipped ftd.
Colors: Almond, mint green, milk glass, crystal w/ruby stain, crystal.
Availability: Mg available, colors or decorations are scarce.
Reproductions: None known.

PG-110 Vase, swung, flat, 15" tall approx. Height varies.
Colors: Milk glass, almond, mint green.
Availability: Mg scarce, colors rare.
Reproductions: Mg w/green & gold hp.

PG-111 Snack server, center handled, 2 tier. Top tier is an 8-1/2" plate, bottom is 10-1/2" dinner plate.
Colors: Almond, mint green, milk glass, crystal velvet, mg w/poinsettia dec., crystal w/ruby stain.
Availability: All scarce.
Reproductions: None known.

PG-112 Basket, nut, 1 handle, crimped rim 5-1/2" diameter.
Colors: Milk glass, almond, mint green, honey amber carnival, ice blue carnival, antique blue mist, dark blue mist, brown mist, green mist, mg mop w/Roses & Bows, mint green mist, almond mist, mg w/Roses & Bows, yellow mist, mg mop, pink mist, antique blue mg, pink pastel.
Availability: Mg difficult, colors very difficult to scarce.
Reproductions: Blue ice carnival, black mg, milk glass, cobalt, black mg w/22kt gold, blue frost, Bermuda Blue, and Stiegel blue opalescent with a reeded handle by Fenton.

PG-113 Candy, 3 footed, crimped & ruffled.
Colors: Milk glass, almond, mint green, almond w/Almond Rose, antique blue mist, dark blue mist, brown mist, green mist, mg w/Roses & Bows, crystal velvet, yellow mist, pink mist, crystal w/ruby stain, mg mop, mg mop w/Roses & Bows, almond w/Dogwood, almond w/Floral Spray, almond mist, mint green mist, amber, brown marble, green marble, honey amber carnival, ice blue carnival, purple marble, antique blue mg, Bermuda Blue, Brandywine Blue.
Availability: Mg available, colors very difficult, hand decorated scarce.
Reproductions: None known.

PG-114 Candy, open, ruffled & crimped, ftd., 4" tall, 6-3/8" diameter.

Colors: Brandywine Blue, antique blue mist, milk glass, dark blue mist, purple marble, green marble, brown marble, green mist, ice blue carnival, honey amber carnival, mg w/Roses & Bows, crystal velvet, yellow mist, pink mist, mg mop w/pastel hp fruit, mg mop, Bermuda Blue, amber.
Availability: Mg available, colors scarce.
Reproductions: None known.

PG-115 Bowl, ruffled & crimped rim, shallow.
Colors: Lilac opalescent.
Availability: Lilac opal available.
Reproductions: None known.

PG-116 Tumbler, water, 8 oz. flat, 4-1/4" tall.
Colors: Milk glass, crystal, mg w/22kt gold.
For Levay: Lilac opalescent carnival (in 1982), lime green carnival (250 sets made), purple carnival, ruby carnival (400 sets made), electric blue opalescent carnival (1000 sets made), electric blue opalescent (100 sets made), aurora cobalt blue carnival (300 sets made in 1981), purple slag carnival (150 sets made), lilac opalescent (500 sets made in 1982).
Availability: Mg and crystal available, all carnival colors and decorated examples are rare.
Reproductions: Summit Art Glass makes a similar tumbler in a light blue carnival. The difference is that this tumbler has a wide rim above the arched panels and the original stops at the arches. These are usually marked with a "V" in a circle.

PG-117 Bowl, ftd., ruffled rim, 6".
Colors: Milk glass, Brandywine Blue, Golden Sunset, Laurel Green, mg w/22kt gold, mg w/Roses & Bows, crystal w/ruby stain.
Availability: Mg available, Brandywine Blue, Laurel Green and Golden Sunset, and 22kt gold very scarce, others difficult.
Reproductions: None known.

PG-118 Basket, 8" tall.
Colors: Milk glass, mg w/dec#32, Brandywine Blue, Golden Sunset, Laurel Green, red carnival (500 made), black carnival (experi-

mental), smoke carnival (factory error), purple carnival, lime green carnival, electric blue carnival, mg w/22kt gold, ice blue carnival, electric blue opalescent (200 made), electric blue opalescent carnival (500 made).
Availability: Mg scarce, any decorated or carnival examples are rare, other colors are very scarce.
Reproductions: None known.

PG-119 Cake salver, 12" dia. flat top, pattern is on the underside of the top. Foot may be belled or skirted.
Colors: Milk glass, Brandywine Blue, Golden Sunset, Laurel Green.
Availability: All very scarce.
Reproductions: None known.

PG-120 Bud vase, scallop ftd., height may vary, pattern is only on bottom of vase, a band between pattern and plain part of vase may not appear on some of these vases.
Colors: Milk glass, Brandywine Blue, Laurel Green, Golden sunset, mg w/22kt gold.
Availability: Mg available, colors and decorated very scarce.
Reproductions: None known.

PG-121 Tid bit tray, center handled, 8", crimped and ruffled.
Colors: Lilac opalescent, crystal mist w/China Rose, crystal mist w/Andrea West Rooster, crystal mist w/Andrea West Country Floral, crystal mist w/wedding bells, mg mop w/Roses & Bows, mg w/Roses & Bows, mg mop, crystal mist w/hp grapes, crystal mist w/strawberry, pink mist, ruby, milk glass, pink pastel, blue pastel.
Availability: Lilac opalescent very difficult, others scarce.
Reproductions: None known.

PG-125 Decanter, flat w/stopper. Decatners were usually matched with the PG-17 wine goblet.
Colors: Crystal, milk glass, Golden Sunset, lime green carnival (1977,100 sets made).

Availability: Mg and crystal very scarce, other colors are rare.
Reproductions: None known.

PG-129 Bon bon, round, 7" dia. low, cupped and crimped rim. See PG-107 for smaller version.
Colors: Mg, crystal w/ruby stain, and crystal.
Availability: Both difficult.
Reproductions: None known.

PG-132 Wall pocket vase, 8" diameter.
Colors: Milk glass, mg w/green and gold hp.
Availability: All are rare.
Reproductions: None known.

PG-133 Bowl or compote, square, 9", square footed. This mold was created at great expense to Westmoreland for the 1967 catalog. With all of the other types of covered compotes, this one did not sell well at all and was produced for a very short time.
Colors: Milk glass.
Availability: Rare.
Reproductions: None known.

PG-134 Bowl or compote, stem ftd., crimped and ruffled. 8-1/2" dia. x 6-1/4" tall.
Colors: Crystal w/ruby stain, mg, mint green or antique green.
Availability: Mg difficult, mint green available, others extremely difficult.
Reproductions: None known.

PG-135 Creamer, 8 oz. ftd. Also marketed as a child's pitcher with PG-102 posing as the child's tumblers.
Colors: Mg, mg w/22kt gold, purple carnival, lime green carnival (500 sets made), ruby carnival, turquoise carnival (300 sets made), Emerald Green Carnival.
Availability: Mg available, decorated scarce, all carnival colors made for Levay are very scarce to rare.
Reproductions: Milk glass w/green and gold hp decoration.

PG-136 Basket, oval, footed, crimped rim.
Colors: Milk glass, possibly others.

Availability: Rare.
Reproductions: None known.

PG-137 Vase, bell, flower pot, flat. See back cover for photo.
Colors: Milk glass.
Availability: Scarce.
Reproductions: None known.

PK-1 Line #6 Peacock creamer, ftd., w/lid, 5" tall. Note example does not show a lid, but the sugar and creamer lid are interchangeable.
Colors: Brandywine Blue Opalescent (for A.A.Importing according to Bob Rupp), milk glass, purple carnival (900 sets made), ruby or cerese, ruby carnival (2000 sets made).
Availability: Mg difficult, other colors very scarce to rare.
Reproductions: None known.

PK-2 Line #6 Peacock sugar, ftd., w/lid, 5" tall. Sugar and creamer lids are interchangeable. The sugar bottom was also made into a rose bowl by cupping the rim.
Colors: Brandywine Blue opalescent (for A.A.Importing according to Bob Rupp), milk glass, purple carnival (900 sets made), ruby or cerese, ruby carnival (2000 made).
Availability: All scarce.
Reproductions: None known.

PL-1 Line #1902 tumbler, flat. This tumbler was produced during the last year of production in black. During my visit to the factory there were several pallets of these tumblers, however they were never shown in a catalog in this color and never made it to retail sales.
Colors: Black milk glass, milk glass, milk glass w/dec#32, mg w/bicentennial decal, dark blue mist w/daisy, green mist w/daisy, crystal mist w/China Rose, crystal mist w/Floral Spray, milk glass w/teddy bears, dogs, squirrels or elephants (these were made to go with the Beaded Edge child's set), pink mist w/daisy, light blue mist w/daisy.

Availability: All scarce with decorated tumblers being very scarce to rare.
Reproductions: None known.

PL-3 Line #1902 soap dish. This items was also manufactured in 1984 in black. This too was not shown in any catalogs or shown to the retail trade in black milk glass.
Colors: Black milk glass, milk glass, mg w/dec#32, dark blue mist w/daisy, green mist w/daisy, crystal mist w/China rose, yellow mist w/daisy, lilac mist w/daisy, brown mist w/daisy, light blue mist w/daisy, pink mist w/daisy, crystal mist w/butterfly.
Availability: All colors very difficult, decorated pieces scarce.
Reproductions: None known.

PL-4 Line #1707 salt & pepper shaker. These were produced in the 1950's and were made to go with any type of pattern.
Colors: Black milk glass, milk glass.
Availability: Both scarce.
Reproductions: None known.

PL-5 Line #700 Water goblet, ftd., 8 oz. This pattern as well as PL-4 through PL-8 did not sell well in the mid-west area. This pattern only sold well in California and New York City, so it may be found more frequently in those areas.
Colors: Black milk glass.
Availability: Scarce.
Reproductions: None known.

PL-6 Line #1802 salad plate, 7-1/2". This pattern was made to intermix with other patterns. See notes in PL-5.
Colors: Black milk glass, black mg w/hp golden peacocks, gold & blue flowers, or gold sheaf of wheat.
Availability: Plain examples are scarce, decorated examples are rare.
Reproductions: None known.

PL-7 Line #1801 Bread & butter plate, 6". This pattern was made to intermix with other patterns. See notes in PL-5.
Colors: Black milk glass.

Availability: Scarce.
Reproductions: None known.

PL-8 Line #1802 dinner plate, 10-1/2". This pattern was made to intermix with other patterns. See notes in PL-5. These plates will also be found with several different scenes from the Bible. These were marketed as Christmas plates and are usually dated with the year. The plates are hand painted in gold.
Colors: Black milk glass, black mg w/Christmas Nativity scenes in gold, black mg w/gold sheaf of wheat, gold peacock or blue & gold flowers, mg w/black m Gregory Deer.
Availability: Black mg scarce, Christmas and decorated versions are rare.
Reproductions: None known.

PL-9 Line #1800 cup & saucer. The cup in this picture was used for the Beaded Edge pattern (also see BE-6) and will be found in those colors and decorations as well as those below.
Colors: Milk glass, black milk glass.
Availability: Black mg scarce, see BE-6 for others.
Reproductions: None known.

PL-10 Line #700 sherbert, footed.
Colors: Black milk glass.
Availability: Scarce.
Reproductions: None known.

PT-1 Peacock tail & daisy plate, scalloped rim, 9-1/2" diameter. Most examples found today are those which were produced for Levay in very limited editions.
Colors: Red carnival (1000 made), black carnival (experimental), amethyst opalescent carnival (25 made).
Availability: All colors are rare, with amethyst opal carnival very rare.
Reproductions: None known.

RB-1 Line #7 Robin on twig nest, 6-1/4" tall footed.
Colors: Apricot mist, dark blue mist, light blue mist, Brandywine Blue, pink mist,

crystal mist, green mist, ruby, ruby carnival (1979, 2000 made), milk glass, mint green, almond, pink carnival (160 made), turquoise carnival, vaseline, purple marble, mg mop, Golden sunset, olive green, Bermuda blue, antique blue, antique blue mist, yellow mist, caramel marble, white carnival, black carnival (experimental), pink.
Availability: Mg available, others scarce, Levay colors rare.
Reproductions: Cobalt, milk glass, mg mop.

RB-2 Line #7/1 Robin, solid glass.
Colors: Crystal, ruby, dark blue mist, green mist, antique blue, almond, pink mist, antique blue mist.
Availability: All slightly difficult.
Reproductions: Cobalt.

RB-5 Rabbit on oval vertical rib base, 5-1/2" long.
Colors: Red carnival (1000 made), black carnival (experimental), milk glass.
Availability: Carnival colors are scarce, mg difficult.
Reproductions: Mg w/hp, mg bottom w/ topaz top, milk glass, cobalt, cobalt carnival, mg mop w/hp, mg mop, sky blue, black milk glass, rubina, crystal & orchid, blue milk glass, vaseline, vaseline carnival.

RH-1 Ring holder, made from the stem of a goblet, possibly from Thousand Eye Line #1000.
Colors: Crystal.
Availability: Very difficult.
Reproductions: A similar ring holder is shown in a 1982-83 L.E.Smith catalog in crystal mist w/red hp rose or blue hp forget-me-nots.

RL-1 Vase, footed, 2 handled, ruffled or plain rim.
Colors: Milk glass, mg w/rose dec#33, Golden sunset, crystal w/ruby stain.
Availability: Mg difficult, dec rare, colors scarce.
Reproductions: Cobalt, pink frost.

RL-2 Bowl, oval, crimped rim.
Colors: Milk glass, mg w/rose dec#33.
Availability: Mg difficult, dec. rare.
Reproductions: None known.

RL-3 Candy w/lid, footed.
Colors: Milk glass, mg w/rose dec#33, crystal w/ruby stain. For Levay: pink carnival in 1978 limited to 500.
Availability: Mg very scarce, crystal w/ruby very scarce, dec. rare, Levay colors very rare.
Reproductions: Cobalt, mg plain and with roses hp with dark orange colors.

RL-4 Basket, oval, plain rim.
Colors: Milk glass, Golden Sunset.
Availability: Mg very scarce, colors rare.
Reproductions: A round version of this basket has also been reproduced in milk glass, black mg w/22kt gold. A square version has been reproduced in pink. Oval reproductions are in pink frost.

RL-5 Bowl, oval, plain rim.
Colors: Milk glass.
Availability: Very scarce.
Reproductions: Round bowls are being reproduced in pink with a plain rim.

RL-6 Vase, decanter style, ruffled rim.
Colors: Milk glass, crystal w/ruby stain.
Availability: Mg scarce, crystal w/ruby rare.
Reproductions: None known.

RL-7 Basket, oval, crimped rim.
Colors: Milk glass, green mist, yellow mist, dark blue mist, brown mist, lilac mist, Bermuda Blue, Brandywine Blue.
Availability: Mg very scarce, colors rare.
Reproductions: None known.

RL-8 Bowl, crimped & ruffled, round.
Colors: Golden Sunset, mg w/rose dec#33, milk glass, crystal w/ruby stain, Bermuda Blue.
Availability: All scarce.
Reproductions: Round plain rim versions are appearing in pink.

RL-9 Candlestick, shaped like a rose blossom.
Colors: Milk glass, mg w/rose dec#33, Golden Sunset.
Availability: All scarce.
Reproductions: Pink frost.

RO-3 Line #2 Rooster on oval 5-1/2" vertical rib base.
Colors: Milk glass, mg w/hp accents, ruby slag carnival (500 made), black carnival (experimental), ruby carnival (1000 made), Aurora cobalt blue carnival (1000 made), purple slag carnival (500 made), purple marble.
Availability: Mg & mg w/hp available, all carnival is rare.
Reproductions: Blue milk glass, cobalt carnival, milk glass, mg mop, topaz, mg w/hp, cobalt, blue ice, Bermuda Blue, mg mop w/hp, cobalt slag, purple slag, vaseline, vaseline carnival. These repros may have the circular "Westmoreland" mark according to the "Towne Crier Newsletter".

RP-1 Bowl, squared, low ftd., 7" dia. x 5" high.
Colors: Milk glass.
Availability: Slightly difficult.
Reproductions: None known.

RP-2 Plate, 8" with depressed center.
Colors: Milk glass, may be found with hand painted parakeet decorations.
Availability: Mg available, decorations difficult.
Reproductions: None known.

RP-3 Bowl, round, low ftd., 8-1/2" dia. x 4-1/2" high.
Colors: Milk glass.
Availability: Available.
Reproductions: None known.

RP-4 Candlestick, 3-1/2". Often used as a base on footed items.
Colors: amber, antique blue mist, apricot mist, light blue mist, dark blue mist, brown mist, almond, green mist, lilac mist, mint green, mint green mist, moss green, yellow

mist, almond mist, pink mist, milk glass, Golden Sunset, Bermuda Blue, olive green.
Availability: Mg common, lilac mist, apricot mist, yellow mist, mint green and almond are scarce. Others difficult.
Reproductions: Stiegel blue opalescent by Fenton.

RP-5 Bowl, square, flat, 11" dia. x 3" high.
Colors: Milk glass.
Availability: Very difficult.
Reproductions: None known.

RP-6 Bowl, flared, low ftd., 10" dia. x 4-3/4" high.
Colors: Milk glass, mint green, almond, Golden Sunset, apricot mist, green mist, dark blue mist, Brandywine Blue, Laurel Green, brown mist, yellow mist, light blue mist, amber, moss green, pink mist, antique blue mist, lilac mist, mint green mist.
Availability: Mg available, colors very difficult to scarce.
Reproductions: Stiegel blue opalescent by Fenton.

RP-7 Cake salver, low footed, 12" dia. x 1-3/4" high. Ribbed foot.
Colors: Milk glass.
Availability: Very scarce. The high footed cake salver is much easier to find.
Reproductions: Stiegel blue opalescent by Fenton.

RP-8 Bowl, crimped, low ftd., 10" dia. x 4-3/4" high.
Colors: Milk glass.
Availability: Scarce.
Reproductions: None known.

RP-9 Banana bowl, high footed, 14" dia. x 9-1/2" high.
Colors: Milk glass. For Levay: Lilac opalescent in 1982 limited to 500.
Availability: Both difficult to scarce.
Reproductions: Cobalt.

RP-10 Cake salver, square, high footed, 11" x 4-1/2" high.

Colors: Milk glass, Brandywine Blue opalescent. For Levay: Lilac opalescent in 1982 limited to 500.
Availability: Mg difficult, colors rare.
Reproductions: None known.

RP-11 Spooner or open sugar, 4-3/8" high.
Colors: Milk glass.
Availability: Difficult.
Reproductions: Cranberry ice, cobalt.

RP-12 Bowl & cover, oval, 6" high. This is also referred to as a butter dish.
Colors: Milk glass.
Availability: Scarce.
Reproductions: Cobalt, cranberry ice.

RP-13 Creamer, 9-1/2 oz.
Colors: Milk glass.
Availability: Difficult.
Reproductions: Cranberry ice, cobalt.

RP-14 Sugar w/lid, 6-1/2" high.
Colors: Milk glass.
Availability: Difficult.
Reproductions: Cranberry ice, cobalt.

RP-15 Bowl, cupped rim, low footed, 7" dia. x 4-3/4" high.
Colors: Milk glass.
Availability: Difficult.
Reproductions: None known.

RP-16 Bowl, bell, low ftd., 12" diameter.
Colors: Milk glass, almond, mint green, Golden Sunset, Laurel Green brown mist, Brandywine Blue, antique blue mist, lilac mist, almond mist, pink mist, amber, moss green, apricot mist, light blue mist, dark blue mist, yellow mist, green mist, Bermuda Blue, olive green, mint green mist.
Availability: Mg available, colors are more difficult to find.
Reproductions: None known.

RP-17 Banana bowl, low footed.
Colors: Milk glass.
Availability: Scarce.
Reproductions: None known.

RV-1 Line #1 mini revolver. This is solid glass. An older version from the depression era will be all crystal with a black fired on color on the grips.
Colors: Crystal, crystal w/black fired on grips, black milk glass.
Availability: Crystal & crystal w/black rare, black mg very scarce.
Reproductions: None known.

RWS-1 Line #1873 Raised wing covered swan. Marketed with an oblong lacy rim base, 6" x 9-1/2" long.
Colors: Black milk glass, milk glass, purple marble, light blue mist, pink mist, ice blue carnival. For Levay: Cobalt carnival (500 made), turquoise carnival, pink carnival (a Levay brochure states that this was experimental, and an ad states that less than 25 complete swans exist), emerald green carnival.
Availability: Pink carnival rare, black mg rare, mg difficult, others scarce to rare.
Reproductions: None known.

SB-1 Vase, footed, belled rim. May be plain or crimped rim, 9-1/2" tall.
Colors: Milk glass, dark blue mist, crystal, Golden Sunset, green marble, green mist, lilac, lilac mist, purple marble, and Brandywine Blue.
Availability: Mg and marbles available, lilac & lilac mist rare, others may be scarce.
Reproductions: None known.

SB-2 Bowl, bell, flat, 10".
Colors: Crystal.
Availability: Very scarce.
Reproductions: None known.

SB-3 Plate, torte, 13".
Colors: Crystal.
Availability: Very scarce.
Reproductions: None known.

SB-4 Bowl or nappy, bell, 6" flat.
Colors: Crystal.

Availability: Scarce.
Reproductions: None known.

SB-5 Bowl, round, 4" flat.
Colors: Crystal.
Availability: Scarce.
Reproductions: None known.

SB-6 Bowl, round, 7" flat.
Colors: Crystal.
Availability: Scarce.
Reproductions: None known.

SB-7 Sugar, open, footed.
Colors: Crystal.
Availability: Scarce.
Reproductions: None known.

SB-8 Creamer, footed.
Colors: Crystal.
Availability: Scarce.
Reproductions: None known.

SB-9 Cup & saucer.
Colors: Crystal.
Availability: Scarce.
Reproductions: None known.

SB-10 Plate, bread & butter, 6".
Colors: Crystal.
Availability: Very difficult.
Reproductions: None known.

SB-11 Tumbler, water, flat, straight rim 8 oz., 4" tall.
Colors: Crystal. For Levay: Ruby/cerise in 1979, ruby carnival in 1979 limited to 1500 sets, purple carnival in 1977-78 limited to 200 sets.
Availability: Crystal very scarce, Levay colors very rare.
Reproductions: None known.

SB-12 Pitcher, flat, 3 pints.
Colors: Crystal. For Levay: Ruby/cerise in 1979, ruby carnival in 1979 limited to 1500 sets, purple carnival in 1977-78 limited to 200 sets.
Availability: Crystal very scarce, Levay

colors very rare.
Reproductions: None known.

SB-13 Comport, turned edge, footed, 7-1/2".
Colors: Crystal.
Availability: Very scarce.
Reproductions: None known.

SB-14 Candlestick, 4".
Colors: Crystal.
Availability: Very difficult.
Reproductions: None known.

SB-15 Basket, round handled, 7".
Colors: Crystal.
Availability: Very scarce.
Reproductions: None known.

SB-16 Candy jar & lid, cone shape, 1/2 lb., 7" tall, ftd.
Colors: Dark blue mist, crystal, Golden Sunset, green marble, green mist, lilac, lilac mist, milk glass, purple marble, Brandywine Blue, crystal w/ruby stain.
Availability: Mg common, marbles slightly difficult, lilac & lilac mist rare, others scarce.
Reproductions: None known.

SB-17 Fan vase or napkin holder, ftd., 6".
Colors: Crystal, Golden sunset.
Availability: Both very scarce.
Reproductions: None known.

SB-18 Tumber, flat, belled rim, 8 oz. See SB-11 for straight rim version.
Colors: Crystal.
Availability: Very scarce.
Reproductions: None known.

SB-19 Goblet, water, 8 oz., footed.
Colors: Brandywine Blue, crystal, Laurel Green, Golden Sunset.
Availability: Crystal scarce, others rare.
Reproductions: None known.

SB-20 Goblet, iced tea, 12 oz. footed.
Colors: Crystal.
Availability: Very scarce.
Reproductions: None known.

SB-21 Cocktail, 3 oz., footed.
Colors: Crystal.
Availability: Very scarce.
Reproductions: None known.

SB-22 Sherbert, low footed.
Colors: Crystal.
Availability: Scarce.
Reproductions: None known.

SB-23 Mayonnaise bowl, footed.
Colors: Crystal, crystal w/ruby stain.
Availability: Both scarce.
Reproductions: None known.

SB-24 Bowl, turned edge, 11", very shallow.
Colors: Crystal.
Availability: Scarce.
Reproductions: None known.

SB-25 Cake salver, 9", footed, 5" tall.
Colors: Crystal.
Availability: Very scarce.
Reproductions: None known.

SB-26 Nappy, heart shaped, 1 handle, 5".
Colors: Crystal.
Availability: Scarce.
Reproductions: None known.

SB-27 Bowl or nappy, belled rim, 1 handle, 6".
Colors: Crystal.
Availability: Scarce.
Reproductions: None known.

SB-28 Basket, triangular handle, 7".
Colors: Crystal.
Availability: Very scarce.
Reproductions: None known.

SB-29 Candelabra, 2 lite. A triple branch version was also produced.
Colors: Crystal.
Availability: Very scarce.
Reproductions: None known.

SB-30 Compote & cover, footed, 6-1/2".
Colors: Crystal, crystal w/ruby accent.

Availability: Crystal available, crystal w/ruby accent very scarce.
Reproductions: None known.

SB-31 Bowl, cupped, 7-1/2".
Colors: Crystal.
Availability: Scarce.
Reproductions: None known.

SB-32 Plate, 7" salad. (Also available in 8",9",10" and 18".)
Colors: Crystal.
Availability: All sizes scarce.
Reproductions: None known.

SB-33 Bowl, round edge, 9-1/2".
Colors: Crystal.
Availability: Scarce.
Reproductions: None known.

SB-34 Vase, flared rim, footed, 8-1/2".
Colors: Crystal.
Availability: Scarce.
Reproductions: None known.

SB-35 Cruet w/stopper.
Colors: Crystal.
Availability: Rare.
Reproductions: None known.

SB-36 Decanter & stopper.
Colors: Crystal.
Availability: Rare.
Reproductions: None known.

SB-37 Comport, rolled edge, footed.
Colors: Crystal.
Availability: Very scarce.
Reproductions: None known.

SB-38 Banana bowl, footed.
Colors: Crystal.
Availability: Very scarce.
Reproductions: None known.

SB-39 Cake salver, candlestick footed.
Colors: Crystal.
Availability: Very scarce.
Reproductions: None known.

SB-40 Mayonnaise set, consists of 7" plate, 6" bell bowl, and #1800 ladle.
Colors: Crystal.
Availability: Very scarce.
Reproductions: None known.

SB-41 Ashtray, square, small.
Colors: Lilac mist, lilac, Brandywine Blue, green mist, dark blue mist, green marble, purple marble.
Availability: Colors scarce.
Reproductions: None known.

SB-42 Compote, open, stem footed.
Colors: Crystal, crystal w/ruby stain.
Availability: Both scarce.
Reproductions: None known.

SB-43 Basket, split handled, round 5" dia., flat.
Colors: Crystal, crystal w/ruby, blue and yellow stain, Golden Sunset.
Availability: Crystal and golden sunset very difficult, stain examples are scarce.
Reproductions: None known.

SF-1 Line #1063 Starfish shaped candlestick. These were marketed with all of the dolphin items, but seem to be less available than the dolphin items.
Colors: Crystal mist, almond, milk glass, mg w/mop, antique blue, antique blue mist.
Availability: All colors scarce.
Reproductions: None known.

SH-1 Line #1 Shell nut dish or bon bon, 6", 3 footed. This piece would look great with fancy soaps also.
Colors: Milk glass, mg w/dec#32, crystal mist, antique blue, almond, antique blue mist, mg w/Christmas dec, mg mop, antique green.
Availability: Mg common, dec#32 difficult, colors difficult to scarce.
Reproductions: Cobalt.

SJ-1 Line #1813 Straw Jar and cover. The bottom of this piece looks like an old wooden bucket with two metal straps holding the

wood planks together. The lid to this piece is the same lid which fits the #1701 Trinket box (TB-1). The straw jar was only produced from 1979 through 1981. Although it will be found plain, it will most often have either a decal or a hand painted decoration.
Colors: Antique blue w/Beaded Bouquet, mint green w/Beaded Bouquet, almond w/Beaded Bouquet, crystal mist w/China rose, black milk glass w/Oriental poppy, brown mist w/daisy decal, crystal.
Availability: All are scarce.
Reproductions: None known.

SP-1 Line #1933 Spiral candlesticks, square base. There are two sizes 7" (which may vary from 6" to more than 7") and 4-1/2". The smaller version is extremely scarce and was produced in milk glass and possibly black.
Colors: 7" almond, mint green, milk glass, black milk glass, Golden Sunset, lilac, purple marble, green marble, brown marble, dark blue mist, green mist, mint green mist, Brandywine Blue, yellow mist, almond mist, mg mop.
Availability: 7" mg available, colors are difficult. 4" are scarce.
Reproductions: None known.

SP-2 Line #1820 Spade coaster/ashtray. This belongs to a set with all four card suits. (See CL-2, DI-1, & HP-2 for others.) Most often these were sold in sets of four different colors.
Colors: Black milk glass, yellow mist, green mist, dark blue mist.
Availability: All colors difficult.
Reproductions: None known.

SR-1 Line #6 Standing Rooster, 2 pc., 8-1/2" tall.
Colors: Brandywine Blue, Laurel Green, Golden Sunset, mg, mg w/hp accents, mg w/Minorca hp (realistic hp feathers), black mg, black mg w/hp accents, antique blue, almond w/hp accents, purple marble, antique blue w/mg head, crystal.
Availability: Mg & mg hp available, Minorca decoration is scarce, other colors very scarce.

Reproductions: Mg mop w/hp feathers, blue milk glass, milk glass, mg mop, topaz, cobalt, black mg, mg mop w/hp accents, cranberry ice, purple slag, light pink, Rhode Island Red (an amberina), cobalt carnival, rootbeer (a brown), Bermuda Blue, cobalt w/hp accents.

SR-2 Line #1891 Spoke & Rim candlestick, 3-1/2" tall.
Colors: Milk glass, mg w/gold accents, black milk glass.
Availability: All colors very scarce.
Reproductions: None known.

SR-3 Line #1891 Spoke & Rim bowl, flared rim, footed. Also available in a flattened rim 10" version.
Colors: Milk glass, mg w/flower decoration, black milk glass, black milk glass w/flower decoration.
Availability: Mg available, all other colors and decorations very scarce.
Reproductions: None known.

ST-1 Compote & cover, footed, 6-1/2". Also will be found in an 8" version.
Colors: 6-1/2": Milk glass, ruby. 8" Golden Sunset, mg.
Availability: Either size is slightly difficult, colors will be difficult.
Reproductions: None known.

ST-2 Covered dish, flat, 6-1/2" dia. x 5" high. The bottom of this candy was sold without the lid as a bowl, but only in milk glass.
Colors: Amber, green marble, lilac, moss green, purple marble, Brandywine Blue, milk glass, Golden Sunset, antique green. For Levay: Aquamarine, ice blue carnival in 1975 and ruby.
Availability: Mg difficult, lilac and marble colors very scarce, others scarce. Levay colors very scarce.
Reproductions: None known.

ST-3 Candlestick, 4-1/2" used as a base on all footed items, as well as a few other patterns. This candlestick is very similar to the Ashburton candlestick (AB-9).

Colors: Milk glass. These were made in other colors when used as bases but there are no references that different colors exist in candlesticks.
Availability: Rare.
Reproductions: None known.

ST-4 Bowl & cover, footed, 9" dia. x 14" tall. Also made into a lamp. (For more information see the Sawtooth explanation in the pattern section of book one). This was affectionately called the "Grandfather's bowl" by the employees who produced it, according to Bob Rupp. The reason for this moniker is that Ira Brainard liked this piece and he was J.H. Brainard's grandfather. Also a 15" tall version was produced.
Colors: Milk glass, Golden Sunset, Brandywine Blue, Laurel Green, mint green, moss green, almond, crystal, olive green, Bermuda Blue, ice blue carnival in 1975, antique green. For Levay: Pink carnival in 1981 only 40 were produced.
Availability: Mg available, Golden Sunset scarce, rare in lamp form, Pink carnival was limited to 40 pieces and hence is very rare. All other colors very scarce.
Reproductions: None known.

ST-5 Banana bowl, footed, 14".
Colors: Milk glass, Golden Sunset and Grossman made a 9-1/2" version in ruby.
Availability: Mg and Golden Sunset are very scarce, ruby scarce.
Reproductions: None known.

ST-6 Cake salver, footed, 14" dia.
Colors: Milk glass, Golden Sunset, Grossman made a 9-1/2" ruby version.
Availability: Mg & Golden Sunset very scarce, ruby scarce.
Reproductions: None known.

ST-7 Bowl, flared, footed, 12". Size may vary.
Colors: Brandywine Blue, Laurel Green, Golden Sunset, milk glass, moss green, Bermuda Blue, olive green, Grossman made a 7" version in ruby.

Availability: Mg available, all colors scarce to rare.
Reproductions: None known.

ST-8 Cake stand, plain plate surface w/candlestick base.
Colors: Crystal.
Availability: Scarce.
Reproductions: None known.

SW-1 Swan vase, flat, w/3 swan necks around the bottom of the vase, 6-1/2" tall. Line #115.
Colors: Milk glass, antique blue milk, lilac opalescent, electric blue opalescent, electric blue opalescent carnival (500 made).
Availability: Mg available, others scarce.
Reproductions: Cobalt, and amberina or ruby.

SW-2 Swan toothpick or cigarette holder.
Colors: Milk glass, antique blue milk, purple marble, lilac opalescent, ice blue carnival, turquoise carnival in 1980, Golden Sunset.
Availability: Mg available, others slightly difficult.
Reproductions: Milk glass, cobalt, pink, cobalt carnival, sapphire blue, sky blue, ruby, ruby carnival, green carnival, amethyst, black milk glass, blue milk glass.

SW-4 Swan on basketweave base, 5-1/2" long. This swan will also be found on a ribbed base. This swan may have an open or closed space where the neck bends in. The closed neck version in considered rarer.
Colors: Milk glass, red carnival (1000 made), black carnival (experimental), caramel marble carnival.
Availability: Mg w/open neck extremely difficult, carnival colors are rare.
Reproductions: Vaseline, vaseline carnival, blue mg, aquamarine/teal, milk glass, cobalt carnival, cobalt, purple slag. Repros may have no markings or a circular "Westmoreland" mark.

TE-1 Plate, dinner 10". Other plates available in 6", 7", 8-1/2", 14" & 18".

Colors: Crystal, crystal w/stain accents.
Availability: Crystal very difficult, stain colors rare.
Reproductions: None known.

TE-2 Salt & Pepper shaker, footed.
Colors: Crystal, crystal w/stain accents.
Availability: Both scarce.
Reproductions: None known.

TE-3 Goblet, water, 9 oz. footed.
Colors: Crystal, crystal w/stain.
Availability: Crystal available, stain colors very scarce.
Reproductions: None known.

TE-4 Goblet, cocktail, 3-1/2 oz. ftd.
Colors: Crystal.
Availability: Scarce.
Reproductions: None known.

TE-5 Cup & saucer. Cups may be flat or footed. Footed version shown on back cover.
Colors: Crystal, crystal w/stain accents.
Availability: Both scarce.
Reproductions: None known.

TE-6 Candlestick, 5".
Colors: Crystal, crystal w/stain accents.
Availability: Crystal available, stain slightly difficult.
Reproductions: None known.

TE-7 Relish set, 1-10", 6 part tray, 1 footed mayonnaise bowl footed, 1-1800 ladle.
Colors: Crystal.
Availability: Very scarce.
Reproductions: None known.

TE-8 Bowl, oblong, crimped, 12" long x 9-1/2" wide.
Colors: Crystal, crystal w/stain accents.
Availability: Both slightly difficult.
Reproductions: None known.

TE-9 Tumbler, iced tea, footed, 12 oz.
Colors: Crystal.
Availability: Slightly difficult.
Reproductions: None known.

TE-10 Parfait, footed.
Colors: Crystal.
Availability: Scarce.
Reproductions: None known.

TE-11 Bowl, belled, 11" dia. x 4" tall, footed.
Colors: Crystal.
Availability: Scarce.
Reproductions: None known.

TE-12 Sugar, footed, open, 5-3/4" tall.
Colors: Crystal, crystal w/stain accents.
Availability: Crystal scarce, stain very scarce.
Reproductions: None known.

TE-13 Creamer, footed, 6-1/4" tall.
Colors: Crystal, crystal w/stain accents.
Availability: Crystal scarce, stain very scarce.
Reproductions: None known.

TE-14 Compote, belled, 5-1/4" dia. x 5-3/8" tall, footed.
Colors: Crystal, crystal w/stain accents.
Availability: Both scarce to very scarce.
Reproductions: None known.

TE-15 Mint compote, flat top, ftd., 4" tall x 6-5/8" dia.
Colors: Crystal, crystal w/stain accents.
Availability: Both scarce.
Reproductions: None known.

TE-16 Bon bon, belled, 1 handle, 7-3/4" dia.
Colors: Crystal, crystal w/stain.
Availability: Both scarce.
Reproductions: None known.

TE-17 Creamer, flat. In the 1970's this item was marketed with a whiskey (TE-24) and sold as a child's pitcher set. This was made for Levay Distributing Co.
Colors: Crystal, crystal w/stain, ruby, ruby carnival (500 sets made).
Availability: Crystal & crystal w/stain scarce, any carnival colors rare.
Reproductions: None known.

TE-18 Sugar, open, flat.
Colors: Crystal, crystal w/stain accents.

Availability: Both scarce.
Reproductions: None known

TE-19 Turtle ashtray.
Colors: Crystal, crystal w/stain, Golden sunset, black milk glass, milk glass, moss green.
Availability: Crystal and crystal w/stain available, Golden Sunset difficult, black mg scarce.
Reproductions: Milk glass, cobalt, sky blue.

TE-20 Turtle cigarette box w/lid. Also used as a candy or mint.
Colors: Crystal, crystal w/stain, Golden Sunset, black milk glass, milk glass, moss green.
Availability: Crystal and crystal w/stain available, Golden Sunset and moss green difficult, black milk glass scarce.
Reproductions: cobalt, orange, milk glass, milk glass mop.

TE-21 Candlestick, these actually belong to line #1067 called "Three Ball." these were most often paired with either Thousand Eye or Della Robbia. Older depression era versions will have a wide base under the three balls.
Colors: Black milk glass, crystal, crystal w/stain accents, Golden Sunset, amber, Bermuda Blue, and Laurel Green.
Availability: Crystal, crystal w/stain & Golden Sunset are available, black mg scarce, other colors are scarce.
Reproductions: None known.

TE-22 Bonbon or covered sugar.
Colors: Purple marble, green marble.
Availability: Marbles are scarce.
Reproductions: None known.

TE-24 Shot glass or child's tumbler, 1-1/2 oz. These were marketed with the TE-17 flat creamer as a child's pitcher set. These were produced in very limited quantities for Levay.
Colors: red carnival (500 sets made), crystal.

Availability: Red carnival rare, crystal scarce.
Reproductions: None known.

VTB-1 Line #275 Victorian Trinket Box, small, square, 4 footed w/lid.
Colors: dark blue mist, green mist, lilac mist, antique blue mist w/Beaded Bouquet, crystal with ruby stain w/Ruby Floral, ruby w/Ruby Floral, mg mop w/Roses & Bows, crystal mist w/Roses & Bows, mg w/Roses & Bows, mg w/red hearts, Roses & bows, crystal mist w/Floral Spray, almond w/Floral Spray, dark blue mist w/Floral Bouquet, brown mist w/Floral Bouquet, crystal mist w/Floral Bouquet, crystal mist w/dogwood, mint green w/dogwood, pink mist w/dogwood, brown mist w/daisy, yellow mist w/daisy, lilac mist w/daisy, green mist w/daisy, dark blue mist w/daisy, crystal mist w/China Rose, mg w/blue Beaded Bouquet, mint green w/Beaded Bouquet, antique blue w/Beaded Bouquet, almond w/Almond Rose, ruby w/white cameo, crystal with ruby stain w/white cameo, pink mist w/white cameo, mg w/purple Beaded Bouquet, almond w/Beaded Bouquet, mg mop, mg mop w/pastel flowers, ruby w/Mary Gregory style, ruby w/Snow flower, mg, almond w/dogwood.
Availability: Colors difficult, decorated examples very difficult to scarce. Be sure to watch the beading on the sides of the bottom of the box. Quite often these have been chipped. Also pay close attention to the condition of the feet.
Reproductions: Cobalt, cobalt w/hp and sky blue, cobalt w/Shirley Temple, Tom Mix or Hopalong Cassidy decals. Others may exist.

WB-1 Wedding bowl & cover, 8".
Colors: Milk glass, mg w/dec#32, crystal w/ruby stain, mg w/purple Beaded Bouquet, milk glass w/gold grapes & leaves, mg w/China Rose.
Availability: Mg common, dec#32 available, ruby stain difficult, all others scarce.
Reproductions: None known.

WB-2 Wedding bowl & cover, 10".

Colors: Crystal mist w/dec#32-1, crystal w/ruby stain & hp rose floral, crystal w/ruby stain, mg w/blue wedding bells, mg w/China rose decal, mg w/dec#32, mg w/gold grapes & leaves, mg w/gold roses & bows, mg w/silver bells anniv., mg w/gold bells anniv., mg w/strawberry decal, milk glass, mg mop w/Roses & Bows, mg w/purple Beaded Bouquet.
Availability: Mg common, dec#32 available, ruby stain difficult, anniversary very difficult, all others very scarce to rare.
Reproductions: Treasured Editions Ltd. owns the rights to this piece but any productions will be hand painted and signed with the dates after the demise of Westmoreland. Very easily recognized.

WB-3 Candlestick, 4-1/2".
Colors: Crystal w/ruby stain, mg w/dec#32, mg w/gold grapes & leaves, milk glass.
Availability: All scarce with decorated items being very scarce.
Reproductions: None known.

WB-4 Box & cover, 6" low footed.
Colors: Milk glass, mg w/dec#32, mg w/gold grapes & leaves.
Availability: All items rare. This box was not preferred by customers due to the lack of height. Not produced for any extensive time.
Reproductions: None known.

WF-1 Sugar, footed, open.
Colors: Crystal.
Availability: Scarce.
Reproductions: None known.

WF-2 Creamer, footed.
Colors: Crystal.
Availability: Scarce.
Reproductions: None known.

WF-3 Finger bowl, 4" footed. This piece was later ruffled at the rim & called a candy (WF-35). It was also the base for the fairy lamp (WF-38).
Colors: Crystal.

Availability: Very scarce.
Reproductions: None known.

WF-4 Compote, bell, low footed, 5". This piece was later crimped and called a sweetmeat, or mint.
Colors: Crystal, crystal w/ruby stain.
Availability: Both very scarce.
Reproductions: None known.

WF-5 Cordial, 1 oz., footed.
Colors: Crystal, crystal w/ruby stain.
Availability: Very scarce.
Reproductions: None known.

WF-6 Goblet, wine, 2 oz. footed.
Colors: crystal, crystal w/ruby stain.
Availability: Both scarce.
Reproductions: None known.

WF-7 Goblet, cocktail, 3-1/2oz., footed.
Colors: Crystal.
Availability: Difficult.
Reproductions: None known.

WF-8 sherbert, low footed.
Colors: Crystal, crystal w/ruby stain.
Availability: Both scarce.
Reproductions: None known.

WF-9 goblet, champagne, belled, high footed.
Colors: Crystal.
Availability: Scarce.
Reproductions: None known.

WF-10 Sherbert, high footed.
Colors: Crystal.
Availability: Scarce.
Reproductions: None known.

WF-11 Tumbler, water, 8 oz. footed.
Colors: Crystal.
Availability: Scarce.
Reproductions: None known.

WF-12 Goblet, water, 10 oz. footed.
Colors: Crystal, crystal w/ruby stain, Golden Sunset, Brandywine Blue, Laurel Green.

Availability: Crystal & stain difficult, others rare.
Reproductions: None known.

WF-13 Tumbler, iced tea, 12-1/2oz., footed. Later made into a vase with a crimped top rim.
Colors: Crystal, crystal w/ruby stain.
Availability: Both scarce.
Reproductions: None known.

WF-14 Plate, 6". Used as a finger bowl liner for flat finger bowl or bread & butter plate.
Colors: Crystal.
Availability: Very scarce.
Reproductions: None known.

WF-15 Finger bowl, flat, round.
Colors: Crystal.
Availability: Very scarce.
Reproductions: None known.

WF-16 Bowl or nappy, cupped rim, flat, 6".
Colors: Crystal, crystal w/ruby stain.
Availability: Stain is more available than plain crystal, both difficult.
Reproductions: None known.

WF-17 Celery bowl, oblong, 12".
Colors: Crystal.
Availability: Rare.
Reproductions: None known.

WF-18 Bon bon, cupped, 1 handled, 6".
Colors: Crystal.
Availability: Difficult.
Reproductions: None known.

WF-19 Mint compote, flat top, high footed, 5-1/2".
Colors: Crystal, crystal w/ruby stain.
Availability: Stain more available than crystal, both difficult.
Reproductions: None known.

WF-20 Compote, bell, 7" footed. May also be found crimped (WF-28), crimped & ruffled (WF-32) and round (WF-21).

Colors: Crystal, crystal w/ruby stain.
Availability: Both are available.
Reproductions: None known.

WF-21 Compote, rounded, 6", footed.
Colors: Crystal.
Availability: Scarce.
Reproductions: None known.

WF-22 Bowl, bell, 12" footed. May also be found lipped, crimped and was also flattened to make a cake salver.
Colors: Crystal, crystal w/ruby stain.
Availability: Both scarce.
Reproductions: None known.

WF-23 Bowl, bell, 12" flat. May be found ruffled, lipped or crimped.
Colors: Crystal, crystal w/ruby stain.
Availability: Scarce.
Reproductions: None known.

WF-24 Candlestick, 6".
Colors: Crystal, crystal w/ruby stain.
Availability: Both scarce.
Reproductions: None known.

WF-25 Bowl, round, 10" flat.
Colors: Crystal.
Availability: Scarce.
Reproductions: None known.

WF-26 Plate, luncheon, 8-1/2". Also found with a center handle with either plain rim or crimped rim.
Colors: Crystal, crystal w/ruby stain.
Availability: Scarce.
Reproductions: None known.

WF-27 Plate, torte, 14".
Colors: crystal, crystal w/ruby stain.
Availability: Both very scarce.
Reproductions: None known.

WF-28 Compote, crimped rim, footed, 7".
Colors: Crystal, Brandywine Blue, Laurel Green, Golden Sunset.
Availability: Crystal common, colors rare.
Reproductions: None known.

WF-29 Bowl, lipped rim, 11-1/2" flat.
Colors: Crystal, crystal w/ruby stain.
Availability: Both are difficult.
Reproductions: None known.

WF-30 Cake salver, 12" low footed.
Colors: Crystal, crystal w/ruby stain.
Availability: Both are difficult.
Reproductions: None known.

WF-31 Candy crimped, high footed. This candy was made from the water goblet.
Colors: Crystal w/ruby stain.
Availability: Slightly difficult.
Reproductions: None known.

WF-32 Compote, crimped and ruffled, high footed.
Colors: Crystal w/ruby stain.
Availability: Slightly difficult.
Reproductions: None known.

WF-33 Vase, crimped rim, footed. This vase was made from the iced tea goblet.
Colors: Crystal w/ruby stain.
Availability: Slightly difficult.
Reproductions: None known.

WF-34 Mint compote, crimped rim, high footed.
Colors: Crystal w/ruby stain.
Availability: Slightly difficult.
Reproductions: None known.

WF-35 Candy, open, crimped, low footed. This candy was made from the finger bowl (WF-3).
Colors: Crystal w/ruby stain.
Availability: Slightly difficult.
Reproductions: None known.

WF-36 Heart shaped bon bon, 1 handle, 8", flat. These were also produced in a 6" version.
Colors: Crystal w/ruby stain.
Availability: 8" and 6" are scarce.
Reproductions: None known.

WF-37 Compote, lipped rim, footed.
Colors: Crystal w/ruby stain.

Availability: Slightly difficult.
Reproductions: None known.

WF-38 Fairy Lite, 2 pieces, footed. These originally came with a crystal candle cup which sat inside the base to hold the candle. These were marketed to try to compete with Fenton's fairy lamps.
Colors: Crystal w/ruby stain, crystal, light blue mist w/hp flowers, yellow mist w/hp flowers, lime green carnival, honey amber carnival, ice blue carnival, Brandywine Blue carnival, ruby, almond w/hp flowers, mint green w/hp flowers, antique blue w/hp flowers, brown mist w/hp flowers, crystal mist w/Roses & Bows, dark blue mist w/hp flowers, antique gold, violet, silver, crystal w/green stain, crystal w/blue stain, pink mist w/hp flowers, green mist w/hp flowers.
Availability: Mint green, almond & antique blue are scarce, crystal w/ruby stain is available, all others range from extremely difficult to scarce.
Reproductions: L.E.Smith has owned this mold since 1985 according to Bob Rupp. In their 1985 catalog these fairy lites are shown in pink, crystal, ice blue and light amber or yellow.

WH-1 Line #1882 Westward Ho water goblet, 8 oz. footed.
Colors: Brandywine Blue, Golden Sunset, Laurel Green, milk glass, purple carnival in 1979 signed "Gateway Carnival Glass Club."
Availability: All very scarce.
Reproductions: Blue ice, cobalt, crystal, blue ice carnival, cobalt carnival.

WI-1 Line #100 winged handle creamer. This item was produced in the 1920's and only three items were produced, a sugar and creamer, and a tray for the sugar and creamer.
Colors: Crystal, pink, green, flashed on jade green with black handles, crystal w/gold handles.
Availability: All colors scarce.
Reproductions: None known.

WL-1 Ivy bowl, 6 pointed, flat, 8".
Colors: Blue pastel mop, lilac mop, crystal, pink mop.
Availability: All colors are difficult.
Reproductions: None known.

WL-2 Bowl, double crimped, flat, 12".
Colors: Blue pastel mother of pearl.
Availability: Available.
Reproductions: None known.

WL-3 Mini lite or candlelamp, 2 piece, 7-1/2" tall. May be found w/candle cup. Bases will be crystal, shades have color.
Colors: Blue pastel, blue pastel mop, crystal, lilac opal, lilac opal mop, pink pastel, royal blue, ruby.
Availability: All colors usually available.
Reproductions: Sapphire blue, crystal, lilac opalescent.

WL-4 Fireball, 2 piece candleholder, 5-1/2".
Colors: Blue pastel, blue pastel mop, crystal, crystal mop, lilac opal, lilac opal mop, pink pastel, pink mop, royal blue, ruby.
Availability: All colors available.
Reproductions: None known.

WL-5 Bowl, double crimped, flat, 9".
Colors: Blue pastel mop, crystal, amethyst opalescent carnival (32 made), amethyst opalescent (for Levay).
Availability: Amethyst opal carnival & plain are rare, others are slightly difficult.
Reproductions: None known.

WL-6 Candlestick, 3".
Colors: Blue pastel mop, crystal.
Availability: Both available.
Reproductions: None known.

WL-7 Basket, oval, 7".
Colors: Crystal, pink mother or pearl, amethyst opalescent carnival (46 made), amethyst opalescent (for Levay), blue pastel mop.
Availability: Amethyst opal carnival & plain are rare, others are available.
Reproductions: None known.

WL-8 Vase, fluted or swung, flat, 11". Note that the height of this vase may vary from 7" to 11"!
Colors: Crystal, pink mop, ruby, blue pastel mop, amethyst opalescent carnival (17 made), amethyst opalescent (for Levay).
Availability: Amethyst opal carnival & plain are rare, others are slightly difficult.
Reproductions: None known.

WL-9 Plate, serving, 11".
Colors: Blue pastel mother of pearl.
Availability: Available.
Reproductions: None known.

WL-10 Bowl, mint, round, 5", flat.
Colors: Pink mother of pearl.
Availability: Available.
Reproductions: None known.

WL-11 Glow Ball, one piece, flat, 4". Also made in a 5" rose bowl only for Levay. Either version may be found w/a candle cup inside.
Colors: 4": Crystal, pink mop, ruby, blue pastel mop. 5": Amethyst opalescent carnival (100 made), amethyst opalescent (for Levay).
Availability: All available.
Reproductions: None known.

WL-12 Basket, double crimped, or star crimped, round, 6" flat.
Colors: Crystal, pink mop, ruby, amethyst opalescent carnival (20 made), amethyst opalescent (for Levay), blue pastel mop.
Availability: Amethyst opal carnival & plain are rare, all others available.
Reproductions: Stiegel blue opalescent by Fenton.

WL-13 Bowl, mint, double crimped, 6" flat.
Colors: Crystal, pink mop, blue pastel mop, ruby.
Availability: All slightly difficult.
Reproductions: None known.

WL-14 Bowl, fruit, round, deep, flat, 9".
Colors: Blue pastel, crystal.

Availability: Both available.
Reproductions: None known.

WL-15 Banana bowl, oval, flat.
Colors: Blue pastel.
Availability: Available.
Reproductions: None known.

WL-16 Bowl, round, 9". Not as deep as the fruit bowl.
Colors: Blue pastel.
Availability: Available.
Reproductions: None known.

WL-17 Serving tray, center handled, 11".
Colors: Crystal.
Availability: Available.
Reproductions: None known.

WW-1 "Woolworth" line #89 creamer. This pattern was an inexpensive line that was sold in Woolworth stores in the 1930's according to Hazel Marie Weatherman's "Colored Glassware of the Depression Era 2". Most items in this pattern will be found occasionally. Mrs. Weatherman states that this pattern was manufactured in pink, blue, green and crystal. Most often pink and green will be found. I have never found any pieces in blue.
Colors: Pink, blue, green, crystal.
Availability: Pink and green available, others may be scarce.
Reproductions: None known.

WW-2 Bowl, 7-3/4", belled. See WW-1 for pattern description.
Colors: Pink, blue, green and crystal.
Availability: Pink and green available, others may be scarce.
Reproductions: None known.

50-1 Line #50 Mayonnaise, flared rim, flat. This pattern is from very early in Westmoreland's history. In 1980 when David Grossman took over the company, he started reissuing quite a number of these old molds.
Colors: Crystal.

Availability: Difficult due to it's recent manufacture.
Reproductions: None known.

61-1 Line #61 Toothpick, flared top rim.
Colors: Crystal, ruby, moss green, Golden Sunset, Bermuda Blue.
Availability: All usually available, colors other than ruby may be difficult.
Reproductions: None known.

101-1 Line #101 Lacy edge plate, 5-1/2" dia.
Colors: Crystal w/ruby & hp cameo, mg w/children's sayings, light blue mist, dark blue mist, some may have Zodiac or the Twelve Days of Christmas decals, mg w/purple Beaded Bouquet, crystal with ruby stain w/Ruby Floral, milk glass w/Kitchen sayings in a cross stitch motif, dark blue mist w/daisy decal.
Availability: All are scarce, Zodiac are extremely scarce.
Reproductions: None known.

208-1 Line #208 Marmalade w/lid & spoon. The spoon sold with this marmalade will always be in crystal. The bottom of this was also marketed as a candle cup.
Colors: As a marmalade: Golden Sunset, moss green, crystal. As a candle cup: Honey amber carnival, ice blue carnival.
Availability: Both versions are very difficult to find.
Reproductions: None known.

229-1 Line #229 Jack-in-the-pulpit small vase 5-1/2" tall approximately. Made during the Grossman era. See #229-2, both pieces are from the same mold.
Colors: Milk glass, ruby, ruby w/snow flower decal, pink mist w/snow flower decal.
Availability: All slightly difficult.
Reproductions: Black mg, fry-like white opalescent, cobalt, blue ice.

229-2 Line #229, bud vase, footed, 4" tall approximately.
Colors: Milk glass, ruby, ruby w/snow flower decal, pink mist w/snow flower decal.

Availability: All slightly difficult.
Reproductions: Since this item and #229-1 are from the same mold reproductions could exist in this form also, although they do not appear in any literature.

240-1 Line #240 Bowl, star crimped, 6" flat.
Colors: Crystal, Golden sunset, moss green.
Availability: All difficult.
Reproductions: None known.

240-2 Line #240 Buzz Star punch set. The set includes a 15", 2-1/4 gallon bowl, base, punch cups and a #1800 punch ladle. This is an older pattern which has also been referred to as line #575, which has been reissued throughout Westmoreland's history. In the later Grossman years, this punch bowl was made for Levay or in experimental colors which are considered rare today.
Colors: Milk glass, crystal, red carnival (500 or less were made), black carnival (experimental, less than 31 made).
Availability: Mg & crystal are scarce, any carnival color is rare.
Reproductions: None known.

300-1 Line #300 Bowl, centerpiece, star shaped. This was Westmoreland's attempt at free form glass. Several other companies tried this type of glass.
Colors: Brandywine Blue, purple marble, lilac, lilac mist, dark blue mist, green mist, green marble, brown marble, green mist w/daisy dec., yellow mist w/daisy dec., dark blue mist w/daisy dec., yellow mist.
Availability: Colors difficult, decorated examples very difficult.
Reproductions: None known.

300-2 Line #300 Irish Waterford bonbon w/cover. Square footed, 4-1/2" dia. x 6" tall with lid. These are most often tagged "English Hobnail" but were never marketed under the #555 line. See EH-151 for candy jar.
Colors: Crystal w/ruby stain and milk glass.

Availability: Both are fairly common.
Reproductions: None known.

300-3 Line #300 Centerpiece bowl, cupped rim.
Colors: Almond, mg mop, possibly others.
Availability: Scarce.
Reproductions: None known.

324-1 Leaf soap dish or mint tray, has four blobs for feet, pattern on bottom. This blends well with #1928 Maple Leaf. Some of the catalogs refer to this as line #1923 and others refer to it as line #324. Dimensions are 4-1/2" wide x 6" long.
Colors: Milk glass, crystal w/red, yellow and blue stain, antique green.
Availability: Mg available, stain colors & antique green difficult.
Reproductions: None known.

340-1 Line #340 Bowl, round, deep. This bowl has a paneled motif with every other panel having a star type pattern with the other panels plain.
Colors: Crystal.
Availability: Difficult.
Reproducitons: None known.

340-2 Line #340 Bowl, round, 8-1/4" dia., deep. This bowl has a paddlewheel or starburst pattern. This may have been originally from Line #575, which was a pattern which dates from early this century.
Colors: Crystal, ruby.
Availability: Crystal difficult, ruby may be more available.
Reproductions: Cobalt, pink lustre.

440-1 Line #440 Basket, 6-1/2" tall. This was produced by Grossman from very old molds. This basket will usually have a reeded handle, although some were produced with a plain handle.
Colors: Blue pastel, pink pastel, pink mist, light blue mist, crystal, lilac opalescent, ruby, cobalt carnival (50 made for Levay).
Availability: All difficult, carnival very scarce.
Reproductions: None known.

575-1 Line #575 Vase, scallop rim, flat. This piece was originally a spooner when it was first produced around the early part of this century. Also see 340-2 for it's companion bowl. The rim of this vase may be pinched or straight.
Colors: Crystal, ruby, lilac opalescent.
Availability: All colors are scarce.
Reproductions: None known.

1067-1 Line #1067 Three Ball Bowl, cupped rim, round bowl.
Colors: Purple marble, green marble.
Availability: Both scarce.
Reproductions: None known.

1085-1 Line #1085 box, round w/4 thumbprint indents in side of box base. Finial has matching indents.
Colors: Dark blue mist w/daisy dec., green mist w/daisy dec., mg w/dec#32, mg w/yellow rose & blue & red forget-me-nots.
Availability: All very scarce.
Reproductions: None known.

1085-2 Line #1085 tumbler w/4 thumbprint indents, flat.
Colors: Dark blue mist w/daisy dec., green mist w/daisy dec., mg w/dec#32.
Availability: All very scarce.
Reproductions: None known.

1211-1 Line #1211 Octagon shaped, candy w/lid, footed, cone shaped.
Colors: Green mist, crystal mist, light blue mist, pink mist, green marble, mg w/gold flower decal, brown marble, purple marble, mg w/dec#32, mg w/gold feather decoration.
Availability: All are scarce, decorated versions are very scarce.
Reproductions: None known.

1512-1 Line 1512 Basket, oval, plain handle, 9". This is another old mold which was revived by David Grossman.
Colors: Crystal. For Levay: Aurora cobalt blue carnival (50 made), butterscotch opalescent in 1983.

Availability: Crystal very difficult, Levay colors are rare.
Reproductions: None known.

1513-1 Line #1513 Rose bowl, 3-3/4". this was produced by Grossman from very old molds.
Colors: Blue pastel, pink pastel, pink mist, lilac opalescent, ruby, crystal, light blue mist, crystal carnival (for Levay), aurora cobalt blue carnival (50 made for Levay).
Availability: All difficult, carnival colors are very scarce.
Reproductions: None known.

1514-1 Line #1514 Compote, crimped & ruffled, ftd. Another old mold revived by David Grossman.
Colors: Crystal.
Availability: Very difficult.
Reproductions: None known.

1515-1 Line #1515 Bowl, crimped, flat, 8-1/2" dia. Another old mold revived by David Grossman.
Colors: Crystal, aurora cobalt blue carnival (50 made for Levay).
Availability: Crystal very difficult.
Reproductions: None known.

1516-1 Line #1516 pitcher, 1 pint, flat. Another old mold revived by David Grossman.
Colors: Crystal, ruby.
Availability: Very difficult.
Reproductions: None known.

1517-1 Line #1517 Compote, flat top, footed. Another old mold revived by David Grossman.
Colors: Crystal.
Availability: Very difficult.
Reproductions: None known.

1518-1 Line #1518 Plate, scalloped rim, 11". Another old mold revived by David Grossman.
Colors: Crystal.
Availability: Very difficult.
Reproductions: None known.

1519-1 Line #1519 Bowl, flared, flat, scalloped rim. Another old mold revived by

David Grossman.
Colors: Crystal.
Availability: Very difficult.
Reproductions: None known.

1520-1 Line #1520 Vase, swung, flat. Height may vary. Another old mold revived by David Grossman.
Colors: Crystal.
Availability: Very difficult.
Reproductions: None known.

1700-1 Line #1700 Candy with lid, tall, footed, colonial style. Production started on this candy in 1973 and continued until 1983. Because of the long duration of production, many examples exist in today's market. These were popular when Westmoreland produced them and they still are even today.
Colors: Mint green w/dogwood, crystal mist w/dogwood, ruby w/Ruby Floral, antique blue w/ Beaded Bouquet, mint green w/Beaded Bouquet, almond w/Beaded Bouquet, crystal mist w/50th anniv., crystal mist w/25th anniv., crystal mist w/Floral Spray, almond w/Floral spray, dark blue mist w/daisies, ruby w/Snow flower, antique blue mist w/Beaded Bouquet, brown mist w/daisy, crystal mist w/Floral Bouquet, brown mist w/Floral Bouquet, pink mist w/dogwood, crystal with ruby stain w/Ruby Floral, lilac mist w/daisy, green mist w/daisy, yellow mist w/daisy, milk glass w/Roses & Bows, black milk glass w/Oriental poppy, dark blue mist w/Floral Bouquet, milk glass w/Wedding decoration, milk glass w/ blue Beaded Bouquet, milk glass w/ Christmas holly, milk glass w/purple Beaded Bouquet, mg mop w/30th anniv., almond plain.
Availability: Rare examples include mint green, almond, black milk glass, antique blue, antique blue mist, lilac mist and yellow mist. All others are only slightly difficult. Scarce decorations include Beaded Bouquet, Christmas holly and Oriental poppy.
Reproductions: None known.

1701-1 Line #1701 Ring Holder, flat w/ upturned sides.
Colors: Crystal.
Availability: Very difficult.
Reproductions: None known.

1800-4 Line #1800 Tid bit tray, scalloped rim with a metal center handle. This is basically an AB/CO-15 plate with a center handle. The tray is 10-1/2" in diameter. This tray was produced during 1981, 1982 and 1983.
Colors: Crystal mist and crystal w/China Rose, strawberry, Andrea West rooster, andrea West Country Floral and grapes; lilac mist w/daisy, green mist w/daisy, yellow mist w/daisy, dark blue mist w/daisy, crystal mist w/wedding bell, crystal mist w/Antique Fruit.
Availability: All are very difficult to find.
Reproductions: None known.
(See Book 2)

1800-5 Punch ladle, line #1800.
Colors: Crystal, milk glass, almond.
Availability: Very scarce to find for sale without a punch set.
Reproductions: None known.

1814-1 Line #1814 vertical ribbed console bowl, round, pedestal footed.
Colors: Green mist, crystal mist, light blue mist, pink mist, Golden Sunset.
Availability: All scarce.
Reproductions: None known.

1814-2 Line #1814 Banana stand, pedestal footed.
Colors: Golden Sunset.
Availability: Scarce.
Reproductions: None known.

1837-1 Line #1837 ladle. This ladle was used with various types of mayonnaise dishes as well as other items needing a ladle.
Colors: Mg, crystal, black mg.
Availability: Black mg scarce all others are usually available.
Reproductions: Cobalt, rubina.

1868-1 Line #1868 Bowl, oval, lacy edge, 2

sides turned upward, 10" x 6-1/2". A flat rim version was also produced, 10" x 7-3/4".
Colors: Lilac mist, dark blue mist, green mist, mg, yellow mist.
Availability: Mg common, colors scarce.
Reproductions: None known.

1872-1 Line #1872 Santa lid on a small sleigh bottom, 5-1/2". The original examples of this are quite lovely and were produced as early as 1962 and as late as 1975. The sleigh was sold without the Santa top. Reproductions abound!
Colors: Brandywine Blue Opalescent, milk glass w/holly on sleigh and hand painted Santa, purple carnival (for Levay in 1977, 246 made), plain milk glass, antique blue mg.
Availability: All colors are rare, with the carnival being the rarest.
Reproductions: Cobalt, amberina, milk glass w/hp Santa, blue mother of pearl (marble like) with hp Santa, ruby, ruby carnival, ruby carnival w/hp Santa, lavendar, green carnival, blue milk glass, milk glass, mg mop, mg mop w/hp, cobalt w/hp, cobalt carnival. All reproductions will bear the "W" with a "G" mark and will also have a "V" inside a circle above the WG marking. This mark is difficult to find because it is so faint.

1877-1 Line #1877 Planter, vertical ribbed, 3 footed, rimed.
Colors: Dark blue mist, brown mist, green mist, milk glass, yellow mist.
Availability: All very difficult.
Reproductions: None known.

1877-2 Line #1877 vertical ribbed, candy, 3 footed w/acorn finial lid.
Colors: Milk glass, Golden Sunset, Antique Blue.
Availability: Mg available, colors very difficult.
Reproductions: None known.

1879-1 Line #1879 Candy, crimped, footed, lacy rim, vertical ribbed sides.
Colors: Apricot mist, dark blue mist, light

blue mist, mint green, crystal mist, green mist, pink mist, mg, antique green.
Availability: All very difficult.
Reproductions: None known.

1900-1 Line #1900 vase, flat, very plain, 6" tall.
Colors: Antique blue mist, black mg w/Oriental poppy decoration, dark blue mist, crystal mist w/antique fruit, crystal mist w/Floral Spray, mg w/blue Beaded Bouquet, almond w/Beaded Bouquet, antique blue w/Beaded Bouquet, dark blue mist w/daisy, green mist w/daisy, brown mist w/daisy, dark blue mist w/Floral Bouquet, brown mist w/Floral Bouquet, crystal mist w/Floral Bouquet, dark blue mist w/Mary Gregory style, ruby w/ruby Floral, crystal mist w/strawberry, crystal mist w/Andrea West Rooster, crystal mist w/Andrea West Country Floral, brown mist plain, crystal w/ruby stain & Ruby Floral, almond w/Dogwood, mg w/Floral spray, crystal mist w/Roses & Bows, mg w/Roses & Bows, crystal mist w/China Rose, mg w/blue wedding bells, mg w/Christmas Bouquet, pink mist.
Availability: All scarce, hand painted decorations are very scarce.
Reproductions: None known.

1900-4 Line #1900 vase, flat, swung, rounded bottom, top is higher in places.
Colors: Dark blue mist, green mist, lilac, lilac mist, green marble, purple marble, Brandywine Blue.
Availability: All are very difficult.
Reproductions: None known.

1900-5 Line #1900 chip & dip set.
Colors: Crystal.
Availability: Scarce.
Reproductions: None known.

1900-6 Line #1900 Bowl, crimped & ruffled, 8-1/4" diameter.
Colors: Green marble, purple marble, lilac, Brandywine Blue, brown marble.
Availability: All difficult.
Reproductions: None known.

1901-1 Dinner plate, scalloped rim. Saucers and other sized plates are available. This dinner plate was most often used with the American Hobnail Pattern.
Colors: Milk glass, possibly others.
Availability: Difficult.
Reproductions: None known.

1902-1 Line #1902 Vase, 6" flat, crimped top.
Colors: Antique blue mist, pink mist w/dogwood, crystal mist w/dogwood, mint green w/dogwood, crystal mist w/25th anniv., crystal with ruby stain w/40th anniv., mg mop w/30th anniv., crystal mist w/50th anniv., mg w/blue wedding bells, mint green w/Beaded Bouquet, antique blue w/Beaded Bouquet, antique blue mist w/Beaded Bouquet, crystal mist w/China Rose, dark blue mist w/daisy, green mist w/daisy, brown mist w/daisy, dark blue mist w/Mary Gregory style, green mist w/Mary Gregory style, mg w/red hearts, roses & bows, crystal mist w/Roses & Bows, milk glass w/Roses & Bows, crystal with ruby stain w/Ruby Floral, brown mist w/Floral Bouquet, dark blue mist w/Floral Bouquet, crystal mist w/Floral Bouquet, almond w/Floral spray, crystal mist w/Floral Spray, mg w/holly, crystal mist w/holly, mg w/purple Beaded Bouquet, crystal mist w/strawberry, brown mist w/Mary Gregory, mg w/blue Beaded Bouquet, brown mist plain, dark blue mist plain, green mist plain, almond w/Beaded Bouquet, pink mist plain.
Availability: All are difficult, with the decorated and decal versions being very difficult.
Reproductions: None known.

1902-2 Line #1902 compote w/lid, stem footed.
Colors: Apricot mist, dark blue mist, light blue mist, crystal mist, green mist, pink mist, crystal mist w/China rose, almond w/almond Rose, mg w/Roses & Bows, ruby w/Ruby Floral, mg w/strawberry, yellow mist, brown mist, light blue mist w/daisy, dark blue mist w/Mary Gregory style, dark blue mist w/daisy, light mist w/Mary Gregory style, pink mist w/Mary Gregory style, pink mist w/daisy, mg w/china rose, crystal w/ruby stain & Ruby Floral.
Availability: All very difficult, but decorated and decal versions are scarce.
Reproductions: None known.

1902-3 Line #1902 Compote, ruffled & crimped, stem footed.
Colors: Apricot mist, dark blue mist, mg w/China rose, mg w/strawberry, green mist, pink mist.
Availability: All are difficult.
Reproductions: None known.

1902-4 Line #1902 Puff box with lid, flat. This puff box is most often mated with the 1902-6 perfume bottles and the 1902-7 oval tray which comprises the #1902 dresser set. This puff box was produced in colors and decorations that were never produced for the entire dresser set. This puff box was produced intermittently from 1971 through 1984. In 1984 the entire dresser set was produced in black milk glass. This black set was never sold to the public through a catalog and was considered experimental.
Colors: Milk glass w/purple Beaded Bouquet, green mist w/daisy, dark blue mist w/daisy, milk glass w/Roses & Bows, brown mist w/floral bouquet, crystal mist w/floral bouquet, dark blue mist w/floral bouquet, brown mist w/daisy, crystal with ruby stain w/Ruby Floral, yellow mist w/daisy, lilac mist w/daisy, black milk glass, crystal mist w/dogwood, mint green w/dogwood, crystal mist w/25th anniv., crystal mist w/50th anniv., milk glass mop w/30th anniv., ruby w/40th anniv., almond w/floral spray, crystal mist w/floral spray, antique blue mist w/Beaded Bouquet, almond w/Beaded Bouquet, pink mist w/dogwood, pink mist w/Snow flower, light blue mist w/daisy, pink mist w/daisy.
Availability: Black milk glass is rare, mint green, almond and antique blue mist is scarce. Scarce decorations include Beaded Bouquet and Roses & Bows. All other examples are slightly difficult.

Reproductions: Black milk glass w/rose decoration, mg w/Roses & Bows, milk glass w/orange floral decoration, pink mist, blue mist, and First Love decoration in crystal mist, milk glass and black milk glass. The First Love decoration is a floral bouquet with a bow. This is a decal. These reproductions were produced by Plum Glass and are usually marked with the "P" in a keystone symbol. Most of the hand painted versions will be artist signed and dated after Westmoreland's closing.

1902-6 Line #1902 Perfume bottle with stopper. This is part of the #1902 dresser set, see 1902-4 for more information. The perfumes were never made separate of the dresser set. The complete set was produced from 1971-1976, although a black milk glass set was produced experimentally in 1984 but never sold to the public via any catalog.
Colors: Mg w/purple Beaded Bouquet, green mist w/daisy, dark blue mist w/daisy, mg w/Roses & Bows, yellow mist w/daisy, lilac mist w/daisy, black milk glass, light blue mist w/daisy, pink mist w/daisy.
Availability: Black mg is rare all others are very scarce.
Reproductions: None known.

1902-7 Line #1902 oval tray for dresser set. the tray appears to be the most difficult item to find in the dresser set. The tray was always plain, never decorated. The tray was also used as a condiment tray for Paneled Grape.
Colors: Black milk glass (1984 experimental), milk glass, dark blue mist, green mist, yellow mist, lilac mist, light blue mist, pink mist.
Availability: All are very scarce but the rare examples include lilac mist and black milk glass.

Reproductions: Black milk glass examples have been found with a Mary Gregory style hand painting. I believe that the glass may have been purchased at the factory auction then hand painted by one of the ex-employees. No other examples of reproductions have been noted in any information that I have in my possession.

1940-1 Vase, 7-1/2" tall, flat.
Colors: Milk glass, mg w/rose decoration, mg w/apple blossom decoration, dark blue mist plain.
Availability: Mg scarce, dec. rare.
Reproductions: None known.

1943-1 Line #1943 Urn & cover, footed, 12-1/2" tall.
Colors: Crystal, crystal w/ruby stain with or without hp flowers, mg, mg w/dec#32, mg w/purple Beaded Bouquet, mg w/gold grapes & leaves, crystal mist w/Roses & Bows.
Availability: Crystal w/ruby stain difficult, all others very scarce.
Reproductions: None known.

1972-1 Line #1972 Ashtray, round, sits on its side.
Colors: Lilac, Brandywine Blue, green marble, purple marble, purple carnival, mint green, ruby.
Availability: All scarce.
Reproductions: None known.

1973-1 Line #1973 Cake cover. Hand blown w/applied handles. This cake cover was shown on several different round cake stands.
Colors: Crystal only.
Availability: Very scarce.
Reproductions: None known.

BIBLIOGRAPHY

Colored Glassware of the Depression Era, 1 by Hazel Marie Weatherman

1984 Supplement & Price Trends to *Colored Glassware of the Depression Era,1* by Hazel Marie Weatherman

Colored Glassware of the Depression Era, 2 by Hazel Marie Weatherman

Supplement & Price Trends to *Colored Glassware of the Depression Era, 2* by Hazel Marie Weatherman

The Encyclopedia of Duncan Glass by Gail Krause

Opaque Glass by S.T. Millard

Handbook of Early American Pressed Glass Patterns by Ruth Webb Lee

Antique Fakes and Reproductions by Ruth Webb Lee

Glass Patents and Patterns by Arthur G. Peterson

A Collector's Guide to Black Glass by Marlena Toohey

American Glass Candy Containers by George Eikelberner & Serge Adadjanian

More American Glass Candy Containers by George Eikelberner & Serge Adadjanian

Yesterday's Milk Glass Today by Regis F. and Mary F. Ferson

Bedroom & Bathroom Glassware of the Depression Years by Kenn & Margaret Whitmyer

First Two Hundred Pattern Glass Pitchers by Minnie Watson Kamm

Second Two Hundred Pattern Glass Pitchers by Minnie Watson Kamm

Third Two Hundred Pattern Glass Pitchers by Minnie Watson Kamm

Fourth Two Hundred Pattern Glass Pitchers by Minnie Watson Kamm

A Fifth Pattern Glass Book by Minnie Watson Kamm

A Sixth Pattern Glass Book by Minnie Watson Kamm

A Seventh Pattern Glass Book by Minnie Watson Kamm

An Eighth Pattern Glass Book by Minnie Watson Kamm

Tiffin Glassmasters by Fred Bickenheuser

Tiffin Glassmasters, Book II by Fred Bickenheuser

Tiffin Glassmasters, Book III by Fred Bickenheuser

Goblets, 1 by S.T. Millard

Victorian Glass by Ruth Webb Lee

Early American Pressed Glass by Ruth Webb Lee

American Historical Glass by Bessie M. Lindsey

Sandwich Glass by Ruth Webb Lee

Milk Glass by E.M. Belknap

Early American Pattern Glass, 1850-1910 by Bill Jenks & Jerry Luna

The Glass Industry in Sandwich ,Volume 4 by Raymond E. Barlow & Joan E. Kaiser

American Pressed Glass and Figure Bottles by Albert Christian Revi

D.C. Jenkins Glass Co. Catalog of Pressed & Blown Glassware

"The Mainline Works" by Maryann Gogniat, an article which appeared in The Laurel Highlands Scene Magazine in March-April 1990.

Westmoreland July 1, 1981 catalog supplement

Westmoreland 1976 "Treasured Gifts" catalog supplement

Westmoreland 1983 catalog and price list

Westmoreland 1984 catalog

Westmoreland 1980 "Gifts of Heritage" catalog

Westmoreland 1981 "Today's Treasures-Tomorrow's Heirlooms" catalog

Westmoreland 1977 catalog

Westmoreland 1978 catalog

Westmoreland's Handmade "English Hobnail Crystal" catalog supplement

Westmoreland "Gifts of Heritage" 1980 fall supplement catalog

Westmoreland "The 1980 Collector's Series" catalog supplement

Westmoreland Catalog supplement No. 3 to Basic Catalog #163

Westmoreland Catalog #75 from 1964

Westmoreland's Handmade, Hand-decorated Crystal catalog supplement

Westmoreland's Handmade "Old Quilt" Pattern catalog supplement

Westmoreland 1969 catalog

Westmoreland 1971 catalog

Westmoreland 1974 catalog supplement

Westmoreland's Handmade "Paneled Grape" pattern catalog supplement

Westmoreland 1967 catalog

Westmoreland 1972 Catalog supplement

Westmoreland 1973 catalog

Westmoreland 1975 catalog

Westmoreland price list to Catalog #173, dated January1, 1963

Westmoreland "Reproductions of Choice Pieces of Early American Glass" catalog dated 1955

Westmoreland "Reflections on Ashburton" brochure

Westmoreland "Gifts of Heritage" 1979 catalog

Westmoreland 1912 Catalog reprinted by Glass Research Press, a division of Heisey Collectors of America

Westmoreland Beaded Grape, Decorated Beaded Grape and Roses & Bows catalog supplement

Westmoreland "America's Finest Handmade Milk Glass" catalog #163 dated 1952

Westmoreland "Handmade Reproductions of choice pieces of Early American Glass" catalog dated 1950

Westmoreland 1970 catalog supplement

Westmoreland 1970 catalog sheet of "Waterford"

Westmoreland catalog sheet & price list dated Jan. 1 through Mar. 31, 1970

Westmoreland catalog sheet & price list dated April 3 through May 20, 1972

Westmoreland catalog sheet & price list dated Jan. 1 through March 31, 1971

China, Glass & Tablewares magazine dated December 1971

China, Glass & Tablewares magazine dated January 1972

China, Glass & Tablewares magazine dated October 1971

China, Glass & Tablewares magazine dated March 1970

China, Glass & Tablewares magazine dated July 1970

Westmoreland "The Remarkable Story of Handmade Glass" 1970 catalog

Westmoreland "America's Finest Handmade Milk Glass" catalog #173 dated 1962

Plum Glass Color catalog and photocopied supplements

Wholesale Glass Distributors Color Catalog and monthly photocopied supplements

Dalzell Viking undated color catalog and photocopied supplements

Summit Art Glass 1989 catalog

The Glass Collector, issue number six, Spring-Summer 1983 by William Heacock

Collecting Glass Volume 3 by William Heacock

Levay Distributing Catalogs and supplements 1973 through 1984

L.G.Wright Master catalog, undated

L.G.Wright and Jennings Red Barn Catalog, undated

Glass Review ad from March 1978 for Amethyst Carnival Butterfly from the Historical Glass Museum Foundation

Glass Review ad from March 1978 for Levay's Electric Blue Carnival

Glass Review ad April 1985 article by Joseph D. Lokay, "Westmoreland Glass"

Glass Review March 1985, Article titled "Who Bought the Westmoreland Molds?" no author given

J.H. Brainard company history and accompaning documents

The Towne Crier Newsletters from the National Westmoreland Glass Collectors Club

The Westmoreland Glass Collector's Newsletter from Volume 1, Number 1 to Volume III , Number 10

Glass Review, February 1981, Article titled "Levay Glass" by Paul Oard & Lee Wilkerson

Westmoreland Brochure titled "Making America's Finest Handmade Milk Glass" undated

Westmoreland catalog titled "Handmade 'Golden Sunset' Crystal" undated

Encyclopedia of Victorian Colored Pattern Glass, Book V, U.S. Glass From A to Z by William Heacock and Fred Bickenheuser

Encyclopedia of Victorian Colored Pattern Glass, Book II, Opalescent Glass from A to Z (edition 2) by William Heacock

March 3, 1888, document from the Commonwealth of Pennsylvania, concerning the formation of the Westmoreland Specialty Company in Pennsylvania; provided by Charles West-Wilson

October 24, 1889, document from the Commonwealth of Pennsylvania, concerning the formation of the Westmoreland Specialty Company in Pennsylvania; provided by Charles West-Wilson

September 1909 document from the Commonwealth of Pennsylvania, concerning the Reorganization of Westmoreland (officers and major stock holders); provided by Charles West-Wilson

February 10,1925, document from the Commonwealth of Pennsylvania, concerning the Westmoreland Specialty Company name change to Westmoreland Glass Company; provided by Charles West-Wilson

August 1967 Dun & Bradstreet report on Westmoreland Glass; provided by Charles West-Wilson

Treasured Editions Limited, undated color catalog and price guide, provided by Mr. Robert Rupp

L.E. Smith Glass Company catalog dated 1986-1987

L.E. Smith Glass Company catalog supplement dated 1987

L.E. Smith Glass Company holiday catalog supplement dated 1985

L.E. Smith Glass Company datalog dated 1982-1983, revised

Butler Brothers Catalog dated 1910

Blackwell Wielandy Company catalog dated 1940-1941

Butler Brothers catalog dated 1905

INDEX